Student's Book

Gateway

2nd Edition

CB128310

David Spencer

macmillan education

A1+

Contents A1+

S Starter unit

Vocabulary

The classroom

1a Work with a partner. Match these words with the objects in the pictures.

bag • board • board rubber • book • chair
computer • desk • dictionary • door • pen
pencil • poster • rubber • ruler • window

1b How do you say the words in your language?

1c LISTENING 01 Listen and repeat.

2 01 Listen and point to the object in your classroom.

Speaking

The alphabet

1 PRONUNCIATION 02 Listen and repeat.

Aa Bb Cc Dd Ee Ff Gg
Hh Ii Jj Kk Ll Mm Nn
Oo Pp Qq Rr Ss Tt Uu
Vv Ww Xx Yy Zz

2a LISTENING 03 Listen and choose the correct alternative.

1 K/Q 3 B/V 5 I/Y 7 G/J
2 E/I 4 A/E 6 V/U 8 A/R

2b Work with a partner. Practise saying all the letters in 2a.

3 SPEAKING Spell a classroom object to your partner. What is the word?

P-E-N-C-I-L

Pencil!

Classroom expressions

1 Look at these classroom expressions. Put them in the correct place in the dialogue. Two expressions are <u>not</u> in the dialogue!

1 How do you spell that?
2 I'm sorry, I don't understand.
3 Can you repeat that?
4 What does 'desk' mean?
5 What's this in English?

Ana: 1 ....?
Teacher: It's a ruler.
Ana: 2 ....?
Teacher: Yes, it's a ruler.
Ana: 3 ....?
Teacher: R-U-L-E-R.
Ana: Thank you!

2 04 Listen and check.

3a SPEAKING Work with a partner. Practise the dialogue in 1.

3b Change the word in red and make new dialogues.

Vocabulary

Colours

1a Match the objects with the words for colours in the box.

black • blue • brown • green • grey • orange • pink • purple • red • white • yellow

1b 05 Listen and repeat.

1 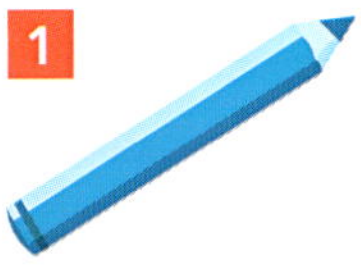
2 

3 
4 
5 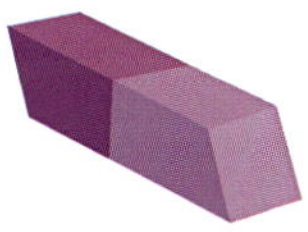
6 
7 
8 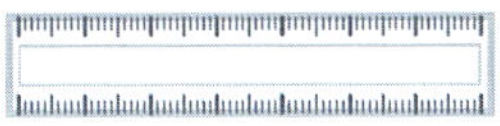
9 
10 
11 

1c Write sentences about the objects.

The pencil is blue.

....

....

....

....

....

2 In your classroom, can you find ...

1 a green desk? Yes/No
2 a red pen? Yes/No
3 a blue door? Yes/No
4 a white board? Yes/No
5 an orange bag? Yes/No
6 a pink pencil? Yes/No
7 a purple book? Yes/No
8 a yellow poster? Yes/No

Vocabulary

Numbers – cardinal and ordinal

1a Put the words in the box in order in the correct column. Write the numbers next to them.

eight • ninth • fifth • ~~first~~ • five • four
fourth • nine • eighth • ~~one~~ • second
seven • seventh • third • sixth • ten
tenth • six • three • two

Cardinal numbers	Ordinal numbers
one – 1	*first – 1st*

1b ▶ 06 **Listen, check and repeat.**

2a Match the ordinal numbers with the words in the box.

eleventh • thirteenth • thirtieth
thirty-first • twelfth • twentieth
twenty-fifth • twenty-first

a 11th c 13th e 21st g 30th
b 12th d 20th f 25th h 31st

2b ▶ 07 **Listen, check and repeat.**

Days and months

3a Put the words in the box in order in the correct column.

April • August • December • February • Friday • ~~January~~
July • June • March • May • ~~Monday~~ • November
October • Saturday • September • Sunday • Thursday
Tuesday • Wednesday

Days	Months
Monday	*January*

3b ▶ 08 **Listen, check and repeat.**

4 SPEAKING **Work with a partner. Look at the calendar. Ask and answer questions.**

January

Su	Mo	Tu	We	Th	Fr	Sa
				1	2	3
4	5	6	7	8	9	10
11	12	13	14	15	16	17
18	19	20	21	22	23	24
25	26	27	28	29	30	31

What day is the 12th?

Monday. What day is the 7th?

5 Answer the questions.

What is …

1 today's day and date? *It's Tuesday the 9th of September.*
2 yesterday's day and date?
3 tomorrow's day and date?

Speaking

Telling the time

1 Match the times with the pictures.

1 five o'clock
2 half past three
3 ten past seven
4 quarter to two
5 quarter past four
6 twenty-five past eight

a ....

b ....

c ....

d ....

e ....

f ....

2 SPEAKING **Work with a partner. Ask and say the times.**

a 6.05   c 3.15   e 6.45   g 5.40
b 7.00   d 11.30   f 10.20   h 3.25

What time is it?

It's five past six.

3 What time is it now?

Language checkpoint: Starter unit

Vocabulary

The classroom bag • board • board rubber • book • chair • computer • desk • dictionary • door • pen pencil • poster • rubber • ruler • window

Colours black • blue • brown • green • grey • orange • pink • purple • red • white • yellow

Numbers – cardinal one • two • three • four • five • six • seven • eight • nine • ten • eleven • twelve thirteen • fourteen • fifteen • sixteen • seventeen • eighteen • nineteen • twenty • twenty-one • thirty forty • fifty

Numbers – ordinal first • second • third • fourth • fifth • sixth • seventh • eighth • ninth • tenth • eleventh twelfth • thirteenth • fourteenth • fifteenth • sixteenth • seventeenth • eighteenth • nineteenth • twentieth twenty-first • thirtieth • fortieth • fiftieth

Days Monday • Tuesday • Wednesday • Thursday • Friday • Saturday • Sunday

Months January • February • March • April • May • June • July • August • September • October November • December

Vocabulary revision

THE CLASSROOM / 10 points

1 Complete the words with vowels (*a*, *e*, *i*, *o*, *u*).

1  b ..... r d

2  d .... s k

3  b .... g

4  p .... s t .... r

5  w .... n d .... w

6  c .... m p .... t .... r

7 

d .... c t ..... n .... r y

8 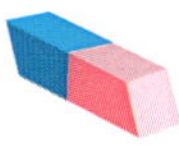 r .... b b .... r

9  p .... n c l

10  c h ..... r

COLOURS / 10 points

2 Write the colours.

1 ....

2  ....

3  ....

4  ....

5  ....

6  ....

7  ....

8  ....

9 ....

10  ....

NUMBERS – CARDINAL AND ORDINAL / 10 points

3 Write the numbers.

a 13 ....
b 30 ....
c 2nd ....
d 21st ....
e 8 ....
f 11 ....
g 20 ....
h 12th ....
i 30th ....
j 3rd ....

DAYS AND MONTHS / 10 points

4 If Monday is the first day of the week and January the first month of the year, write the …

1 third day: ....
2 second month: ....
3 twelfth month: ....
4 seventh day: ....
5 sixth day: ....
6 sixth month: ....
7 second day: ....
8 tenth month: ....
9 fourth day: ....
10 fifth month: ....

Total: / 40 points

1 My ID

Vocabulary

Countries

1a Look at this map. What is different about it?

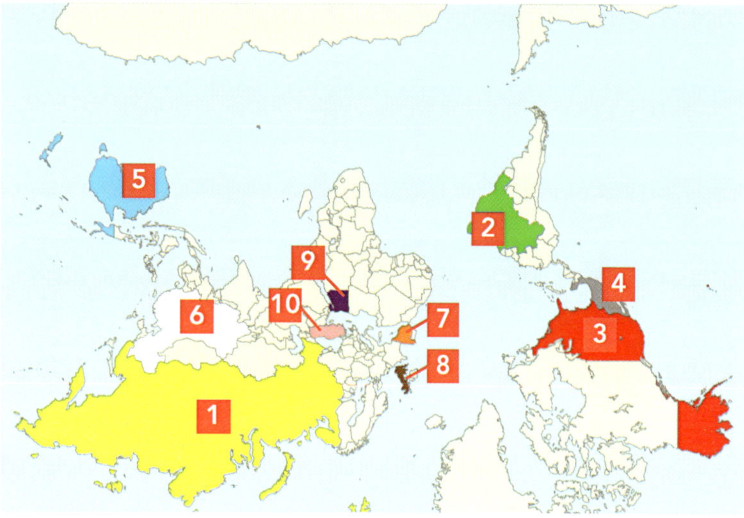

1b Work with a partner. Match the country names to the map.

Australia • Brazil • China • Egypt • Mexico • Russia
Spain • the UK • the US • Turkey

2 ▶ 09 **Listen, check and repeat.**

3 SPEAKING **Work with a partner. Look at the map. Say a colour. What is the country?**

Green?

Brazil. Red?

the US

Nationalities

4 Match the countries in 1b with these nationalities.

American • Australian • Brazilian • British
Chinese • Egyptian • Mexican • Russian
Spanish • Turkish

Australia – Australian

5a PRONUNCIATION ▶ 10 **Listen to the words and choose the correct alternative.**

1 a American b American
2 a Australian b Australian
3 a Brazilian b Brazilian
4 a British b British
5 a Chinese b Chinese
6 a Egyptian b Egyptian
7 a Mexican b Mexican
8 a Russian b Russian
9 a Spanish b Spanish
10 a Turkish b Turkish

5b ▶ 10 **Listen again and repeat with the correct word stress.**

6a Write down the name of one famous person for the nationalities in 4.

Australian – Hugh Jackman

6b SPEAKING **Work in small groups. Take it in turns to say the names from 6a. What is the correct nationality?**

Rafael Nadal.

Spanish.

Yes!

7 LISTENING ▶ 11 **Work with a partner. Listen to people saying *hello* in their language. What nationality from 4 do you think they are?**

1 .... 4 ....
2 .... 5 ....
3 .... 6 ....

Is number 1 Egyptian?

No, I think it's Chinese.

1a **Work with a partner. Who are the people in the photos? Do you know?**

a 
b 
c 

1b READING **Read the texts quickly and complete the table. Which photo in 1a does each mention?**

Name	Photo (a, b or c)	Nationality	Hobby
1 Tom			
2 Elena			
3 Murat			

2 **Read the text again and choose the best answer.**

1 Tom is interested in …
   a five or six different football clubs.
   b a football club from London.
   c a Brazilian football club.

2 Bruno is the name of Elena's …
   a favourite singer.
   b best friend.
   c favourite singer and her cat.

3 Elena's cat is …
   a a fan of vanilla ice cream.
   b a white or yellow colour.
   c her favourite pet.

4 Chris Hemsworth is …
   a a famous American actor.
   b the little brother of Liam Hemsworth.
   c a superhero in the cinema.

3 CRITICAL THINKING

Think! Then compare ideas with your class.

- In your country, are young people interested in the things in the text?
- In your opinion, are today's young people all around the world interested in similar things?

4 **What do the underlined words in the text mean? Guess and then check in your dictionary.**

5 SPEAKING **What about *you*?**

1 What is your favourite hobby?
2 Who is your favourite football player and/or singer?
3 What is your favourite ice cream?

My favourite hobby is tennis. What about you?

My favourite hobby is swimming.

21ST CENTURY KIDS

Who are they? What are their likes? Are they all interested in the same things?

We ask kids from around the world to tell us about their hobbies.

1 I'm Tom. I'm 12 and I'm British. I live in London. My hobby is football. London is an important city for football. I think five or six London clubs are in the Premier League now. One of them is Chelsea. I'm a big Chelsea fan! My favourite football player is Oscar. He isn't British, he's Brazilian.

2 My name is Elena. My best friend is Irina. We're 13 years old. We're from Samara in Russia. We are in a choir. Our favourite songs in choir are pop songs. Irina and I are big fans of British and American pop music. My favourite singer is Bruno Mars. That's why my dog's name is Bruno! My cat is called Vanilla because she's the colour of vanilla ice cream, my favourite type of ice cream.

3 My name is Murat and I'm from Izmir, a big city in Turkey. I'm really interested in making films. I go to a film club every Saturday. My favourite types of films are superhero or action films. My favourite actors are Liam and Chris Hemsworth. They're brothers. They aren't American. They're from Australia. Liam Hemsworth is in *The Hunger Games* and Chris is in *Thor*. Chris is about 32 and Liam is 26.

Flipped classroom: watch the grammar presentation video.

to be – affirmative and negative

1a Look at the sentences and complete the verb table.

1. I'm Tom.
2. He isn't British.
3. He's Brazilian.
4. They aren't American.
5. They're from Australia.
6. We're 13 years old.

Affirmative
I (a) .... British.
You're British.
He/She/It's British.
We (b) .... British.
They (c) .... British.
Negative
I'm not Brazilian.
You aren't Brazilian.
He/She/It (d) .... Brazilian.
We (e) .... Brazilian.
They (f) .... Brazilian.

1b Match the long forms and their contractions.

Long forms: **1** *are* **2** are not **3** is **4** am **5** am not **6** is not
Contractions: **a)** 'm **b)** *'re* **c)** 's **d)** 'm not **e)** aren't **f)** isn't

GRAMMAR REFERENCE ➤ PAGE 20

2a Write sentences using the words and nationalities.

1 I *I'm British.*
2 We ....
3 She ....
4 They ....
5 You ....
6 He ....

2b Now make the sentences in 2a negative.

I'm not British.

3 Choose the correct alternative.

1. Katy Perry isn't/aren't Australian.
2. Katy Perry and Bruno Mars is/are from the US.
3. You and I am/are British.
4. My best friend is/are Jack.
5. Chelsea and Arsenal isn't/aren't Spanish teams.
6. They is/are 14 years old.

4 Complete the sentences with the correct form of the verb *to be* in the affirmative or negative.

SCOTT, 13, LOS ANGELES, THE US.

My name (a) .... Scott. I (b) .... 14 yet. I (c) .... only 13. My best friends (d) .... Jim and Neil. Jim, Neil and I (e) .... from the US but we (f) .... from New York. We (g) .... from Los Angeles. Los Angeles (h) .... really big. I love it – I (i) .... very happy here!

5 Work with a partner. Use the words to write six grammatically correct sentences.

is	I	am
the UK	not	are
Marisa	We	Brazilian
from	aren't	isn't

I am from the UK.

....

to be – questions and short answers

6 Look at the sentences and complete the verb table.

1 **Are** you a football fan?
2 **Are** they interested in the same things?
3 No, they **aren't**.
4 **Is** he Brazilian?
5 **Yes**, he **is**.

Questions	Short answers
Am I American?	Yes, I **am**./No, **I'm not**.
(a) .... you American?	Yes, you **are**./No, you **aren't**.
(b) .... he/she/it American?	Yes, he (d) ..../ No, he **isn't**.
Are we American?	Yes, we **are**./No, we **aren't**.
(c) .... they American?	Yes, they **are**./No, they (e) ....

GRAMMAR REFERENCE ➤ PAGE 20

7 Complete the sentences with the correct form of the verb *to be*.

Interviewer: (a) .... you from the UK?
Sasha: No, I (b) ....
Interviewer: (c) .... you from the US?
Sasha: Yes, I (d) ....
Interviewer: (e) .... your house in New York?
Sasha: No, it (f) .... It's in Washington D.C.
Interviewer: (g) .... Barack, Michelle and Malia members of your family?
Sasha: Yes, they (h) ....

8 LISTENING ▶ 12 Look at the table. Then listen and read the dialogue. Who is the person?

Australia								US							
Sydney				Canberra				Los Angeles				Chicago			
Big School		Small School		Big School		Small School		Big School		Small School		Big School		Small School	
Clark	Davis	Taylor	Adam	Green	Scott	Hill	White	Brown	Cook	Reed	Perry	Long	Evans	Lee	Bell

A: Are you from the US?
B: Yes, I am.
A: Are you from Chicago?
B: Yes, I am.
A: Are you at a big school?
B: No, I'm not.
A: Is your name Bell?
B: No, it isn't.
A: Is your name ....?
B: Yes, it is!

9 SPEAKING Work with a partner. Choose a person from the table in 8. Can your partner discover who you are?

Vocabulary

The family

1a Look at the family tree. Complete the text with these words. Check that you understand all the words in red.

aunt • brother • cousins • father
grandfather • grandparents • mother
nephew • uncle

My family by Ava Morgan

I've got one (a) .... His name is Liam. He's good to me because I'm his little sister. My (b) .... is called Sandra and my (c) .... is called Jack. My parents are the best!

Harry and Amie are my (d) ....
I love them. My grandmother is really special, and her husband, my (e) ...., is great. Henry is my (f) .... His wife, my (g) ...., is called Anne.

Henry and Anne are really good to me and Liam because I'm their only niece and Liam is their only (h) .... They have two children. They're my (i) .... and they're called Oliver and Sophie.

1b ▶ 13 Listen and check.

2a Write down the names of six people in your family.

2b SPEAKING Look at your partner's names. Guess who the people are.

Is Lisa your mother?
No, she isn't.
Is she your aunt?
Yes, she is!

Understanding STATISTICS

LIFE SKILLS OBJECTIVES	KEY CONCEPTS
■ To match diagrams and statistics ■ To read and understand statistics ■ To find and present different statistics	**average [adj, n]:** *The average of 5, 7 and 15 is 9 (5+7+15(÷)3).* **thousand [n]:** *Two thousand = 2,000* **million [n]:** *Two million = 2,000,000* **over/under [prep]:** *Over 100 people = 101, 102, etc. Under 100 people = 99, 98, etc.* **population [n]:** *population = all the people who live in a particular area* **per cent [n]:** *50% = 1/2*

1a READING **Look at this information about the UK. Match the information and the pictures.**

1 The average number of people living in a UK home is 2.4 people.
2 943,000 people are from the Czech Republic, Estonia, Poland, Hungary, Latvia, Lithuania, Slovakia and Slovenia.
3 There are 3.5 million children under 5 in England.
4 27.6 million: Male population.
5 28.5 million: Female population.
6 1 in 6 people in the UK is over 65.
7 The average age of the population is 39.
8 Ethnic population is 12% of the UK population (= 7.5 million).

1b **Work with a partner. Compare and explain your answers.**

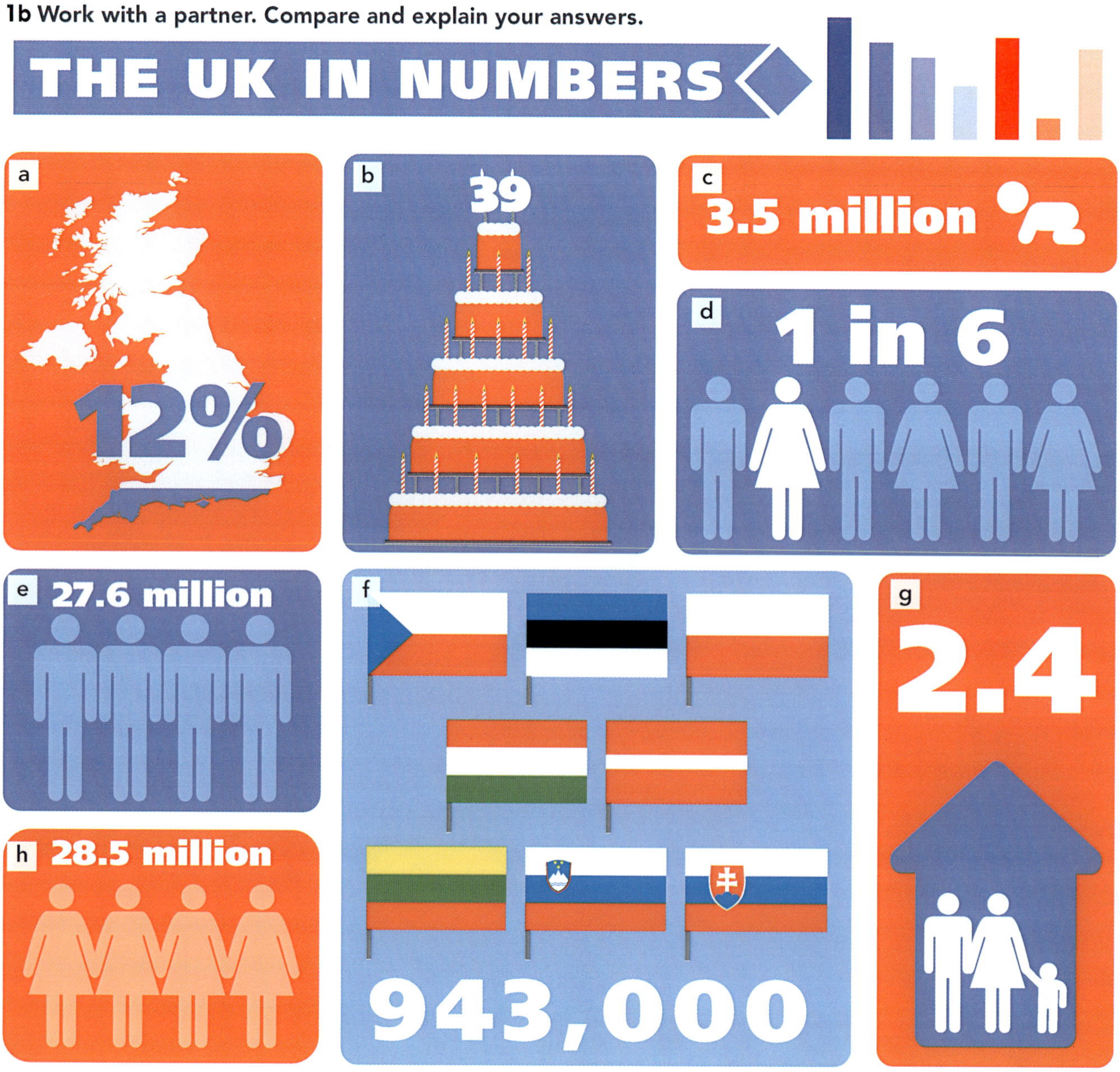

2 Look again at the information. Are these sentences True (T) or False (F)?

1. There are over 28 million men and boys in the UK. T/F
2. The average age in the UK is just under 40. T/F
3. 7.5 million is 12% of the total UK population. T/F
4. The average number of people living in a house or flat in the UK is under two. T/F
5. Under 20% of the UK population is over 65. T/F
6. There are three and a half million children under 5 in the UK. T/F
7. The male and female population is over 55 million. T/F
8. 943,000 people in the UK are from four countries in Eastern Europe. T/F

3 Work with a partner. In your opinion, which statistics in 1 are interesting or surprising?

4 LISTENING ▶ 14 **The video shows statistics about the Australian population. Watch or listen. One statistic is the same as in the UK. Which?**

5 ▶ 14 **Watch or listen again. Match the numbers and information.**

1. 23.4 million
2. 85%
3. 1
4. 4.4 million
5. 19 million
6. 27%
7. 448,610
8. 1 in 6
9. 37.3

A. people in Australia from Italy, Germany and Greece
B. average age of the Australian population
C. number of people in every 2.9 km^2 in Australia
D. people in the East of Australia
E. people in Australia
F. per cent of people born outside Australia, living in Australia now
G. people in the West of Australia
H. people in Australia's population over 65
I. per cent of people live on or near the coast of Australia

6 SPEAKING **Work with a partner. What do you think? Are the statistics for Australia similar to the statistics for your country? Why/Why not?**

LIFE TASK

Work with a partner. Follow this plan:

1. *Choose a country. Find different statistics about the population of the country. For example, find out:*
   - **a** *the total population*
   - **b** *the average age of the population*
   - **c** *the number of children under 5*
   - **d** *the number of people over 65*
   - **e** *multicultural statistics*
   - **f** *the male and female population*
   - **g** *other information*
2. *Make or find pictures to present the statistics.*
3. *Present the statistics to the class. Can they identify the country?*

Listening

1 **Work with a partner. What can you see in the pictures below?**

✔ EXAM SUCCESS

Read the instructions in 2a. Why is it a good idea to look at the pictures before you listen?

➤ EXAM SUCCESS page 151

2a LISTENING ▶ 15 **Listen to three dialogues and tick (✓) the correct picture.**

1 Which is the picture of Mark and his family?

A

B

2 What is a good present for Helen?

A

B

3 Which is Joe's bag?

A

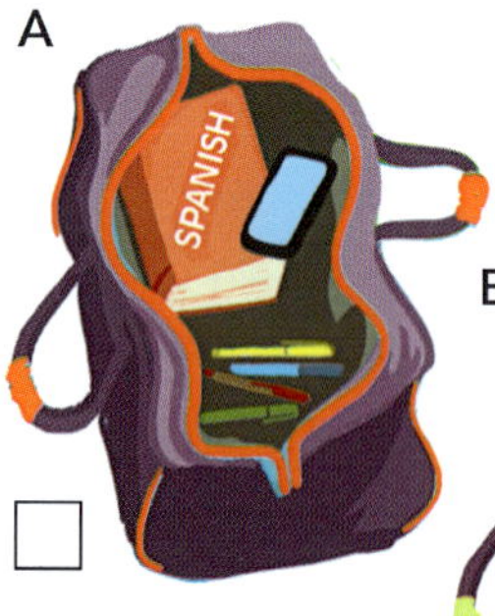

B

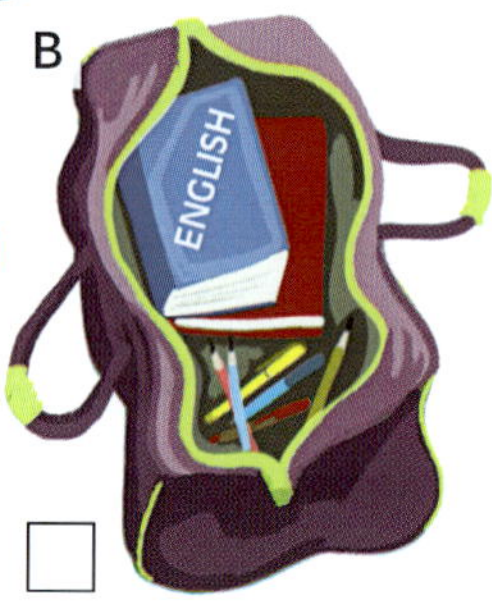

2b ▶ 15 **Listen again and check your answers.**

Grammar in context

have got

1a **Look at the sentences and complete the verb table.**

1 Sarah**'s got** a dog.
2 **Have** you **got** a dog?
3 No, I **haven't**.
4 She **hasn't got** a DVD.

Affirmative
I/You/We/They**'ve got** three cousins.
He/She/It (a) .... brown eyes.
Negative
I/You/We/They **haven't got** three cousins.
He/She/It (b) .... brown eyes.
Question form
(c) .... I/you/we/they .... three cousins?
Has he/she/it **got** brown eyes?
Short answers
Yes, I/you/we/they **have**./ No, I/you/we/they (d) ....
Yes, he/she/it **has**./No, he/she/it **hasn't**.

1b **Match the contractions and the long forms.**

Contractions: **a)** *'s got* **b)** 've got **c)** hasn't got **d)** haven't got
Long forms: **1** has not got **2** *has got* **3** have not got **4** have got

GRAMMAR REFERENCE ➤ PAGE 20

2 **Look at the table. Write complete sentences with the correct affirmative or negative form of *have got*.**

Zoe	✓	✗	✗
Alex	✗	✓	✓
Lucy	✗	✗	✓

1 Zoe/a cat. *Zoe's got a cat.*
2 Lucy/a bike. ....
3 Alex and Lucy/mobile phones. ....
4 Alex and Lucy/cats. ....
5 Alex/a bike. ....
6 Zoe/a mobile phone. ....

3a SPEAKING **Memory test! Work with a partner. Your partner closes their book. Ask questions about the table in 2.**

Has Lucy got a bike?

No, she hasn't.

Correct! Have Zoe and Alex got bikes?

3b Ask your partner about the things in the table.

Have you got a cat?

Yes, I have./ No, I haven't.

4a Put the words in order to make questions.

1 got a or sister Have you brother?
2 Has family got your car a?
3 pet a you Have got?
4 a favourite got Have you singer?
5 grandfather phone a mobile your Has got?
6 an dictionary you Have English got?

4b SPEAKING **Work with a partner. Ask and answer the questions.**

5 Complete the text with the correct forms of *to be* and *have got*.

Nicole Kidman (a) ...... a famous actress. She (b) ...... a famous husband. Her husband (c) ...... a singer called Keith Urban. They (d) ...... two children. Their names (e) ...... Sunday Rose and Faith Margaret. Nicole (f) ...... a brother, but she (g) ...... a sister called Antonia. Nicole and Keith (h) ...... houses in Sydney, Los Angeles and Nashville.

Possessive adjectives

6 Look at the sentences. Write the possessive adjectives next to the correct subject pronouns.

1 I've got **my** mobile phone.
2 Who's **her** favourite band?
3 What about **your** mobile phone?
4 She's often at **our** house.
5 **Its** name is Max.
6 She's got all **their** CDs.

a I ......
b you ......
c it ......
d she ......
e we ......
f they ......

GRAMMAR REFERENCE ➤ PAGE 20

7 Choose the correct alternative.

1 Hello. I/My name's Katie.
2 Anne has got a brother. Her/His name is Robert.
3 Our/We names are Wayne and Liam.
4 His/Their names are Jake and Abby.
5 I've got a sister. Her/His name is Olivia.

8 Complete the text with these words.

her • his • its • my • my • our • their

Hello. (a) ...... name is William.

This is (b) ...... brother. (c) ...... name is Michael.

We've got one cousin. (d) ...... cousin is called Lily.

She's got a cat. (e) ...... cat is really big. (f) ...... name is Misty.

She's also got two dogs. (g) ...... names are Bella and Duke.

Personal questions – 1

1 LISTENING 16 **Carlos has a new English tutor. His tutor asks him questions. Listen and complete his answers.**

1 My first name is Carlos and my surnames are García ....
2 Yes. It's T-O-.......-R-E-S.
3 I'm Mexican. I'm from ....
4 I'm ....
5 I'm really interested in ....
6 Yes. It's carlos.......................................@mexmail.com.

2a LISTENING 17 **Listen to three people spelling names. Write the names down.**

1 ....
2 ....
3 ....

2b SPEAKING **Work with a partner. Practise spelling the words in 2a. Use 'double' when necessary.**

✔ EXAM SUCCESS

Why is it important to know the alphabet in English when you answer personal questions?

➤ EXAM SUCCESS page 151

3 16 **Listen to the dialogue in 1 again and complete the questions in the Speaking bank.**

SPEAKING BANK

Useful questions to ask for personal information

- What's your **(a)** ....?
- **(b)** .... you spell that?
- Where are you **(c)** ....?
- How **(d)** .... are you?
- What are your **(e)** ....?
- Have you got an email **(f)** ....?

4a **Invent new personal information.**

Name: ....
Surname: ....
Nationality and home town/city:
....
Age: ....
Hobby/Hobbies: ....
Email address: ....

4b SPEAKING **Work with a partner. Prepare new dialogues using the questions in the Speaking bank and your information from 4a. Remember to ask your partner to spell their name or surname.**

5 **Write down other personal questions.**

Have you got any brothers or sisters?

PRACTICE MAKES PERFECT

6 SPEAKING **Work with a partner. Ask and answer the questions in the Speaking bank and your questions in 5. Give true answers.**

What's your name?

My name's Tatyana and my surname's Solovyova.

Can you spell that?

A personal profile

1 READING **Read this personal profile. Complete the Fact File with information from the profile.**

PERSONAL PROFILE

Hello. My name is Becky Davidson. I'm British. I'm from Liverpool. At the moment I'm 12, but my birthday is in January.

My father is called Thomas and my mother is Gemma. She's from Spain. I've got one brother. His name is Jamie and he's at university at the moment. I haven't got pets but I love animals.

I'm really into music. My favourite singers are Emeli Sandé and Ed Sheeran.

FACT FILE

NAME: (a) ....

SURNAME: (b) ....

FROM: (c) ....

AGE: (d) ....

FAMILY – PARENTS: (e) ....

FAMILY – BROTHERS AND SISTERS:
(f) ....

PETS: (g) ....

HOBBIES: (h) ....

2a Look below at the rules for using capital letters in English. Find an example of each rule in Becky's personal profile.

WRITING BANK

Using capital letters in English

We use capital letters for:

- The pronoun *I*

Example: ....

- The start of a sentence

Example: ....

- Names of people, cities, etc.

Example: ....

- Countries

Example: ....

- Nationalities/languages

Example: ....

- Months/days

Example: ....

WRITING BANK ➤ PAGE 156

2b Are the rules for using capital letters different in your language? Give examples.

3 Read this personal profile. There are no capital letters. Rewrite the text correctly using capital letters.

PROFILE

hi. my name's raul vega. i'm 13 years old. my birthday is in october. i'm from cholula. cholula is a small city near puebla in mexico.

my mother's name is susana and my father is called josé. i've got a brother called francisco and a sister called adriana. and i have a dog called rocky.

my hobby is going to the cinema. my favourite film is *the hobbit*. i think martin freeman is a very good actor. what about you? are you interested in american or british films?

4 Complete the Fact File with information about yourself.

FACT FILE

Name: (a) ....

Surname: (b) ....

From: (c) ....

Age: (d) ....

Family – parents: (e) ....

Family – brothers and sisters:
(f) ....

Pets: (g) ....

Hobbies: (h) ....

5 PRACTICE MAKES PERFECT **Write your own personal profile using the information in your Fact File in 4. When you finish, use the information in the Writing bank to check your use of capital letters.**

Language checkpoint: Unit 1

Grammar reference

to be

FORM

Affirmative	I'm (am) Tom. You're (are) British. He/She/It's (is) American. We're (are) from Spain. They're (are) 13.
Negative	I'm not (am not) Mia. You aren't (are not) Turkish. He/She/It isn't (is not) from Australia. We aren't (are not) British. They aren't (are not) 16.

Question form	Am I late? Are you OK? Is he/she/it from the UK? Are we late? Are they Mexican?
Short answers	Yes, I am./ No, I'm not. Yes, you are./No, you aren't. Yes, he/she/it is./ No, he/she/it isn't. Yes, we are./No, we aren't. Yes, they are./No, they aren't.

USE

- We use *to be* to describe a person's nationality, age, appearance, etc. *She is Spanish.*
- We do not use contractions ('m, 're, 's, etc.) in affirmative short answers. *Yes, I'm I am.*

have got

FORM

Affirmative	I've got (have got) a pen. You've got (have got) two sisters. He/She/It's got (has got) a brother. We've got (have got) an English dictionary. They've got (have got) a phone.
Negative	I haven't got (have not got) a bike. You haven't got (have not got) two cats. He/She/It hasn't got (has not got) a calculator. We haven't got (have not got) a red pen. They haven't got (have not got) a Spanish dictionary.

Question form	Have I got your email address? Have you got a phone? Has he/she/it got a name? Have we got our books? Have they got bikes?
Short answers	Yes, I have./No, I haven't. Yes, you have./No, you haven't. Yes, he/she/it has./No, he/she/it hasn't. Yes, we have./No, we haven't. Yes, they have./No, they haven't.

USE

- We use *have got* to talk about the things we possess.

Possessive adjectives

FORM

Singular	Plural
my	our
your	your
his/her/its	their

USE

My name is Claire.
Is this your bag?
Their mother is Egyptian.

Vocabulary

Countries Australia • Brazil • China • Egypt • Mexico • Russia • Spain • the UK • the US • Turkey

Nationalities American • Australian • Brazilian • British • Chinese • Egyptian • Mexican • Russian • Spanish
Turkish

The family aunt • brother • cousin • father • grandfather • grandmother • grandparents • husband • mother
nephew • niece • parent • sister • uncle • wife

Other words and phrases ➤ page 141

Grammar revision

to be — / 8 points

1 Complete the dialogue with the correct form of the verb *to be*.

Alice: (a) .... you from the US?

Frank: No, I (b) ....

Alice: Oh! (c) .... you and Ben from Australia?

Frank: Yes, we (d) .... We (e) .... from Sydney.

Alice: (f) .... Sydney the capital of Australia?

Frank: No, it (g) .... The capital (h) .... Canberra.

have got — / 7 points

2 Choose the correct alternative.

1 I <u>has/have</u> got a mobile phone.

2 Tom and Gina <u>has/have</u> got three cousins.

3 We <u>hasn't/haven't</u> got a music DVD.

4 <u>Has Daniel got/Has got Daniel</u> a sister?

5 Yes, he <u>has/has got</u>.

6 <u>Has/Have</u> you got a pet?

7 Yes, I <u>have/'ve</u>.

Possessive adjectives — / 5 points

3 Write the correct possessive adjective in each space.

1 I've got a cat. .... cat is black.

2 I've got a cousin. .... name is William.

3 Kate and Jim have got a Spanish grandmother. .... name is Maria.

4 Ethan and I have got a dictionary. .... dictionary is red.

5 I've got an English text book. .... title is *Gateway*.

Vocabulary revision

COUNTRIES — / 6 points

1 Where are these cities? Write the name of the country.

1 Rio de Janeiro ....

2 London ....

3 Cairo ....

4 Istanbul ....

5 New York ....

6 Moscow ....

NATIONALITIES — / 6 points

2 Complete the nationalities with the correct vowels (*a*, *e*, *i*, *o*, *u*).

1 C h .... n .... s ....

2 .... s t r .... l .... n

3 .... g y p t .... n

4 T .... r k .... s h

5 M .... x .... c .... n

6 B r .... z .... l .... n

THE FAMILY — / 8 points

3 Put the letters in the correct order to make a member of the family. Then say if the person is male (M), female (F), or if there is no difference (ND).

1 nosuci .... M/F/ND

2 cenie .... M/F/ND

3 trises .... M/F/ND

4 fiew .... M/F/ND

5 nardgrapten .... M/F/ND

6 tuna .... M/F/ND

7 phewen .... M/F/ND

8 clune .... M/F/ND

Total: / 40 points

2 School days

Vocabulary

School subjects

1a Work with a partner. Match the school rooms (a–e) with the correct word or phrase. Use a dictionary if necessary.

art • English • French • geography • history
ICT (Information and Communication Technology)
maths • music • PE (Physical Education) • science

a

b

c

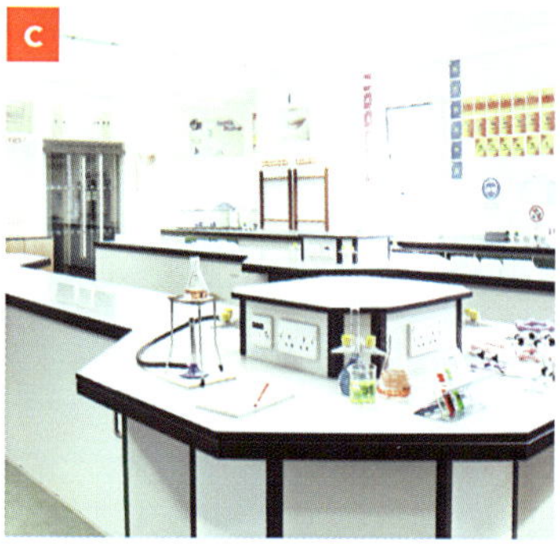

d

e

1b 18 Listen and repeat.

2 SPEAKING Work with a partner. What subjects have you got today?

We've got maths at quarter to nine.

Then we've got English.

Everyday objects

3a Look at the picture. Which of the words in the box are *not* in the photo? Check that you understand all the words. Use a dictionary if necessary.

calculator • folder • laptop • marker pens
mobile phone • MP3 player • pencil case
snack • tablet • trainers

3b 19 Listen and repeat.

4 LISTENING 20 Listen to four students. What have they got in their bags today? What lesson is it for?

	Object	Lesson
1		
2		
3		
4		

5 SPEAKING Work with a partner. Say which of the objects in 3 you have got in your bag now and why.

I've got my trainers.

Why?

I've got football practice after school.

home news about message board sign in

BRING YOUR OWN TECHNOLOGY (BYOT) TO SCHOOL

The idea is simple. In some schools, students take their personal smartphone, tablet or laptop to school and use it in class. But is that a good idea? What's your opinion?

In some schools they have a BYOT system, but not in mine. In my best friend's school, students take their smartphones to use in class. But then they send texts, play games, watch videos or take photos. That's OK at home, but not at school. Reply Like

New technology is expensive for schools. But my students all have smartphones at home. Now I bring mine to class and they bring theirs. It's very useful in many different school subjects. A smartphone has a calculator for maths, a dictionary for English or French, maps for geography, and videos for history, science … Reply Like

I've got two daughters. At my daughters' school, they have a BYOT system. But the children aren't happy. Now there's a big difference between students in class. Some students have got brilliant new laptops or tablets. Some have got old laptops. And for some it isn't easy to buy a computer. I don't think it's fair. Reply Like

1 **Work with a partner. Have you got a phone and a tablet or laptop? Do you take any of them to school with you? Why/Why not?**

2 READING **Read the Internet forum and answer the questions.**

1 What is 'BYOT to school'?

....

2 Who thinks 'BYOT to school' is good?

a Mia Jones Yes/No

b Brad Simmons Yes/No

c Angela Hughes Yes/No

3 **Are the statements True (T) or False (F)?**

1 It's necessary for Mia to take her phone to class. T/F

2 In Mia's opinion, students learn a lot with phones in class. T/F

3 In Brad's opinion, it's difficult for schools to buy laptops and tablets. T/F

4 In Brad's opinion, smartphones are only useful for science. T/F

5 In Angela's daughters' school, the BYOT system is not popular with the students. T/F

6 In Angela's daughters' classes, the students have all got similar technology. T/F

✓ EXAM SUCCESS

To do exercise 3, is it a good idea to read the text quickly or slowly? Why?

➤ EXAM SUCCESS page 151

4 **CRITICAL THINKING**

Think! Then compare ideas with your class.

- When is it important to have a mobile phone or smartphone?
- When is it important to switch it off?

5 **What do the underlined words in the text mean? Guess and then check in your dictionary.**

6 SPEAKING **What about *you*?**

When do you use a mobile phone or smartphone? Why?

When do you use a tablet and/or laptop? Why?

Grammar in context

Flipped classroom: watch the grammar presentation video.

Possessive 's

1 Look at the sentences (a–c) and then match 1 to 4 with A to D.

a In my best friend's school, it's OK to take a phone.
b I've got two daughters. At my daughters' school, it's OK to take smartphones.
c In Mia and Angela's opinion, technology isn't always good.

1 We use the apostrophe (') …
2 After singular names or nouns …
3 After plural nouns ending in -s …
4 When we name more than one person …

A we just add an apostrophe (').
B to show possession.
C we add 's.
D the 's goes after the last person.

GRAMMAR REFERENCE ➤ PAGE 32

2 Look at the people and their possessions. Write sentences.

1  Harry ➤ mobile phone
It's Harry's mobile phone. 

2  my dad ➤ bag
It's ……………………………… 

3  the teachers ➤ computer
It's ……………………………… 

4  my sisters ➤ marker pens
They're ……………………………… 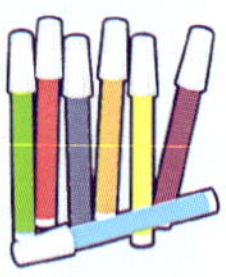

5  Emma ➤ MP3 player
It's ……………………………… 

6  the students ➤ books
They're ……………………………… 

7  Alex and Amy ➤ tablets
They're ……………………………… 

3 Are the sentences correct? Rewrite the incorrect sentences.

1 They've got tablets at William's and Dana's school.
2 Is Jacks pencil case blue?
3 My friend's names are Oscar and Ellie.
4 My music teachers' names are Paula and Eve.
5 Our schools' head teacher is in favour of mobile phones.
6 It's my grandparents' house.
7 I think they're Matt and Joe's bags.

4 SPEAKING Work in a small group. Point to an object in the classroom. Whose is it?

It's Katie's calculator.

Possessive pronouns

5a Look at sentences a to c and complete 1 to 3 with the correct possessive pronouns.

a It's OK to take a phone, but she doesn't take hers.
b In some schools they take smartphones, but not in mine.
c I bring my phone to class and the students bring theirs.

This is my phone. = This phone is (1) ………………
This is your phone. = This phone is yours.
This is his phone. = This phone is his.
This is her phone. = This phone is (2) ………………
This is our phone. = This phone is ours.
This is their phone. = This is phone is (3) ………………

5b The words in red are possessive pronouns. What type of words are the words in blue?

GRAMMAR REFERENCE ➤ PAGE 32

6 Choose the correct alternative.

1 She's my/mine best friend.
2 Are they your/yours pens?
3 The red pencil case is my/mine.
4 They're our/ours bags, not your/yours.
5 I think the laptop is their/theirs.
6 Whose trainers are they? Are they her/hers?
7 I think they're Matt's trainers. Yes, they're his/theirs.

7 **Answer the questions using possessive pronouns.**

1 Are they Vanessa's books? Yes, *they're hers*
2 Is it your MP3 player? Yes, ...
3 Is it Ethan's dictionary? Yes, ...
4 Is it your brothers' tablet? Yes, ...
5 Are they our pencil cases? Yes, ...
6 Is it my snack? Yes, ...

Regular and irregular plural nouns

8 **Look at the two lists. Which are regular plural nouns? Which are irregular?**

List 1: Regular/Irregular	List 2: Regular/Irregular
man ➤ men	boy ➤ boys
woman ➤ women	girl ➤ girls
child ➤ children	friend ➤ friends
person ➤ people	family ➤ families
	country ➤ countries

GRAMMAR REFERENCE ➤ PAGE 32

9 **What can you see? Write sentences about the pictures using numbers and the singular or plural form of the word.**

The Johnson family

The Henderson family

I can see …

1 *two girls* (girl)
2 .... (family)
3 .... (boy)
4 .... (woman)
5 .... (man)
6 .... (person)
7 .... (child)

Describing faces

1a **Work with a partner. Say the words in the box and touch the different parts of your face.**

ear • eye • hair • mouth • nose • teeth

1b 21 **Listen and repeat.**

2 SPEAKING **Work with a partner. Look at the adjectives in the box. What part(s) of the face can we describe with each adjective? One word cannot describe a part of the face. Which one? Use your dictionary to help you if necessary.**

big • blue • brown • curly • dark • fair • green
grey • long • red • short • small • straight • tall

I think curly is for hair.

3 **Read the description of the boy in the photo. Find three mistakes.**

He's got long, fair hair. His hair is curly. He's got brown eyes. His eyes are big. His ears and mouth aren't very big or small – they're average.

4a **Write a description of yourself.**

....
....
....
....
....
....
....

4b **Give your description to your teacher. They will read out a description to the class. Who is it?**

Organising your STUDIES

LIFE SKILLS OBJECTIVES

- To think about where and when to study
- To see how other students organise their time and space
- To create a weekly study plan

KEY CONCEPTS

school timetable [n]: *On a school timetable you have all the days and times of your classes.* **shelf/shelves [n singular/plural]:** *Put the books on the shelf, in the correct section.* **study planner [n]:** *With a study planner, you write all the things you do in a day, at school and after school.* **time management [n]/manage your time [phrase]:** *Time management helps you to use your time in a good, efficient way.*

1 **Work with a partner. Look at this questionnaire. Take it in turns to ask and answer all the questions.**

2 READING **Read about study spaces and then evaluate your own study space. Is it good or bad? Why?**

STUDY SPACE – Some tips

- It's useful to have a special place to study. It's easy to have everything organised and ready there.
- If you haven't got a private place to study, ask your family and friends not to disturb you when you are busy.
- It's ideal to have good light when you read and write. It's important for your eyes. Light from the window is best in the day. But a reading lamp is important for the evening and night.
- Open your window. Fresh air is good, too.
- A comfortable chair is important. If you aren't comfortable, it's difficult to concentrate.
- It's important to organise your books in a clear and logical way. Have a special shelf for your school books.
- Use different folders for different subjects. Put separate sections in your folders for different topics. Now it's easy for you to find information quickly.
- Have you got a TV/games console/mobile phone/tablet in your room? Turn them off when you study.

Your study space

Where do you usually study – in your bedroom, in another room at home, in a library …?

....

Have you got a comfortable chair?

....

Have you got a place where you can write?

....

Has the place got a lot of light?

....

Is it quiet?

....

Where are all your books? Is it easy to find the things you need to take to school each day?

....

Is it easy to find all your notes for different subjects and topics? How are they organised?

....

3 **Work with a partner. Look at the picture. Using the information in the text in 2, what is good and bad about this study place? Make two lists: Good/Bad.**

4 LISTENING ▶ 22 **Students are giving advice about time management. Watch or listen. Put the advice in the order they mention it.**

Tip 1 .... Tip 2 .... Tip 3 ....

A the importance of parents having a copy of your study planner

B the importance of knowing your school timetable

C the importance of using a study planner

5 ▶ 22 **Listen/Watch again. Match the sentence halves.**

1 Know …
2 Have one copy of your school timetable at school …
3 On a study planner, write down your school timetable …
4 With a study planner …
5 Give a copy of your study planner …
6 It's important to plan …

a and activities after school.
b to your parents.
c your school timetable.
d it's easy to plan study and homework.
e and one copy at home.
f your rest periods.

6 **What is your opinion of the advice in 5 – ✓✓ very good, ✓ good, or ✗ not very good?**

7 **Look at this study planner. Is this student's week similar to yours? What is similar and what is different?**

MY WEEKLY STUDY PLANNER

	Mon	Tues	Wed	Thurs	Fri	Sat	Sun
7–9 am	Breakfast	Breakfast	Breakfast	Breakfast	Breakfast	Breakfast	Rest
9–10 am	French	PE	Geography	ICT	Geography	Volleyball match	Breakfast
10–11 am	English	PE	History	ICT	Maths		Piano practice
11–12 am	Science	English	English	Maths	English		
12–1 pm	Science	Music	French	Maths	Spanish		
1–2 pm	Lunch	Lunch	Lunch	Lunch	Lunch	Lunch	Lunch
2–3 pm	Art	Maths	PE	Science	History		
3–5 pm	Art club	Choir	Volleyball practice	Piano lesson	Rest		
5–6 pm	Homework	Homework	Homework	Homework	Homework	Piano practice	Homework
6–7 pm	Dinner	Dinner	Dinner	Dinner	Dinner	Dinner	Dinner
7–8 pm	Homework	Piano practice	Homework	Homework	Homework		Homework
8–9 pm	Rest	Rest	Rest	Rest	Rest		

LIFE TASK

Create your own study planner in English. Follow this plan:

1 *Copy the table in 7.*
2 *Put in your school timetable.*
3 *Add other activities after school and at the weekend.*
4 *Add times when it's easy and convenient to study and do homework.*
5 *Compare and comment on your study planner with other students. Have you got ideas to make their study planners better?*

Listening

1 **Look at the photo of a 'Studio School'. Is it similar to your school? Why/Why not?**

2a Read the questions.

1 The age of students at Studio Schools is between ...
   a 14 and 18.
   b 14 and 19.
   c 15 and 19.
2 Studio Schools are small because ...
   a the classrooms aren't very big.
   b the students have got a lot of problems.
   c it's important for the students to have personal attention.
3 Studio Schools are different because ...
   a the classes are very practical.
   b they've got unusual subjects.
   c the students decide their school subjects.
4 At Studio Schools, the students ...
   a are always in classrooms.
   b do real work outside school.
   c do work on Saturday or Sunday.
5 Harry ...
   a hasn't got homework.
   b has got a lot of homework every day.
   c is happy with his homework.
6 The idea of Studio Schools is to ...
   a help students to study and work.
   b teach students to be artists and inventors.
   c help students to be the next Leonardo Da Vinci.

2b LISTENING 23 **Listen and choose the correct answers.**

3 SPEAKING **What about *you*?**

What is your opinion of this school?

Grammar in context

Question words

1a Look at the questions and check that you understand the question words.

1 How old are you?
2 Where are your classes?
3 How many students has this school got?
4 Who is your personal coach?
5 Which subjects are typical here?
6 How much homework have you got?
7 What is a personal coach?
8 When/What time are lessons?
9 Why are they called Studio Schools?
10 How do you study?

1b Match each question in 1a with the correct answer below.

a Usually from 9 to 5.
b It depends, but not much usually.
c I'm 15.
d Here, in the classrooms at school.
e It's a teacher who helps us.
f There are 300.
g Maths, English and science.
h Because of the studios of the past, in Italy.
i Miss Feldman.
j For example, working in teams.

GRAMMAR REFERENCE ➤ PAGE 32

2a Complete the sentences with the correct question words.

1 .... long is this lesson?
2 .... do you prefer – art or science?
3 .... old is your best friend?
4 .... many students are in this class?
5 .... is your father from?
6 .... is your favourite singer?
7 .... is your birthday?
8 .... time is the next break?

2b SPEAKING **Work with a partner. Ask and answer the questions.**

this, that, these, those

3a Match each sentence with the correct picture.

1 This school is old.
2 That school is new.
3 These students have got school uniform.
4 Those students haven't got school uniform.

3b Which of the words in blue are …

1 singular/plural?
2 for things that are distant from the speaker?
3 for things that are close to the speaker?

GRAMMAR REFERENCE ➤ PAGE 32

4 Look at the pictures and complete the sentences with *this*, *that*, *these* or *those*.

1 .... are my books.

2 .... is my book.

3 .... are my books.

4 .... is my book.

5 Choose the correct alternative.

1 *This/These* phone is Julia's.
2 *This/That* is my dictionary, here in my hand.
3 I think *that/those* pens are mine.
4 *These/Those* boys in the other room are my friends.
5 *This/These* are my favourite school subjects.
6 I think *this/that* is my tablet, but it's difficult to see from here.

Articles

6a Match each rule (a–e) with one of the sentences (1–5).

1 Harry's Studio School is a new school.
2 It's an interesting school.
3 The school is in the UK.
4 The students there have personal coaches.
5 – Students in the UK have got maths and English.

a We use an when the next word begins with a vowel (*a*, *e*, *i*, *o*, *u*) sound.
b We use a/an the first time that we talk about something.
c We use no article when we talk about something in general.
d We use the when we talk about something for the second or third time.
e We use the when we talk about specific things or people.

GRAMMAR REFERENCE ➤ PAGE 32

6b Complete the sentences with *a*, *an*, *the* or *–*.

1 I've got .... English textbook. .... book is called *Gateway*.
2 I think .... geography is interesting.
3 She's got .... cat. .... cat is black and white.
4 It's OK to use .... mobile phones here.
5 .... computers in my classroom are new.

7 Complete the dialogues with the correct responses.

1 Is that your school?
 a Yes, it's a school.
 b Yes, this is your favourite school.
 c No, mine is very modern.
2 What have you got in your bag, Sophie?
 a Yes, I've got the tablet and my marker pens.
 b Just my books today. And you?
 c Have you got your laptop today? I haven't.
3 How old are the students in your class?
 a I think we've got 24 or 25 in English.
 b I think they're 13, but maybe one or two are 14.
 c I'm not sure but I think it's a very old school.
4 What's your opinion of the school?
 a I think school is really important.
 b The teachers are very good here.
 c Teachers and new technology are both important.

✔ EXAM SUCCESS

Look at the incorrect answers in 7. Is the grammar wrong? Or are they answers to different questions?

➤ EXAM SUCCESS page 151

Describing people

1 LISTENING ▶ 24 **Look at the class photo. Listen to two people talking about it. Which person in the photo is Karen and which is Tom?**

2a ▶ 24 **Complete these sentences from the dialogue. Listen again if necessary.**

1 ………… her hair light brown or fair?

2 She's quite ………….

3 He isn't very ………… actually.

4 He ………… short hair.

5 Tom's hair is a bit ………….

6 He's got really brown ………….

2b Look at the information in the Speaking bank. Choose the correct alternative.

SPEAKING BANK

Useful language for describing people

- With just an adjective, we use _be/have got_, e.g. Sentence 5.
- With a noun (with or without an adjective), we use _be/have got_, e.g. Sentence 4.
- To make an adjective extreme, we add _not very/a bit/quite/very/really_. (Choose two)
- To make an adjective soft, we add _not very/a bit/quite/very/really_. (Choose three)
- We say 'He has got _–/a_ short brown _hair/hairs_.'

3 Complete the sentences with the correct form of *be* or *have got*.

1 My sister ………… red hair.

2 He ………… quite short.

3 His eyes ………… green.

4 She ………… a small mouth.

5 They ………… fair hair.

6 ………… her hair brown?

PRACTICE MAKES PERFECT

4 SPEAKING **Work with a partner. Student A, turn to page 154. Student B, turn to page 155. Then take it in turns to describe and identify the people in the photo. Remember to use the information in the Speaking bank.**

Developing writing

An informal email

1 READING **Read the email from James. Find James in the photo below. Which one is Connor?**

Hi Luis!

My name's James Farrell. I'm your new e-pal. I'm from Galway in Ireland. Here's a photo of me with my two brothers. I'm the one with blue eyes and light brown hair. My hair's quite long. I'm not tall, but my brother Connor is. He's very tall! He's the one in the green T-shirt.

My school is called Manor Park. It isn't a very big school. It's only got 400 students. My favourite subjects are maths and science. I've got maths on Monday and Wednesday and science on Tuesday and Friday. I also like ICT. At school we've got a special computer room.

After school we've got a lot of homework. But I've also got time for other activities. For example, I'm in the school drama club. At the weekend I've got guitar lessons.

Write back soon and tell me about yourself.

All the best

James

2 **Read the email again. What are James's answers to these questions?**

1 What's the name of your school?

....

2 Is your school big or small?

....

3 How many students has your school got?

....

4 What are your favourite subjects?

....

5 When have you got maths?

....

6 Have you got a computer room at school?

....

7 Have you usually got a lot of homework?

....

8 Have you got any special hobbies or activities after school?

....

3 **Look at James's email again and complete the expressions in the Writing bank.**

WRITING BANK

Writing informal emails

- Start with .... *(Luis)* or *Dear (Luis)*. Only write the person's first name *(Luis)*, not their surname.
- Use contractions when possible, e.g. *We* .... *got a special computer room.*
- To finish, write *Write* .... *soon*, ... *the best*, or *Best wishes*.

4 **Answer the questions in 2 about yourself. Make notes.**

PRACTICE MAKES PERFECT

5 **Imagine that you are James's new e-pal. Write back to James with information about yourself. Follow this plan.**

Paragraph 1: *Give your name, say where you are from, give a basic physical description of yourself.*

Paragraph 2: *Give information about your school, including your timetable and your favourite subjects.*

Paragraph 3: *Write about homework and other activities.*

Use expressions from the Writing bank to start and end your email.

WRITING BANK ➤ PAGE 156

Grammar reference

Possessive 's

FORM

Joe's laptop
Pete and Mark's classroom
My parents' car

USE

- We use *'s* to indicate possession.
- When there is more than one person named, we put *'s* after the last person.
- When a noun is plural and ends with an *-s*, we just add an apostrophe (').

Possessive pronouns

FORM

Singular	Plural
mine	ours
yours	yours
his/hers/its	theirs

USE

We use possessive pronouns when we do not repeat the noun.
My name is Robert and hers is Helen.
My school is in the city centre. Where is yours?
Their trainers are new. Mine are really old.

Regular and irregular plural nouns

FORM

To make regular plural nouns, we add *-s*:
book ➤ books trainer ➤ trainers
Some nouns end in consonant + *y*. The plural form ends *-ies*:
country ➤ countries family ➤ families
Some nouns have irregular plural forms:
child ➤ children person ➤ people
man ➤ men woman ➤ women

Question words

USE

We use ***how many*** to ask about quantities (countable).
We use ***how much*** to ask about prices and quantities (uncountable).
We use ***what*** to ask about things.
We use ***what time*** to ask about times of the day.
We use ***when*** to ask about time in general.
We use ***where*** to ask about places.
We use ***which*** to ask about specific things.
We use ***who*** to ask about people.
We use ***why*** to ask for explanations.
We use ***how*** to ask about the way we do things.

this, that, these, those

FORM

Singular	Plural
This is my father.	*These are my parents.*
That is my brother.	*Those are my cousins.*

USE

- We use ***this*** and ***these*** for people and objects which are close to the speaker.
- We use ***that*** and ***those*** for people and objects that are distant from the speaker.

Articles

A/An

- We use ***a/an*** when we mention something for the first time, or to say that the person or thing is one of a number of things or people. ***An*** comes before a vowel sound. *I've got a cousin.*

The

- We use ***the*** to talk about something or somebody mentioned before. *This is a good school. The school is not very big.*
- We also use ***the*** to talk about a specific thing. *The book on the table is mine.*

No article

- We do not use an article when we are talking about things in general. *I like history.*

Vocabulary

School subjects art • English • French • geography • history • ICT • maths • music • PE • science
Everyday objects calculator • folder • laptop • marker pens • mobile phone • MP3 player • pencil case snack • tablet • trainers
Describing faces ear • eye • hair • mouth • nose • teeth
Adjectives big • blue • brown • curly • dark • fair • green • grey • long • red • short • small • straight • tall
Other words and phrases ➤ page 142

Grammar revision

Possessive 's and possessive pronouns — / 6 points

1 Complete the sentences with the words in the box. There are eight words but only six spaces.

her • hers • mine • my • sister's • sisters' • their • theirs

1 I've got a tablet. ➤

That's (a) .... tablet. That tablet is

(b) ....

2 My sister has got a tablet. ➤

It's my (c) .... tablet. That tablet is

(d) ....

3 My sisters have got a tablet. ➤

It's my (e) .... tablet. That tablet is

(f) ....

Regular and irregular plural nouns — / 4 points

2 Write the plural form of the words.

1 parent ....

person ....

2 child ....

family ....

3 nephew ....

boy ....

4 woman ....

girl ....

Question words — / 6 points

3 Choose the correct alternative.

1 Which/Why is my bag?
2 How much/old is your grandfather?
3 What time/When is your birthday?
4 Where/Why isn't Maria at school today?
5 What/Who is your maths teacher?
6 How/What many subjects have you got today?

this, that, these, those and articles — / 6 points

4 Complete the text with *this*, *those*, *a*, *an*, *the*, or – (no article). Use each word once only.

'We've got (a) .... old house. (b) .... house is quite small. We've also got (c) .... cat. Look. Here it is. (d) .... is my cat. I love (e) .... cats in general, except (f) .... my friend's cat. It's not very friendly!'

Vocabulary revision

SCHOOL SUBJECTS — / 6 points

1 What are the school subjects?

You study …

1 numbers. ....
2 things from the past. ....
3 computers, the Internet, etc. ....
4 sports. ....
5 gravity, plants, $E = mc^2$. ....
6 different countries, the weather, maps, rocks, etc. ....

EVERYDAY OBJECTS — / 6 points

2 Find six everyday objects and write them below:

markerplayertrainerscasetopphoneMP3penslappencilmobile

1 .... 4 ....
2 .... 5 ....
3 .... 6 ....

DESCRIBING FACES — / 6 points

3 Complete the description with parts of the face and adjectives.

'This man's hair is (a) ...., (b) ...., and (c) .... He's got big (d) .... His (e) .... is long. He's only got three (f) ....!'

Total: / 40 points

Reading

➤ TIP FOR READING EXAMS

In *True/False* activities, remember …
First read the text quickly and then read the *True/False* sentences. After that, read the text again, slowly.

➤ EXAM SUCCESS page 151

1 READING **Read about three schools. Match the schools and the photos.**

1 ………… 2 ………… 3 …………

2 **Read the text again. Are these sentences True (T) or False (F)?**

1 Antarctica has just one primary school. T/F
2 The teachers in Antarctica are Spanish. T/F
3 The students in Pumaqangtang school are in the school in the day and at night. T/F
4 The only unusual thing about the school in Pumaqangtang is that it is very cold. T/F
5 The old Gulu village school is very far from the children's village. T/F
6 The students from the old Gulu village school have a new teacher. T/F

3 SPEAKING **What about *you*?**

Which is your favourite school in the text? Why?

Use of English

➤ TIP FOR USE OF ENGLISH

In activities where you choose correct responses in dialogues, remember …
The response must be grammatically correct AND logical.

➤ EXAM SUCCESS page 151

4 **Complete the five dialogues. Choose the correct responses.**

1 What are your hobbies?
a Yes, they are. b I'm into sport.
c My cousin is interested in superhero films.

2 What's this in English?
a I'm sorry, I don't know. b How do you spell that?
c Yes, it's a notebook.

3 Where is Fiona from?
a I think this is Irish.
b The US, I think. Or maybe Canada.
c I don't know. Maybe she's from school.

4 Is that your tablet?
a No, it's my mum's. b My mum's got a tablet.
c Which tablet is yours?

5 What do you think of this album?
a I love music, especially pop.
b The singer is great.
c No, I think it's my brother's.

INCREDIBLE SCHOOLS!

1 There are schools in very cold places! Esperanza Base is an Argentinian army base in Antarctica. There are about ten families. The base has got a primary school, and two teachers. Antarctica has got one other primary school. It's in Villa Las Estrellas, a Chilean army base. Villa Las Estrellas has got approximately 15 students and two teachers. The teachers in the Antarctic are from Argentina and Chile so the classes are in Spanish.

2 Pumaqangtang is a town with about 1,000 people in it. It's in Tibet, in the Himalayas. It's got a primary school. The school is very, very high. It's at an altitude of approximately 5,500 metres! The school has got about 105 students. Their home is in the school. One problem there is the temperature. Some days it's minus 40°C! The school is about 30 years old. The classes are in Chinese and in Tibetan.

3 Gulu village is in China. The old primary school is in a spectacular place in a National Park. But it's very difficult to get there, and very dangerous! And it's a long journey, because it's a five-hour walk! The school has got five classrooms but just one teacher. They haven't got computers. There's a place to play basketball but it isn't easy to play basketball high in the mountains. So now the students have got a new school in a different place. The school is big and it's easy to get to class. Their old teacher is with them in the new school.

Listening

➤ TIP FOR LISTENING EXAMS

In picture activities, remember …

Look at the pictures BEFORE you listen. They can give you an idea of what comes in the dialogues.

➤ EXAM SUCCESS page 151

5 Work with a partner. What is in the pictures?

6a LISTENING ▶ 25 **Read the questions. Listen to three dialogues and tick (✓) the correct picture.**

1 What day and time is it now for Liam and Carla?

a Tuesday

b Wednesday

c Tuesday

2 Where is Mason from?

a

b

c

3 Which is Mark's uncle?

a

b

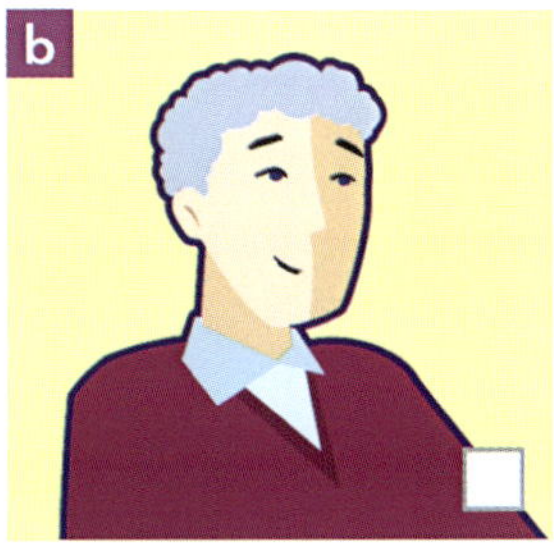

c

6b ▶ 25 **Listen again and check your answers.**

Speaking

➤ TIP FOR SPEAKING EXAMS

In speaking exams, remember …

It's important to know how to spell things such as your first name, your surname or your address.

➤ EXAM SUCCESS page 151

7a Work with a partner. Student A, turn to page 154. Spell the names to your partner. Student B, write down the names. When you finish, check the spelling.

7b Now change roles. Student B, turn to page 155. Spell the names to your partner. Then check.

8 Work in a small group. Individually, choose a new word from Units 1 and 2. Spell the word. Who is the first to guess the word? Now it is their turn. When you finish, play again.

'CAN DO' PROGRESS CHECK UNITS 1–2 — CEF

1 How well can you do these things in English now? Give yourself a mark from 1 to 4.

1 = I can do it very well.
2 = I can do it quite well.
3 = I have some problems.
4 = I can't do it.

a I can name different countries and nationalities. ☐
b I can ask for and give basic personal information using *to be* and *have got*. ☐
c I can talk about my family. ☐
d I can understand simple texts giving basic personal information. ☐
e I can write a short personal profile. ☐
f I can talk about a basic school day. ☐
g I can use question words to ask basic questions. ☐
h I can understand simple texts about school life. ☐
i I can give basic physical descriptions. ☐
j I can write a short informal email. ☐

2 Now decide what you need to do to improve.

1 Look again at my book/notes.
2 Do more practice exercises. ➤ WORKBOOK Units 1 and 2
3 Ask for help.
4 Other: ....

3 24/7

Vocabulary

Everyday activities

1a Work with a partner. Match the pictures with some of these phrases.

do homework • finish school • get up • go home go to bed • go to school have a shower • have breakfast • have dinner have lunch • start school

1

2

3

4

5

6

1b Pictures 1 to 6 are in a logical order. Continue the everyday activities. Use all the phrases. Use your dictionary if necessary.

get up ➤ have a shower ➤ have breakfast ➤ go to school ➤ ?

1c ▶ 26 Listen and check your answers.

1d ▶ 26 Listen again and repeat.

2 SPEAKING Work in small groups. Take it in turns to talk about a typical day.

I get up at quarter past seven.

I have a shower first. Then I have breakfast.

I go to school by bus.

Free-time activities

3a Work with a partner. Match the photos with some of the free-time activities in the box.

chat online • do sport • draw • go out with friends listen to music • paint • play computer games play the guitar/piano • read • surf the Internet watch films/TV

1 – chat online, surf the Internet …

1

2

3

4

5

6

7

3b ▶ 27 Listen and repeat.

4a Put the free-time activities in order for you. 1 = great, 10 = boring.

1 = go out with friends, 2 = chat online …

4b SPEAKING Work with a partner. Compare your lists. Are they similar?

5 LISTENING ▶ 28 Listen to people talking about their everyday and free-time activities. Match the speakers (1–5) with the activities (a–e).

1	Speaker 1	a	do sport
2	Speaker 2	b	have lunch at home
3	Speaker 3	c	have dinner with the family
4	Speaker 4	d	play computer games
5	Speaker 5	e	watch TV until 10.30 pm

1 READING **Read this article from a school magazine. It's about two teenagers and their hobbies. What do they get for doing their free-time activities?**

Charlotte: ....

Nick: ....

Hobbies that give you something else!

Charlotte Sandison

When Charlotte Sandison finishes school, she goes home, does her homework and then she immediately starts reading. 'When I finish a book, I go online and I write a review of it. I have a book club. We're a group of friends and we chat online about the books we like.' Because Charlotte is passionate about reading, authors send her their books and ask her to write about them on the book club website. 'Not every book is great. But one day I want to be a writer and you learn from every book you read.'

Nick Tyler

Nick Tyler loves computer games. 'I don't play during the week because of homework and football, but at the weekend I play a lot.' Nick is a computer games tester. Games studios pay him to play new games. They don't pay him much, but they also give him the games. 'You don't just play. You answer questions online and write your opinion.' He doesn't like all the games. 'Sometimes they send games for really young kids! But it's cool when I play a new game and my best friend doesn't know about it!' Is he interested in making games himself one day? 'I play football, but I don't want to be a professional footballer! It's the same with computer games.'

2 **Read the text again. Is this information about Charlotte (C), Nick (N) or both (B)?**

1 They enjoy doing sport. C/N/B
2 Their hobby is connected to a job that they are interested in. C/N/B
3 Writing is a part of their free-time activity. C/N/B
4 They do their hobby on Saturday and Sunday only. C/N/B
5 There is a part of their hobby that they think is bad. C/N/B
6 They need the Internet for a part of their free-time activity. C/N/B

3 **CRITICAL THINKING**

Think! Then compare ideas with your class.

- Are computer games good or bad for you? Why?

4 **Match the underlined words in the text with these definitions.**

1 a text where you give your opinion of something
2 make something go from one place to another or from one person to another
3 somebody who does things to see if something is good or bad
4 without waiting
5 a place on the Internet where you find information about something

5 SPEAKING **What about *you*?**

1 Which of the two hobbies do you prefer? Why?
2 Which of your hobbies do you recommend to other people? Why?

Present simple – affirmative

1a Look at the sentences. When do verbs in the present simple finish in *-s*/*-es*?

1 Some hobbies **give** the opportunity to do more.
2 When she **finishes** school, she **goes** home and she **does** her homework.
3 When I **finish** each book, I **go** online and I **write** a review.
4 She immediately **starts** reading.
5 We **chat** online.
6 You **learn** from every book you **read**.
7 He **loves** computer games.
8 They **give** him the games.
9 It **seems** interesting.

1b Are these sentences True (T) or False (F)?

1 We use the present simple to talk about regular or routine actions. T/F
2 We use the present simple to talk about things that are always or usually true. T/F

GRAMMAR REFERENCE ➤ PAGE 46

2a PRONUNCIATION ▶ 29 Listen. Which of the words have the /ɪz/ sound at the end?

1	finishes	6	does
2	goes	7	studies
3	reads	8	teaches
4	has	9	cries
5	watches	10	washes

2b ▶ 29 Listen again and practise saying the words.

2c Choose the correct alternative in the spelling rules.

1 We add _-s/-es_ to the verbs *go* and *do*.
2 The *he/she/it* form of *have* is _regular/irregular_.
3 To verbs that end in *-sh* or *-ch*, we add _-s/-es_ and pronounce it /ɪz/.
4 With verbs that end in consonant + *y*, the *he/she/it* form is _-ys/-ies_.

3 Choose the correct alternative.

1 They _play/plays_ football on Friday.
2 My friends _read/reads_ comics.
3 Dylan and Matt _study/studies_ German.
4 Our teacher _has/have_ her own blog.
5 Katie and I _go/goes_ to school by bus.
6 My sister _watch/watches_ TV after school.

4 Complete the sentences with the present simple form of the correct verb in the box.

ask • do • finish • go • hate • love • play • write

1 My friend .... five different musical instruments.
2 My friends .... ten messages every day.
3 She .... her homework at the weekend.
4 I .... English. It's my favourite subject.
5 My sister .... sports. In her opinion, they're all bad.
6 When school .... at four o'clock, we .... home.
7 My teacher .... a lot of questions.

Present simple – negative

5 Look at the sentences and complete the rules with *don't* or *doesn't*.

a I **don't play** during the school week.
b They **don't pay** him much.
c You **don't** just **play**.
d They send him games that he really **doesn't like**.
e It's cool when I play a new game that my best friend **doesn't know** about!

1 After *he/she/it* we use ....
2 After *I/you/we/they* we use ....
3 After ***don't*** or ***doesn't*** we use the verb without *-s/-es*.

GRAMMAR REFERENCE ➤ PAGE 46

6 Complete the sentences with *don't* or *doesn't*.

1 I .... get up at 5 am.
2 Megan and Lucy .... watch football on TV.
3 Andy .... play football.
4 His father .... go to work by car.
5 You .... walk to school.
6 Ryan and I .... do our homework on Sunday.
7 That student .... listen to the teacher.

7 **Make these sentences negative.**

1 My grandmother plays computer games.
My grandmother doesn't play computer games.
2 I go to school in a sports car.
3 My cousin reads ten books a day.
4 Her parents watch TV at 7 am.
5 I speak Chinese.
6 Sam and Leo go to bed at ten o'clock.
7 His brother makes the dinner.
8 She watches TV in the afternoon.

8a **Look at the words in the table. You have five minutes to write as many correct sentences as possible with the words. Use each word at least once.**

don't	to	we	go
Stephanie	and	play	watch
watches	computer games	goes	school
doesn't	you	TV	I

8b **Write one long sentence with the words. How many words are there in your sentence?**

9a **Are the sentences true for you? If not, add *don't*.**

1 I .... play computer games during the school week.
2 I .... watch TV before school.
3 I .... get up at 7 am on Saturday.
4 I .... listen to music when I do my homework.
5 I .... go out with my friends at the weekend.
6 I .... play the guitar.

9b SPEAKING **Say the sentences to your partner. How many are the same?**

9c **Tell the class about your partner.**

Amanda doesn't play computer games during the school week.

Places in a town

1a **Work with a partner. Match the pictures with the words in the box.**

cinema • library • museum • park • restaurant
shopping centre • sports centre • swimming pool

1b 30 **Listen and repeat.**

2 **What place or places in 1 do you associate with these words?**

1 books
2 trees and flowers
3 pizzas
4 water
5 rackets and balls
6 money and credit cards
7 films
8 old objects

3 SPEAKING **Work with a partner. Which of the places in 1 have you got in your town or city?**

We've got two cinemas.

Where are they?

On London Road and on Park Street.

Attitudes to TV

LIFE SKILLS OBJECTIVES

- To think about how much TV you watch
- To consider how TV influences us
- To consider other things to do apart from watching TV

KEY CONCEPTS

TV programme [n]: *My favourite TV programme is on every Friday at 7 pm.* **turn on/off [v]:** *When your programme finishes, turn the TV off.* **advert/advertisement [n]:** *After the programme, they have three minutes of adverts.* **positive/negative influence [n]:** *A positive influence of TV is that you know what is new in the world.*

1a READING **Look at the TV survey below. Complete it with your answers. When your answer is *Yes*, give details.**

1b Compare your answers with the rest of the class. Are your answers similar? What are the top answers?

2a The questions in 1 are from a survey of high school students from the US. Here are the results below. Are they similar to your class?

TV SURVEY

Please tell us if you:

		YES	NO
1	watch TV before you go to school in the morning.		
2	have a TV in your bedroom.		
3	watch TV with your parents.		
4	think TV in general is very violent.		
5	like to have the TV on when you study.		
6	have a favourite TV show that you just can't miss.		

Now tell us how many:

1. TV programmes (30–60 minutes) you watch in a typical week.

....

2. TVs you have in your home.

....

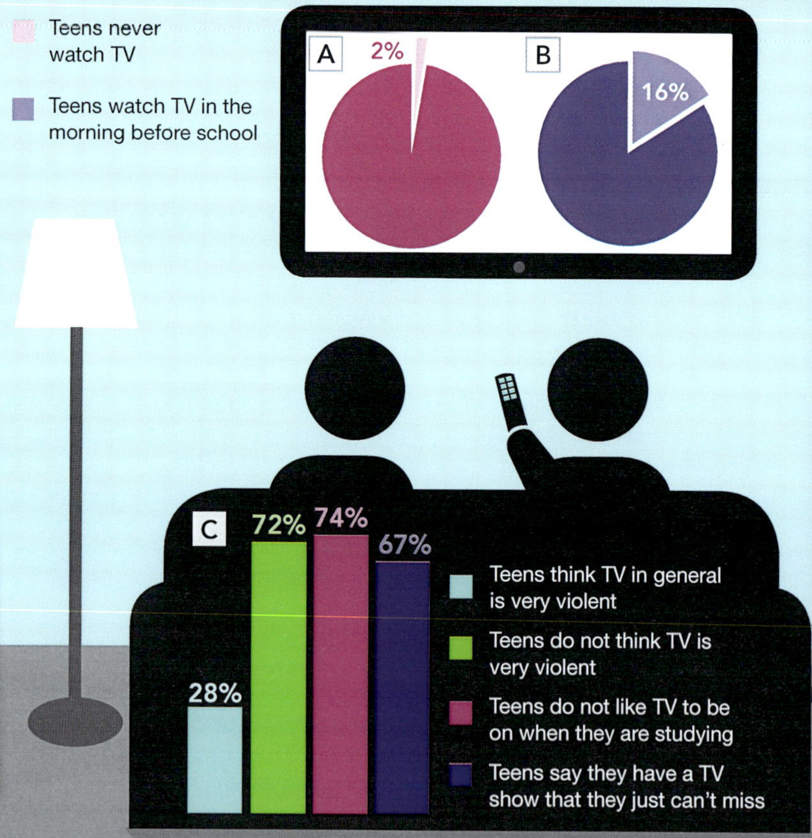

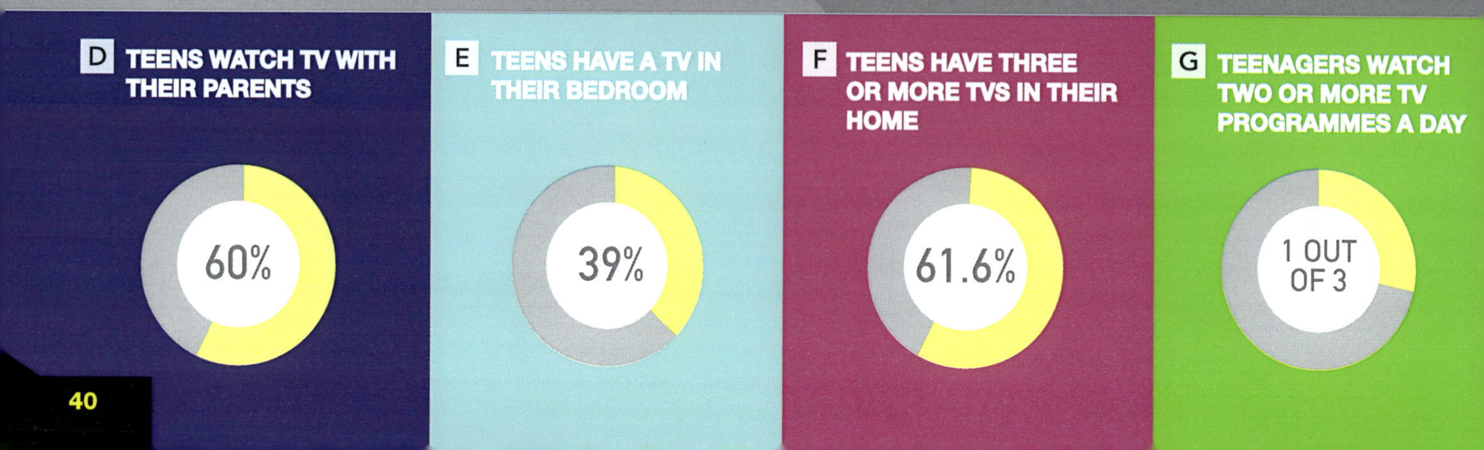

2b SPEAKING **Work with a partner. What is your opinion of these results? Is each statistic good, bad, interesting, surprising, normal …?**

I think chart A is surprising.

Why?

All of my friends watch TV sometimes.

3a READING **Look at these comments about the influence of TV. Decide if each one talks about a positive influence (✓) or a negative influence (✗).**

WHAT DO YOU THINK OF TV?

Rory — THREAD

♥ Add friend

Watching TV relaxes me. When I watch, I don't think about school, or homework, or exams. TV takes me to a different place.

REPLIES EXPAND ALL

Tania

On TV all the actors and presenters are perfect. They're tall and beautiful, with white teeth. Why haven't they got a mix of all types of people on TV? The adverts are the same. It's a perfect world that doesn't exist.

♥ Like ➥ Reply < Share

Hugo

The problem with TV is that when you watch, you don't do anything. You don't use your brain and you don't use your body. I prefer reading, doing sport, and going out with friends.

♥ Like ➥ Reply < Share

Rose

When I watch my favourite TV programmes, I learn things. Sometimes I learn a piece of information about the world, and sometimes I learn about people. The important thing is to find good programmes to watch.

♥ Like ➥ Reply < Share

Jared

When I watch a TV programme, the next day at school I talk about it with my friends. We give our opinions about it. It's another thing that my friends and I have in common.

♥ Like ➥ Reply < Share

Helen

In our house the TV is on all the time. When we have dinner, we watch TV. After dinner, we watch TV. We don't talk, we just watch the TV. Our TV is a member of the family.

♥ Like ➥ Reply < Share

3b Which of the comments are true for you? Discuss the comments with a partner.

3c Have you got any other ideas about the positive or negative influence of TV?

4 LISTENING ▶ 31 **A teenager called Megan is talking about TV in her video diary. Watch or listen. Are the sentences True (T) or False (F)?**

1. This week is a typical week for Megan. T/F
2. Megan is not happy this week. T/F
3. Megan usually watches a lot of TV. T/F
4. Megan is very creative this week. T/F
5. Megan feels good when she watches TV. T/F
6. Megan wants people to do the same as her. T/F

5a Look at these ideas for things to do instead of watching TV. Give each one a mark from 1 (you don't like it) to 5 (you love it).

1. Draw or paint
2. Learn to play a musical instrument
3. Visit a local museum
4. Go for a walk in the park
5. Learn a new sport at a sports centre

5b SPEAKING **Work with a partner. Compare your answers.**

LIFE TASK

Imagine that next week is No TV Week. Work in a small group and follow this plan:

1. *Make a list of ideas for things to do instead of watching TV. Use ideas from 5 and add your own ideas.*
2. *Choose your favourite five activities. Add important details to help somebody who wants to do one of the activities (what, where, how …).*
3. *Make a poster with your five activities.*
4. *Display your posters. Find good ideas from the other posters.*
5. *Try to spend a week without TV! Write down what you do instead of watching TV. Share your experiences with the rest of the class.*

Listening

1 SPEAKING **Work with a partner. Ask and answer the questions.**

1 What music do you like? Rock, pop, jazz, classical, hip-hop ...?
2 When do you listen to music?
3 Do you sing or play a musical instrument? Which instrument(s) do you play?

✔ EXAM SUCCESS

The next exercise is a *True/False/Not Mentioned* listening activity. When a piece of information is not in the listening text, is the correct answer False or Not Mentioned?

➤ EXAM SUCCESS page 151

2a LISTENING ▶ 32 **Listen to a radio programme about a young musician called Kiran Leonard. Are these sentences True (T), False (F), or is the information Not Mentioned (NM)?**

1 Kiran's new album is his first album. T/F/NM
2 He plays the violin. T/F/NM
3 His songs are all very long. T/F/NM
4 He listens to different types of music. T/F/NM
5 He makes his music in a studio in his house. T/F/NM
6 Music is just a free-time activity for Kiran. T/F/NM
7 He wants to study music at university one day. T/F/NM

2b ▶ 32 **Listen again and check your answers.**

3 SPEAKING **What about *you*?**

1 Do you know any young musicians or singers?
2 Do you listen to British or American music or music from your country?
3 Do you buy albums or listen to music on the Internet?

Grammar in context

Present simple – yes/no questions and short answers

1a **Look at the questions and short answers. Match the questions (1 and 2) with the answers (a and b).**

1 Do you know Kiran Leonard?
2 Does he write his own songs?

a Yes, he does./No, he doesn't.
b Yes, I do./No, I don't.

1b **Are these sentences True (T) or False (F)?**

1 We use does with *he/she/it* and do with the other subject pronouns. T/F
2 In questions, do or does comes before the subject. T/F
3 In short answers, we repeat the main verb (e.g. *know, write* ...). T/F

GRAMMAR REFERENCE ➤ PAGE 46

2a **Complete the questions and answers with *do, does, don't* or *doesn't*.**

1 .... you walk to school?
Yes, I ....
2 .... your last class finish at 3 pm?
No, it ....
3 .... your grandparents like hip-hop?
No, they ....
4 .... the students in your class come to class on time?
Yes, they ....
5 .... you watch TV at the weekend?
Yes, we ....

2b SPEAKING **Work with a partner. Ask and answer the questions in 2a. Give true answers.**

3a SPEAKING **Look at these activities. Prepare questions to ask people in your class.**

1 get up at six o'clock *Do you get up at six o'clock?*
2 watch TV before school ....
3 play tennis at the weekend ....
4 sing songs in English ....
5 go to school by car ....
6 study on Sunday ....
7 listen to hip-hop ....
8 go out with friends on Friday ....
9 do sport on Monday ....

3b **Ask different people in the class the questions. Find a different person for each activity.**

Flipped classroom: watch the grammar presentation video.

Present simple – wh- questions

4 Look at a–c and answer the questions below.

a Where does he get his ideas from?
b What kind of music does he play?
c Who do you want to tell us about?

1 Where do the question words (e.g. *where, why, how*) go?
2 How do we answer these questions – with *yes/no* or with a long answer?

GRAMMAR REFERENCE ➤ PAGE 46

5a Put the words in the correct order to make questions.

1 and your Where live do you family?
2 play How instruments many he does?
3 How come to you do school?
4 What family your have time dinner does?
5 home for does Susanna go Why lunch?
6 do on does brother What your Saturday?

5b Match the answers to the questions in 5a.

.... a He plays football.
.... b In Manchester.
.... c Because she lives near the school.
.... d Five, including the piano.
.... e I walk.
.... f It depends, but usually at half past seven.

6a Complete the questions.

1 Where .... you .... lunch during the week? (have)
2 What time .... your family .... dinner at the weekend? (have)
3 What .... you and your friends .... during the break? (do)
4 Why .... people .... English in your country? (study)
5 Which TV programmes .... you .... during the week? (watch)

6 Why .... people .... playing computer games? (like)

6b SPEAKING Work with a partner. Ask and answer the completed questions in 6a.

Adverbs of frequency

7a Look at the sentences. The words in blue say how often we do something. Are sentences 1 to 6 in order from 'Very frequent to not frequent' or from 'Not frequent to very frequent'?

1 Elliot always tells us about interesting new artists.
2 Kiran usually writes the music first.
3 He often listens to his mum and dad's CDs.
4 His dad sometimes plays music.
5 You don't often find musicians who play 20 different instruments.
6 He never plays other people's songs.

7b Look at the sentences below and decide if the rules below are True (T) or False (F).

a He's often in the studio.
b She never plays classical music.
c They're usually here on time.

1 Adverbs of frequency go after the verb *to be*. T/F
2 Adverbs of frequency go after the main verb (e.g. *play, listen, write*). T/F

GRAMMAR REFERENCE ➤ PAGE 46

8 SPEAKING Work with a partner. Ask and answer the questions. Answer with *Yes* or *No*, and an adverb of frequency.

1 Do you go to the theatre? *Yes, sometimes.*
2 Do you walk to school?
3 Do you play football?
4 Do you go to bed at 11 pm?
5 Do you make your breakfast?
6 Do you do homework on Sunday?
7 Do you go to the library?

9 Look at the key and write sentences using the correct form of the verbs given.

Key: 0 = never
★ = sometimes
★★ = often
★★★ = usually
★★★★ = always

1 My sister/sing in the shower. ★★★★
My sister always sings in the shower.
2 My friends and I/go out on Sunday. ★
3 You/be late. 0
4 We/speak English in class. ★★★
5 I/be happy. ★★★★
6 We/go to school at the weekend. 0
7 She/study in the evening. ★★

Giving directions

1 SPEAKING **Work with a partner. Match the pictures with the phrases.**

> Go past (the cinema). • Go straight on.
> It's between (X and Y). • It's on the corner (of X and Y).
> It's on your left. • It's on your right.
> It's opposite (the cinema). • Turn left. • Turn right.
> Walk along (X).

a 
b 
c 
d 
e 

f 
g 
h 
i 

j 

2 LISTENING ▶ 33 **James is inside the bus station. Look at the map and listen. Where does he want to go?**

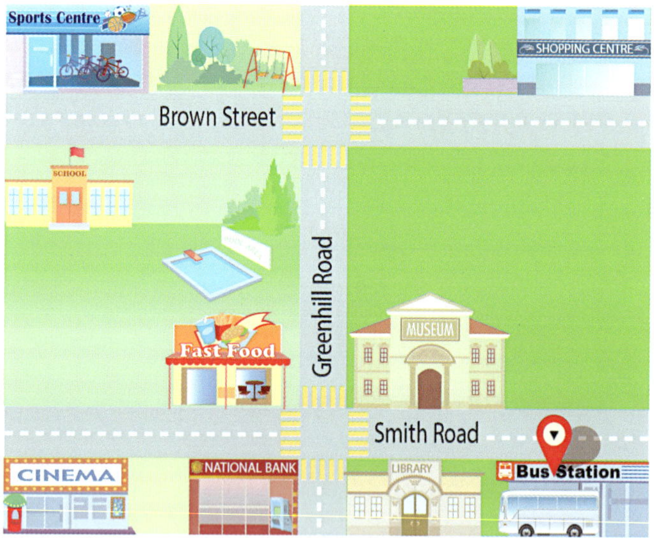

3a Work with a partner and complete the dialogue.

James: Excuse me. Can you tell me how to get to the ______, please?

Woman: When you go out of the bus station, turn **(a)** .... Walk along Smith Road and then turn **(b)** .... at Greenhill Road. Go **(c)** .... Walk **(d)** .... the museum. Then turn **(e)** .... at Brown Street. Go past the **(f)** .... and the ______ is on your right, opposite the **(g)** ....

James: Thanks!

3b ▶ 33 **Listen again and check your answers.**

4a Use the map in 2. Prepare directions from the bus station to a different place in the town.

4b SPEAKING **Work with a partner. Give your directions, but don't say the name of the place. Can your partner say which place it is?**

When you go out of the bus station, turn left. Go straight on. Walk past Greenhill Road and the bank. It's on your left.

It's the cinema.

5 Look at the useful expressions in the Speaking bank. Which expressions are 'Giving directions' and which are 'Asking for directions'? Check that you understand all the expressions.

SPEAKING BANK

Useful expressions to ask for and give directions

....

- Can you tell me how to get to …, please?
- Excuse me, do you know where … is?
- Is there a … near here?

....

- Turn right/left.
- Walk along …
- Go straight on.
- Go past …
- It's on the right/left.
- It's on the corner (of … and …).
- It's between … and …
- It's opposite …

PRACTICE MAKES PERFECT

6a SPEAKING **Work with a partner. Do this role-play using expressions from the Speaking bank to help you.**

Student A: You are at the bus station and want directions. Look at page 154.

Student B: You are at the bus station and want directions. Look at page 155.

6b Act out your dialogues for the class.

A short note – 1

A

CALLING ALL STUDENTS!

We want to organise a school music festival next month. We need information!

What music do you like?

Do you play an instrument or sing?

Which songs do you want to hear at the music festival?

Write a note and send it to Jan (Class 7A)

B

HELLO!

I NEED INFORMATION ABOUT THE SCHOOL ART CLUB. I KNOW THAT THE CLUB MEETS AFTER SCHOOL, BUT WHICH DAY OR DAYS DOES IT MEET? WHERE ARE THE MEETINGS? WHAT EXACTLY DOES THE CLUB DO WHEN IT MEETS?

PLEASE WRITE ME A NOTE WITH THE INFORMATION.

THANKS,

CINDY (CLASS 6B)

C

A MESSAGE TO MEMBERS OF THE COMPUTER CLUB

This year we want to enter the 'Computer Games Designers of the Future' competition. We want you to give us ideas. Please answer these questions.

- Which computer games do you like?
- What type of world and characters are your favourites?

Have you got time to help us to create a new game for this competition?

Please write to Chris (Class 4D) with your ideas.

1 READING **Look at these notices from a school notice board. Answer these questions about each one.**

1 Who is each notice from?
2 How many questions do they ask?
3 Why do they ask these questions?

1 Jan from Class 7A
2 Three
3 They want information to organise a school music festival.

2 Look at this note replying to Cindy's notice. Find Laurence's answers to Cindy's questions and underline them. Does he give all the necessary information?

Hi Cindy,

My name's Laurence. I'm in class 5C and I'm a member of the Art Club. We meet on Mondays and Wednesdays after school, at four o'clock. We don't meet in the Arts and Crafts Room because they have special lessons there on those days. But Room 12 has all the things we need. It's free then, so we meet there. Mrs Stewart is in charge of the Club. She gives us ideas for things to do but you're free to do what you want. Generally, one week is painting and the next is drawing. Come to the club next Monday and see what we do!

See you,

Laurence

3 Look at the note again. Find an example of each of these words. Then write the words in the correct place in the Writing bank.

1 because 2 and 3 but 4 so

WRITING BANK

Useful words for linking ideas

- Addition: (a) ....
- Contrast: (b) ....
- Reason: (c) ....
- Consequence: (d) ....

4 Complete the sentences with *and*, *but*, *because* or *so*.

1 I play the piano .... I play the guitar.
2 I like playing computer games .... I don't like this one.
3 She doesn't go to the Art Club .... she isn't interested in art.
4 We love computers .... we want to be members of the Computer Club.
5 I sing .... I don't want to be in the music festival.
6 My friend hasn't got time .... he never plays computer games.
7 I don't play football computer games .... I hate football.

PRACTICE MAKES PERFECT

5a Choose to reply to either Jan or Chris's notice. Plan your answers to their questions. Write down your ideas.

5b Write your note. Give all the necessary information. Use the words from the Writing bank in your note.

WRITING BANK ➤ PAGE 156

✓ EXAM SUCCESS

In this type of writing task, how important is it to know who you are writing to and what information to include? Why?

➤ EXAM SUCCESS page 151

Grammar reference

Present simple – affirmative

FORM

Affirmative	I/You/We/They **start** at 11 o'clock. He/She/It **starts** at 11 o'clock.

Spelling rules for the third person singular form

- We usually add -s to the verb.
  Examples: like – likes walk – walks
- We add -es to verbs that end in *-s, -sh, -ch, -x*.
  Examples: watch – watches wash – washes kiss – kisses
- We add -es to the verbs *go* and *do*.
  Examples: go – goes do – does
- With verbs that end in *consonant* + *y*, we omit the *y* and add -ies.
  Examples: study – studies cry – cries
- With verbs that end in vowel + y, we add -s.
  Examples: play – plays say – says
- The third person singular form of *have* is irregular.
  Example: have – has

USE

We use the present simple to talk about:

1 regular habits and routines.
  We walk to school every day.
2 things that are always or usually true.
  The bus arrives at half past eight.

Present simple – negative

FORM

Negative	I/You/We/They **don't (do not) start** at 11 o'clock. He/She/It **doesn't (does not) start** at 11 o'clock.

- After ***don't*** or ***doesn't*** we use the base form of the verb (without -s), e.g. *go, walk, start*.

Present simple – yes/no questions and short answers

FORM

Yes/no questions	**Do** I/you/we/they **start** at 11 o'clock? **Does** he/she/it **start** at 11 o'clock?
Short answers	Yes, I/you/we/they **do**. No, I/you/we/they **don't**. Yes, he/she/it **does**. No, he/she/it **doesn't**.

- ***Do*** and ***Does*** come before the subject (e.g. *the book, I, it*).
- In short answers we do not repeat the main verb (e.g. *work, go, play* …).

Present simple – wh- questions and question words

FORM

wh- questions	**When** do I/you/we/they start? **Why** does he/she/it start at 11 o'clock?

- *Wh-* questions contain question words like *who, what, which, where, when, why, how.*
- The question word comes at the start of the question.

Adverbs of frequency

100%
always
usually
often
sometimes
never
0%

USE

- We use adverbs of frequency to say if something happens often or not.
- The usual position for adverbs of frequency is before the main verb.
  I usually surf the Internet.
- Adverbs of frequency go after the verb *to be*.
  I'm always here.
  He's often at his friend's house.

Vocabulary

Everyday activities do homework • finish school • get up • go home • go to bed • go to school • have a shower • have breakfast • have dinner • have lunch • start school

Free-time activities chat online • do sport • go out with friends • listen to music • paint/draw • play computer games • play the guitar/piano • read • surf the Internet • watch films/TV

Places in a town cinema • library • museum • park • restaurant • shopping centre • sports centre • swimming pool

Other words and phrases ➤ page 143

Grammar revision

Present simple – affirmative and negative

/ 7 points

1 Write sentences using the affirmative or negative form of the present simple.

1 Usain Bolt/not/play tennis. ....
2 My grandfather/watch TV all day. ....
3 I/not/get up at 5 am. ....
4 My sister/finish school at 3.30 pm. ....
5 My parents/not/do homework. ....
6 My friends and I/go to school on Friday. ....
7 My teacher/have lunch at school. ....

Present simple – questions and short answers

/ 7 points

2 Choose the correct alternative.

Tim: (a) You go/Do you go home by bus?
Jeff: Yes, I (b) do/go. How (c) do you go/go you home?
Tim: (d) Yes, I do./I walk.
Jeff: (e) Do you/Do you do your homework when you get home?
Tim: No, (f) I don't./I don't do.
Jeff: When (g) do you/you do it?
Tim: After dinner.

Adverbs of frequency

/ 5 points

3 Put the adverb of frequency in the correct place in the sentence. Then order the adverbs from 1 (very frequent) to 5 (not frequent).

1 I read comics. *sometimes* ....
2 My sister listens to hip-hop. *always* ....
3 I'm late for school. *never* ....
4 She has music lessons at the weekend. *usually* ....
5 I go out with my friends. *often* ....

Vocabulary revision

EVERYDAY ACTIVITIES

/ 7 points

1 Complete the everyday activities with vowels.

1 h .... v .... s h .... w .... r
2 g .... t .... b .... d
3 h .... v .... b r .... k f .... s t
4 d .... h .... m .... w .... r k
5 g .... t .... p
6 f .... n .... s h s c h l
7 g .... h .... m ....

FREE-TIME ACTIVITIES

/ 7 points

2 Match the words to make free-time activities.

1 chat	with friends
2 play the	online
3 surf the	music
4 go out	Internet
5 listen to	films
6 do	piano
7 watch	sport

PLACES IN A TOWN

/ 7 points

3 Complete the sentences with the correct place in a town.

1 You go to a .... to see films.
2 You go to a .... to walk, meet your friends or play with a ball.
3 You go to a .... to eat.
4 You go to a .... to do sport.
5 You go to a .... to swim.
6 You go to a .... to buy things.
7 You go to a .... to find and read books.

Total: / 40 points

4 Home time

Vocabulary

Rooms

1 **Work with a partner. Match the rooms (1–6) with these words.**

bathroom • bedroom • dining room
hall • kitchen • living room

2a PRONUNCIATION **34 Listen. Mark the stress with a circle.**

bathroom

2b **34 Listen again and repeat the words with the correct stress.**

Furniture

3a **Work with a partner. Match the objects (a–m) in the picture with the words.**

bath • bed • chair • cupboard • fridge • radiator
shelf • shower • sink • sofa • table • toilet • wardrobe

3b **35 Listen and repeat.**

4 LISTENING **36 Listen to somebody describing a similar flat to the one in 1. Circle six differences in the picture.**

5a **Draw a simple plan of your house or flat. Mark on your plan where the furniture in 3 is.**

5b SPEAKING **Work with a partner. Show your plan and explain it to your partner.**

Our house has got five rooms. This is my bedroom. It's got …

1 **Work with a partner. Describe the photos.**

2 READING **Read the article. Match these questions with the correct parts of the text.**

a What about the bathroom?
b Are there places to cook your own food?
c Is your bedroom big?
d What is there in your bedroom?
e How many people are there in your bedroom?

STUDYING ABROAD

Carla Vega is a 13-year-old student from Spain. This year she is at a boarding school in the UK. Here she tells us about accommodation at the school.

1 ....

'Sometimes there are two or three students in the same bedroom. This year I've got an individual bedroom. But we all use the same living room.'

2 ....

'No, not really! But there's everything you need for studying. There's also a small en suite bathroom. That's nice!'

3 ....

'Well, there's a bed, of course. That's in the corner. Above that I've got a notice board where I put posters and my timetable and stuff. There's a big desk and in front of the desk is my chair. Behind one part of the desk there's a window. That gives me light. Above the desk, on the other side, there are bookshelves. There's a reading lamp on the desk, and a wardrobe next to the desk. The wardrobe isn't enormous, but I've got space under my bed to put things. And near the bed, there's a radiator.'

4 ....

'There isn't a bath, just a shower, a toilet and the sink. There aren't shelves in the bathroom. That's a bit inconvenient.'

5 ....

'We've got a small kitchen to make snacks. There's a cooker, a fridge and a sink for washing the dishes. But we always have breakfast, lunch and dinner in the school canteen. It's good to eat together.'

✔ EXAM SUCCESS

In this type of exercise, why is it useful to first read the whole text before you look at the titles?

➤ EXAM SUCCESS page 151

3 **Read the article again. Does it describe the same place as in the photos? Give reasons for your answer.**

4 **CRITICAL THINKING**

Think! Then compare ideas with your class.

- From the photos and description, do you think this is a good place to study and live? Why/Why not?

5 **Match the underlined words in the text with these definitions.**

1 very big
2 things in general
3 making problems
4 place where two walls meet
5 with other people
6 a school where the students also live
7 a place to live
8 a bathroom that joins a bedroom
9 equipment for serving and eating food
10 equipment for cooking

6 SPEAKING **What about *you*?**

Would you like to study abroad one day? Why/Why not?

Grammar in context

Flipped classroom: watch the grammar presentation video.

There is/There are

1 Look at the sentences and answer the questions.

1 There's a bed.
2 There are shelves for my books.
3 There isn't a bath.
4 There aren't shelves in the bathroom.
5 Are there places to cook your own food?
6 Yes, there are.
7 No, there aren't.

Which sentence(s) is/are …
a affirmative?
b negative?
c singular?
d plural?
e in the question form?
f short answers?

GRAMMAR REFERENCE ➤ PAGE 58

2a Look at the picture and complete the sentences with *is*, *isn't*, *are* or *aren't*.

1 There .... a fridge.
2 There .... four chairs.
3 There .... two pizzas.
4 There .... a sofa.
5 There .... two radiators.
6 There .... three shelves.
7 There .... a table.
8 There .... a wardrobe.
9 There .... two cupboards.
10 There .... a bath.

2b ▶ 37 Listen, check and repeat.

3 Complete the questions and short answers about the picture. Use the correct form of *there is* or *there are*.

1 Q: .... three pizzas?
A: ....
2 Q: .... three chairs?
A: ....
3 Q: .... a burger?
A: ....
4 Q: .... a radiator?
A: ....
5 Q: .... shelves?
A: ....
6 Q: .... a cupboard?
A: ....

4 SPEAKING Memory test! Work with a partner. Student A, close your book. Student B, ask questions about the picture. Can your partner remember? After four questions, change roles.

Are there three chairs?

Yes, there are.

Prepositions of place

5 Read the sentences and match with diagrams a–h to show that you understand the meaning of the prepositions.

1 Above the bed I've got a notice board. ....
2 Behind the desk there's a window. ....
3 There's a reading lamp on the desk. ....
4 There's a wardrobe next to the desk. ....
5 I've got space under my bed to put things. ....
6 Near the bed, there's a radiator. ....
7 There are three students in the bedroom. ....
8 In front of the desk is my chair. ....

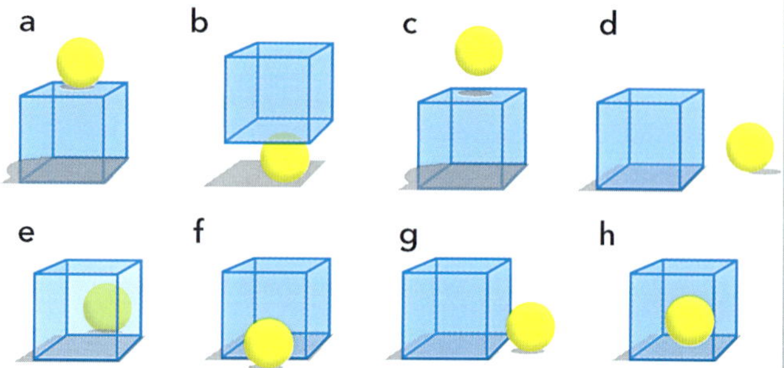

GRAMMAR REFERENCE ➤ PAGE 58

6 Look at the pictures. Choose the correct alternative.

1

There are two people in/on the room.

2

There is a cat next to/in front of the TV.

3

There are two books above/under the table.

4

There's a tablet in/on the table.

5

There's a lamp behind/in front of the sofa.

6

There's a chair near/next to the sofa.

7

There are two people above/on the sofa.

8

There's a shelf under/above the sofa.

7a Use prepositions to write five sentences about the position of objects in the pictures in 6. Make two sentences false.

There's an English dictionary on the shelf.
There's a cat on the chair.

7b SPEAKING Work in a small group. Read out your sentences. Can other students identify the false sentences?

Food and drink

1

2

3

4

5

6

7

8

9

10

11

12

13
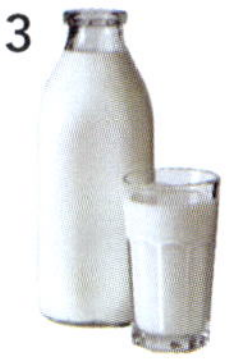
14

15

16

17

18

19

20

1a Work with a partner. What food can you see in the photos? Use the words in the box to help you.

apple • banana • biscuit • bread • burger • butter • cake
cheese • chicken • chips • coffee • egg • fish • honey
ice cream • jam • lemonade • meat • milk • orange juice
pizza • salad • salt • strawberry • sugar • tea • tomato
water • yoghurt

1b Use your dictionary to check that you understand all the words in the box.

1c 38 Listen and repeat.

2 Which words in 1 are …

a types of fruit?
b drinks?
c sweet?
d dairy products (made from milk)?

3 SPEAKING Work with a partner. Find out which food and drink your partner likes and dislikes.

Do you like apples?

Yes, I do. And you?

Not much.

Choosing healthy FOOD

LIFE SKILLS OBJECTIVES

- To learn how to read food labels
- To think about our food choices
- To analyse what we eat and decide if it is healthy or not

KEY CONCEPTS

healthy/unhealthy [adj]: *I think apples are healthy – they're really good for you* **amount [n]:** *It's important to eat the right amount – not too much or too little.* **serving [n]:** *This breakfast cereal has 16 servings so I can eat it every morning for 16 days.* **saturated fat [n]:** *Burgers, whole milk, cream and butter all contain lots of saturated fat.* **fat [n]:** *Some foods, like nuts, contain fats which are not as bad as saturated fats.* **nutrient [n]:** *We eat because our body needs the nutrients from food for energy.*

1 Work with a partner. Look at the different types of food. Do you think each type of food is healthy (H), unhealthy (U), or it depends (D)?

1 apples

2 breakfast cereals

3 eggs

4 chips

5 orange juice

6 burger

2 When experts talk about food, they often talk about Reference Intake. The Reference Intake shows us approximately how much food it is OK to eat in one day. Look at this table. What is the total number of calories for *you*?

REFERENCE INTAKE

Age	Energy Calories (kcal)	Fat (g)	Saturated Fat (g)	Sugar (g)	Salt (g)
11-14	2200	85	25	110	6
	1850	70	25	90	6
15-18	2750	105	35	140	6
	2100	80	25	105	6
19+	2500	95	30	120	6
	2000	70	20	90	6

Male/Female

3a Look at this food label from a breakfast cereal packet. In your opinion, is the cereal healthy, unhealthy or in the middle? Why?

per 30g cereal:

16 SERVINGS	ENERGY	FAT	SATURATES	SUGARS	SALT
	493kJ 116kcal	0.8g LOW	0.3g LOW	11g HIGH	0.2g MED
	6%	6%	6%	6%	6%

% of an adult's reference intake.
Typical values per 100g: Energy 1639kJ/387kcal

3b READING **Read and match A–D with 1–4 below.**

A ◯ Food labels show the amount of each nutrient: fat, saturated fat, sugar and salt in a serving, in grams. The colour is important. They use a traffic-light system. If the amount is high, it's red. That means 'Stop!' You need to be careful. If it's medium, it's amber (orange). If it's low, it's green. That means 'Go!' It's good for you.

B ◯ The people who produce the food decide what is a normal 'serving', i.e. the normal amount of food for one person to eat at one time. But it's important to see what they consider is normal. In this case, the serving is 30g of breakfast cereal. But many people eat over 30g.

C ◯ Food labels usually measure energy in kilojoules (kJ) and kilocalories (Kcal – often called calories). Labels give the amount in 100g (100ml for drinks) or the amount in a serving, or both. Read the label carefully – there's often a big difference in calories between a serving and 100g.

D ◯ These percentages (%) show the amount of your Reference Intake that comes from one serving. It's important to remember that the Reference Intake is usually a maximum limit. The idea is that you don't go above these amounts.

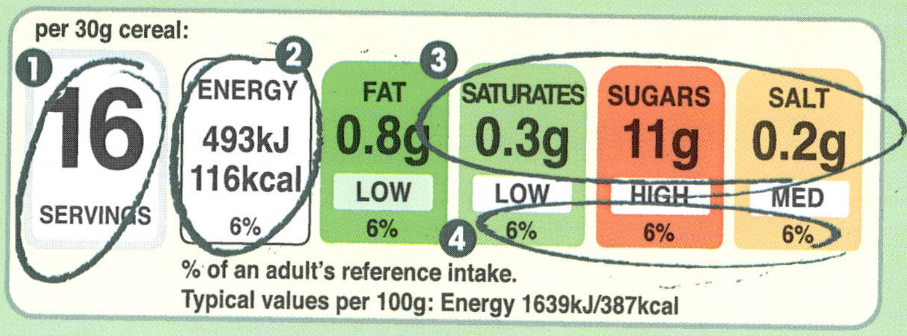

4 Read texts A to D again and mark the statements True (T) or False (F).

1 The colour amber is similar to orange. T/F
2 When you see a nutrient marked in red, it's bad. T/F
3 A serving is always 30g. T/F
4 30g of cereal is not a lot for many people. T/F
5 The number of calories is always per 100g. T/F
6 It is bad to go above your Reference Intake. T/F

5a Look at this food label. Do you think this food is healthy or unhealthy? Give reasons for your answer.

ENERGY	FAT	SATURATES	SUGARS	SALT
450kJ 107kcal	5.3g	3.3g	10.4g	0.03g
	HIGH	HIGH	HIGH	LOW
5%	8%	17%	12%	1%

5b Do you think this comes from a pizza packet or a chocolate bar? Why?

6 LISTENING ▶ 39 **A teenager is talking about what he eats. Watch or listen. What do you think of his diet?**

7 ▶ 39 **Watch and listen again and answer the questions.**

1 What does the boy usually have for breakfast?
2 What does he have for lunch?
3 Why does he buy his lunch at school?
4 Does he think he has a healthy diet?
5 Does his diet worry him? Why/Why not?

8 SPEAKING **Do you think the boy's diet is typical of teenagers in your country? Why/Why not?**

LIFE TASK

Do you have a healthy diet? Find out. Follow this plan:

1 *Write an eating diary for the last three days. Make a list of the contents of your breakfast, lunch and dinner, plus any other snacks.*

2 *Circle each type of food or drink on your list with a colour. Green means it hasn't got much sugar, fat or salt. Amber (orange) means it's medium. Red means it's got a lot!*

3 *Work with a partner. Look at the colours in your eating diary. What are the good and bad things about your diet/your partner's diet? If you have a lot of red marks, think about healthy alternatives!*

Listening

1 Match the photos with these words.

bowl • cake tin • food processor • spoon

a

b

c

d

2 You are going to listen to a food programme. Look at the ingredients needed for today's recipe. Check that you know what all the ingredients are. What do you think the recipe is for?

a low-fat cream cheese
b butter
c sugar
d honey
e biscuits
f strawberries

3 LISTENING 40 **Listen to the programme. What is the recipe for? In what order do you hear the ingredients in 2?**

1 ....
2 ....
3 ....
4 ....
5 ....
6 ....

4a 40 **Read this description of the recipe. Find seven mistakes. Listen again if necessary.**

For this recipe, you need 300g of low-fat cream cheese. You also need two spoonfuls of honey and one of sugar. You mix them together in a cake tin. For the base you need 300g of biscuits and 50g of butter. You mix them using a food processor. Then you put that mixture in a cake tin and add the cream cheese mixture. You put it in the fridge. At the end you put strawberry jam on top. In about 30 minutes it's ready to eat!

4b Correct the mistakes.

5 SPEAKING **What about *you*?**

1 Would you like to eat this recipe? Why/Why not?
2 Do you think this recipe is easy to make? Why/Why not?
3 How often do you cook? What do you make?

Grammar in context

Countable and uncountable nouns

1 Look at the sentences and the word in blue in each sentence. Is it possible to count this word or not? Write C (Countable) or U (Uncountable).

1 I've got real **strawberries**.
2 I've got a **spoon**.
3 You mix it with the **honey** and the **sugar**.
4 We need 100 grams of **butter**.
5 We put the **biscuits** in a food processor.

GRAMMAR REFERENCE ➤ PAGE 58

2 Put the food and drink in the correct place.

~~apple~~ • banana • biscuit • bread • burger • butter • chip • egg • honey • jam • lemonade • meat • milk • orange juice • salt • strawberry • sugar • tomato • water

Countable

apple

Uncountable

3 SPEAKING **Work with a partner. Look around the classroom. Try to find three countable things and three uncountable things.**

some, any, a/an

4 Look at the sentences and complete the rules with *some*, *any* or *a/an*.

a I've got a spoon.
b We need some sugar.
c Have you got any strawberry jam?
d We need some biscuits.
e Have we got a cake tin?
f I haven't got any jam.
g There isn't an egg in this recipe.

1 We use .... with singular countable nouns (*apple*, *chip*), in affirmative and negative sentences and questions.

2 We use .... with plural countable nouns (*apples*, *chips*) and uncountable nouns (*milk*) in affirmative sentences.

3 We use .... with plural countable nouns (*apples*, *chips*) and uncountable nouns (*milk*) in negative sentences and questions.

GRAMMAR REFERENCE ➤ PAGE 58

5 Choose the correct alternative.

1 Have you got *a/any* water?
2 There isn't *any/some* milk in the fridge.
3 We've got *a/some* bread in the kitchen.
4 Is there *an/any* orange juice in the bottle?
5 I think there are *any/some* strawberries.
6 There's *a/some* chip under the table.
7 We need to buy *a/some* butter tomorrow.

6 Look at the photo and decide if the statements are True (T) or False (F).

1 There are three men at the table. T/F
2 There are some glasses. T/F
3 There's an orange on the table. T/F
4 There aren't any spoons. T/F
5 There aren't any children there. T/F
6 There are dishes on the table. T/F

7 Complete the sentences about the picture in 6 with *is*, *are*, *isn't* or *aren't* and *some*, *any*, *a* or *an*.

1 There .... honey.
2 There .... orange juice.
3 There .... apples.
4 There .... people with dark hair.
5 There .... old man.
6 There .... milk.
7 There .... bread.
8 There .... burgers.

8a Complete the dialogue with the correct form of *there is* or *there are* and *a*, *an* or *any*.

A: Can I ask you some questions about your school?
B: Yeah, sure.
A: (a) .... canteen at your school?
B: Yes, (b) ....
A: (c) .... information about healthy eating on posters?
B: Yes, (d) ....
A: (e) .... fridges or cupboards where students can keep food or drinks?
B: No, (f) ....
A: (g) .... place where you can buy food or drinks?
B: Yes, (h) .... There's a little shop.
A: (i) .... healthy snacks there?
B: Yes, (j) .... You can buy fruit there, for example.

8b ▶ 41 Listen and check.

8c SPEAKING Work with a partner. Ask and answer the questions in 8a about your school.

Making and replying to offers

1a SPEAKING **Work with a partner. What can you see in the photo?**

1b Answer the questions.

1 How often do you invite friends to your house?
2 How often do you visit friends' houses?
3 What do you do when you visit friends?

2 LISTENING 42 **Listen to the people in the photo. Are the statements True (T) or False (F)?**

1 Andy and Joe go into the living room. T/F
2 Joe visits Andy to watch a film at his house. T/F
3 Andy offers Joe something to eat and to drink. T/F
4 Joe is thirsty. T/F
5 Joe offers to turn the TV on. T/F

3a 42 **Listen again and complete the Useful expressions in the 'Making offers' section of the Speaking bank.**

SPEAKING BANK

Useful expressions for making and replying to offers

Making offers

- Can I **(a)** ....?
- Have a **(b)** ....
- Would you like **(c)** ....?
- How about **(d)** ....?
- Shall I **(e)** ....?

Replying to offers

- Yes, sure.
- Thanks./Thank you./Cheers.
- That'd be great.
- No, thanks/thank you.
- No, I'm fine, thanks.
- No, it's OK.

3b 43 **Listen, check and repeat.**

4 Complete the dialogue. What does Holly say to Olivia?

Olivia: Hi Holly. Come in!
Holly: **(a)** ....
Olivia: Thanks. Shall I take your coat and your bag?
Holly: **(b)** ....
Olivia: Can I put it here on the table?
Holly: **(c)** ....
Olivia: Yes. Would you like anything to eat or drink?
Holly: **(d)** ....
Olivia: No, sorry, I don't think I have. How about lemonade?
Holly: **(e)** ....
Olivia: Here you are. And the glasses are in that cupboard behind you.

1 Yes, sure. I'm really thirsty!
2 Thanks. What a lovely dress!
3 That'd be great. Have you got any orange juice?
4 OK … Is that the kitchen?
5 Yes, thanks. But be careful because I've got my laptop in there.

EXAM SUCCESS

In this type of exercise, is it important to read the whole dialogue when you finish? Why/Why not?

➤ EXAM SUCCESS page 151

PRACTICE MAKES PERFECT

5a SPEAKING **Work with a partner. Prepare a dialogue. Include two offers in your dialogue.**

Student A: You are at home and your friend comes to visit you.
Student B: You visit your partner's house to play computer games.

5b Practise the dialogue.

5c Act out your dialogue for the class.

A description of a place

1a SPEAKING **Work with a partner. Imagine your dream bedroom. Would you like to have these objects in it? Give a mark from 0 to 5 for each object (0 = I don't want it, 5 = I really want it).**

1 posters/paintings ....
2 a computer ....
3 a games console ....
4 a TV ....
5 musical instruments ....
6 a sofa ....

1b Are there any other objects you would like? Which?

2 READING **Three teenagers describe their dream bedrooms. Read the descriptions. Who wants the bedroom in the picture?**

Jasmine

My dream bedroom has got pink walls. There are famous paintings on the walls. Next to my bed, there's a beautiful old table and chair. I usually sit at the table in the morning, open my notebook and write stories. When I open the windows I always hear birds singing because in front of my bedroom windows there's a big park. I'm always happy and relaxed in my bedroom!

Charlie

My dream bedroom is big. On the walls of my room I've got posters of my favourite bands. There's always music in my room. I've got a really cool guitar. When my friends come and visit me, we play music for hours. I've also got a big desk in my room, where I do my homework. In front of the bed there's a sofa. It's really comfortable! In front of the sofa there's a big TV and a games console. When my friends and I finish playing music, we play computer games there.

Emma

My dream bedroom is a cinema. I've got a really comfortable bed and I watch films from there. On the wall there's an enormous TV. Next to my bed, there's a fridge with cold drinks. There's also a machine to make hot popcorn! My bedroom has also got enormous windows and a great view of a big swimming pool.

3 SPEAKING **Work with a partner. Tell them which bedroom you like and which bedroom you don't like. Explain your decisions.**

I like Charlie's bedroom because I like music and computer games.

I really like the cinema bedroom. I love films and popcorn.

4 Look at the texts again. Write a list of adjectives that appear in the descriptions. Remember that adjectives help us to write interesting descriptions.

famous, beautiful ...

5 Look at the Writing bank and the texts in 2. Choose the correct alternative in the rules for word order.

WRITING BANK

Basic word order

- Adjectives usually come after/before the noun they describe.
- Adjectives usually come after/before the verb *to be*.
- Adverbs of frequency come after/before the main verb.
- Adverbs of frequency come after/before the verb *to be*.

6 Is the word order correct in these sentences? If there is a mistake, correct it.

1 The walls are red and there are paintings big and colourful.
2 I write sometimes stories and songs in my bedroom.
3 I don't usually listen to music in my room.
4 The bed and sofa are very big and comfortable.
5 My friends often are at my house.
6 I've got a desk beautiful next to the window.

PRACTICE MAKES PERFECT

7a Look at the task.

An English magazine wants teenagers to describe their ideal bedrooms. Write an article about your ideal bedroom. Include information about the furniture and other objects.

7b Write your article. Remember to check the word order in your description.

WRITING BANK ➤ PAGE 156

Grammar reference

There is/There are

FORM

	Singular	Plural
Affirmative	**There's** a cupboard.	**There are** two cupboards.
Negative	**There isn't** a sofa.	**There aren't** two sofas.
Questions	**Is there** a cupboard?	**Are there** two cupboards?
Short answer	Yes, **there is.**/No, **there isn't.**	Yes, **there are.**/No, **there aren't.**

Prepositions of place

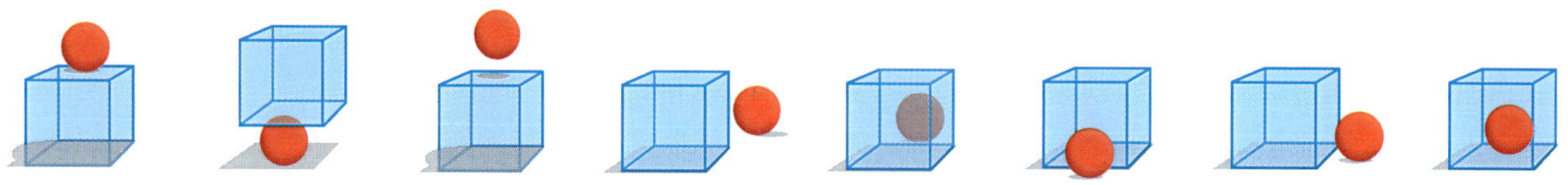

on under above near behind in front of next to in

Countable and uncountable nouns

- We can count *apples*, *bananas*, *eggs*, *burgers*, *chips* and so there is a singular and plural form. *Apple*, *banana*, *egg*, *burger*, and *chip* are all examples of **countable** nouns.
- We cannot count some things (for example liquids) and so we do not usually use a plural form. For example *milk*, *water*, *bread*, *salt*, and *cheese*. These are examples of **uncountable** nouns.

some, any, a/an

USE

- We use **some** with uncountable nouns and with plural countable nouns, in affirmative sentences.

  I've got some chips. *We've got some lemonade.*
- We use **any** with uncountable nouns and with plural countable nouns, in negative sentences and questions.

  I haven't got any sugar.

  He hasn't got any eggs.

  Have you got any water?

  Are there any tomatoes?
- We use ***a**/**an*** with singular countable nouns in affirmative and negative sentences and in questions. ***An*** goes before a vowel sound.

  I haven't got a dish.

  He's got an orange.

Vocabulary

Rooms bathroom • bedroom • dining room • hall • kitchen • living room

Furniture bath • bed • chair • cupboard • fridge • radiator • shelf • sink • shower • sofa • table toilet • wardrobe

Food and drink apple • banana • biscuit • bread • burger • butter • cake • cheese • chicken • chips coffee • egg • fish • honey • ice cream • jam • lemonade • meat • milk • orange juice • pizza • salad • salt strawberry • sugar • tea • tomato • water • yoghurt

Other words and phrases ➤ page 144

Grammar revision

There is/There are / 6 points

1 Choose the correct alternative.

1 There *is/are* 25 people in that class.
2 There *are/aren't* two 't's in the word 'writing'.
3 There *isn't/aren't* computers in the library.
4 There *is/are* a big desk there.
5 There *isn't/aren't* time to do the exercise now.
6 *Are/Is* there 11 people in a football team?

Prepositions of place / 5 points

2 Complete the sentences with a preposition.

1  The keys are .... the book.

2  The bottle is .... the computer.

3  The rubber is .... the desk.

4 

The dictionary is .... the shelf.

5  The light is .... the table.

Countable and uncountable nouns / 4 points

3 Write C (countable) or U (uncountable) after each word.

1 milk ....
2 lemonade ....
3 banana ....
4 bread ....
5 biscuit ....
6 meat ....
7 bottle ....
8 dish ....

some, any, a, an / 6 points

4 Complete the sentences with *some, any, a* or *an*.

1 Have you got .... sugar?
2 There isn't .... salt in this.
3 You've got .... orange to eat after your lunch.
4 I've got .... cheese for the pizza.
5 There isn't .... bread to make a sandwich.
6 Is there .... tomato in the bag?

Vocabulary revision

ROOMS / 5 points

1 Put the letters in the correct order to make rooms.

1 neckith ....
2 modrobe ....
3 ginnid ormo ....
4 lahl ....
5 broomhat ....

FURNITURE / 7 points

2 Write the names of the objects.

1 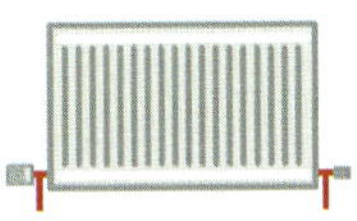 ....

2  ....

3 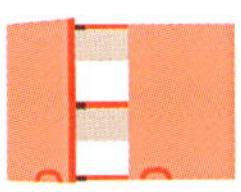 ....

4  ....

5  ....

6 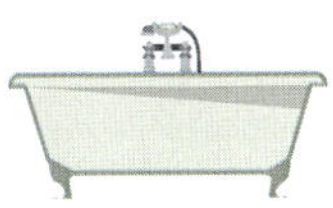 ....

7 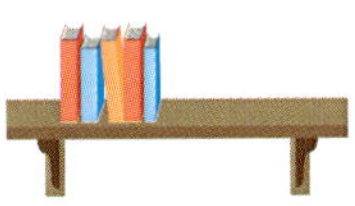 ....

FOOD AND DRINK / 7 points

3 Complete the words.

1 A popular drink in the UK: t ....
2 Made from strawberries, for example: j ....
3 A dairy product: b ....
4 Green and healthy: s ....
5 You put it on food like chips: s ....
6 People sometimes put it in drinks to make them sweet: s ....
7 Cold and sweet: i ....

Total: / 40 points

Reading

➤ TIP FOR READING EXAMS

In matching activities, remember …
Read the whole text first to get a general idea before you answer very specific questions.

➤ EXAM SUCCESS page 151

1 READING **Read this interview with a teenage girl. What is her favourite free-time activity? Why is the book *The Hunger Games* special for her?**

2 Match these questions with the correct parts of the text.

a Why is the book expensive?
b Why do you collect books?
c Does your copy of *The Hunger Games* have your name in it?
d Emma, what's your special free-time activity?
e Have you got a favourite book in your collection?
f How do you know that a book is a first edition?

3 SPEAKING **What about *you*?**

1 Do you collect anything? What? What is your favourite thing in your collection?
2 Would you like to collect something? Why?/Why not?

My special free-time activity

1 ☐
My dad and I collect books.

2 ☐
Because I love them. I read a lot.

3 ☐
Yes, I've got a copy of *The Hunger Games* by Suzanne Collins. People pay thousands of dollars for this book now.

4 ☐
Because it's very popular, especially because of the film. But this copy isn't easy to find. It's a first edition. It's got the author's signature. Now there are millions of copies of *The Hunger Games* in the world. But there aren't millions of copies of the first edition, or thousands of copies with the author's signature.

5 ☐
On one of the first pages, English or American books usually have a list of numbers. For example, 10 9 8 7 6 5 4 3 2 1, or 2 4 6 8 10 9 7 5 3 1. When the list has the number 1, it's a first edition.

6 ☐
No, it doesn't. When a book has a name in it, other people don't want it. But that isn't very important to me. This book is special for me because I love the story. I only collect books that I love.

Writing

➤ TIP FOR WRITING EXAMS

In writing exams, remember …
When you write a short note, it is essential to know who you are writing to and what information to include.

➤ EXAM SUCCESS page 151

4 Look at this notice from a school notice board. Who is the notice from? What three pieces of information do they want?

Hi!
I need information about the school Book Club.
Which day or days does it meet? Where are the meetings? What exactly does the club do when it meets?
Please write back and tell me!
Thanks,
Stephanie (Class 2B)

5 Write a reply to Stephanie's note. Give all the necessary information. Invent it.

Use of English

➤ TIP FOR USE OF ENGLISH

In activities where you have to complete the dialogue, remember …
Read the sentences before and after each space to decide the correct answer.

➤ EXAM SUCCESS page 151

6 **Indira is asking Sam for directions. Complete the dialogue. There are six sentences but only four spaces.**

Indira: Excuse me. Can you tell me how to get to the museum?
Sam: 1 ....
Indira: What's the name of the street?
Sam: 2 ....
Indira: Is it opposite the library?
Sam: 3 ....
Indira: Ah, OK. Thank you.
Sam: 4 ....
Indira: Yes, that'd be great!

A Yes. Go straight on and then turn right.
B No, it's opposite the art gallery.
C Is it on the corner of Parker Road?
D No, sorry, I don't.
E Would you like me to show you the route on my phone?
F I think it's Hazel Street.

Listening

➤ TIP FOR LISTENING EXAMS

In *True/False/Not Mentioned* activities, remember …
Read the statements before you listen. They can give you an idea of what you are listening for.

➤ EXAM SUCCESS page 151

7 LISTENING 44 **Listen to a man called Mike answering questions about where he lives. Are these sentences True (T), False (F), or is the information Not Mentioned (NM)?**

1 Mike's home has six big bedrooms. T/F/NM
2 Mike often reads in his bedroom. T/F/NM
3 There are 52 computers in Mike's home. T/F/NM
4 Sport is important for Mike and the others. T/F/NM
5 Mike and the others don't eat meat. T/F/NM
6 Mike and the others like drinking lemonade. T/F/NM
7 Mike hasn't got a favourite room. T/F/NM
8 Mike doesn't live on the Earth. T/F/NM

8 **What about *you*?**

Would you like to live in this place? Why/Why not?

'CAN DO' PROGRESS CHECK UNITS 3–4 — CEF

1 **How well can you do these things in English now? Give yourself a mark from 1 to 4.**

1 = I can do it very well.
2 = I can do it quite well.
3 = I have some problems.
4 = I can't do it.

a I can talk about basic routine actions using the present simple. ☐
b I can say how often I do things using adverbs of frequency. ☐
c I can talk about what I do in my free time. ☐
d I can ask for and give directions. ☐
e I can write short notes. ☐
f I can talk about houses and rooms using *There is/There are*. ☐
g I can talk about quantities with *some, any, a/an*. ☐
h I can name different food and drink. ☐
i I can make and reply to offers. ☐
j I can write a short description of a room. ☐

2 **Now decide what you need to do to improve.**

1 Look again at my book/notes.
2 Do more practice exercises.
➤ WORKBOOK Units 3-4
3 Ask for help.
4 Other: ....

5 Connected

Vocabulary

Computers

1 Work with a partner. Look at the photos. How many of the objects can you name?

a

b

c

d

e

f

g
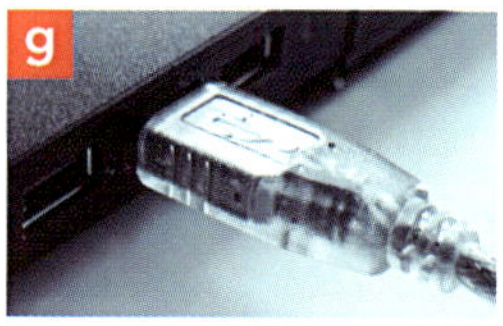

h

i
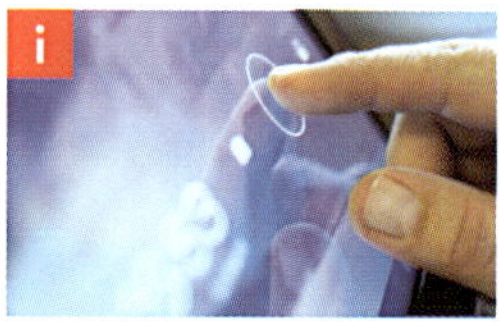

j

k
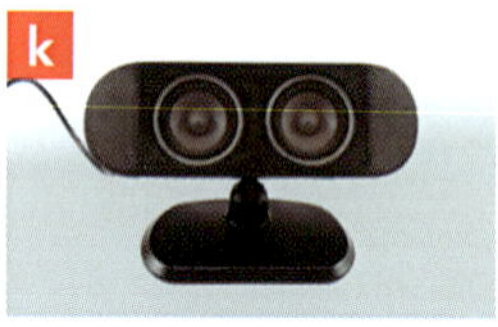

2a Look at the words in the box. Can you name all the objects in 1 now?

keyboard • monitor/screen • mouse
printer/scanner • screensaver • speaker
touchpad • touch screen
USB cable and port • webcam

2b 45 Listen and repeat.

3 Play a game. A student draws one of the objects in 1 on the board. Can you identify the object?

Using computers

4 Match the words and icons.

click on • copy • cut and paste • download • log on/off
print • save • send an email

5 46 Listen and repeat.

6 Complete the sentences with words from 4.

When you …

1 .... a document, you make a second document that is the same as the original.
2 .... data, you transfer it from another computer or via the Internet to your computer.
3 .... something with your mouse, you make it work.
4 .... something on a computer, you keep the information that you put into it.
5 .... a document, you make a copy on paper, using a printer.
6 ...., a message goes from your computer to another computer.
7 .... something, you move words or pictures on a computer screen from one place to another.
8 ..../......, you start/finish using a computer system or programme by giving some information (e.g. your name).

7a LISTENING 47 Listen to a student answering these questions. What does she say?

1 How often do you use a computer?
2 What do you use computers for?
3 Do you download things onto your computer? If so, what?
4 Do you send emails? If so, how often?
5 How often do you print or scan things? What do you print or scan?
6 When and why do you use a webcam?
7 Have you got a screensaver? What is it?

7b SPEAKING Work with a partner. Ask and answer the questions in 7a. Give true answers.

Reading

1 READING **Read the articles. Think of a good title for each article.**

TEEN TECH WORLD
BRILLIANT TECH IDEAS!

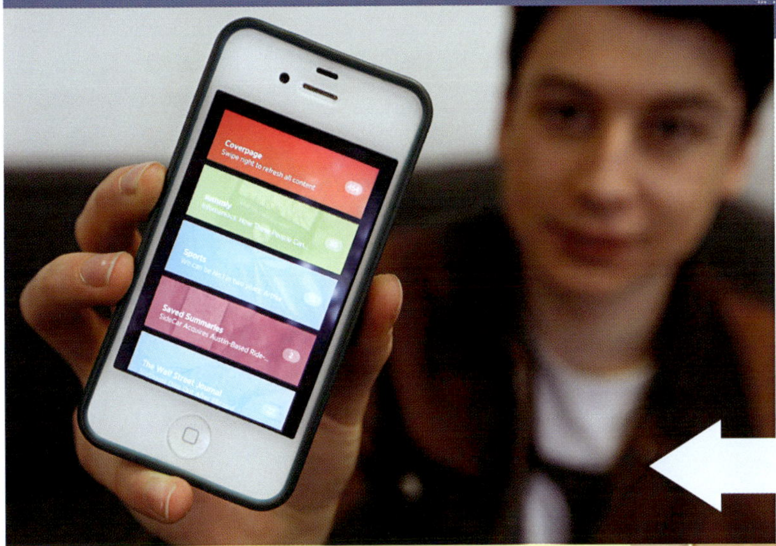

A

A student from London called Nick D'Aloisio is already a millionaire thanks to his mobile app invention, **Summly**. With more than a million downloads, Summly is obviously a popular app. But what exactly can you do with it? Basically, Summly changes long news stories into three paragraphs. This means that the story fits perfectly onto a phone screen. Today, people need to get information quickly and easily. They can't read every news story because they don't have time. But with Summly they can get information fast, clearly and concisely. So, plan well and work hard like Nick and you can become a tech millionaire too!

B

Americans Eric Rosenbaum and Jay Silver are the inventors of an amazing new gadget called **Makey Makey**. With their invention, you can make any object into a touchpad, keyboard or mouse. You just connect the object (a banana, pasta ... a human body!) to the Makey Makey board. This is connected to your computer via a USB cable. When you touch the object, you make a connection. Makey Makey sends a keyboard message to the computer and it believes that Makey Makey is a keyboard! You can't use objects that don't conduct electricity. But apart from that, the only limit is your imagination. A piano made with bananas? Why not?!

2 **Read the text again and complete the table.**

	Text A	Text B
1 Name of the inventor(s)		
2 Nationality of the inventor(s)		
3 Name of the invention		
4 Main aim of the invention		

3 **Answer the questions.**

1 Why is the Summly app useful in today's world?
2 How is Nick's life different now thanks to Summly?
3 How do you make the Makey Makey gadget work?
4 What objects don't work with the Makey Makey gadget?

4 **CRITICAL THINKING**

Think! Then compare ideas with your class.

- How useful do you think these inventions are? Why?

5 **What do the underlined words in the text mean? Guess and then check in your dictionary.**

6 SPEAKING **What about *you*?**

1 Would you like to have a Makey Makey board? Why/Why not?
2 What's your favourite gadget or app? Why do you like it?

can/can't

1 Look at the sentences and choose the correct alternative.

a You **can** make any object into a touchpad.

b You **can't** use objects that don't conduct electricity.

c What **can** you do with it?

d **Can** you use water?

e Yes, you **can**./No, you **can't**.

1 We use <u>can/can't</u> in affirmative sentences.

2 We use <u>can/can't</u> in negative sentences.

3 We <u>use/don't use</u> **do** to make questions with **can**.

4 We <u>repeat/don't repeat</u> the main verb in short answers.

5 We <u>use/don't use</u> **can** to talk about ability.

GRAMMAR REFERENCE ➤ PAGE 72

2a PRONUNCIATION 48 Listen to the sentences. Notice that *can* is short, but *can't* is long.

1 I **can** draw.

2 I **can't** draw.

2b 49 Listen. Underline the alternative which you hear.

1 She <u>can/can't</u> sing.

2 He <u>can/can't</u> play the guitar.

3 They <u>can/can't</u> swim.

4 We <u>can/can't</u> speak Spanish.

5 She <u>can/can't</u> understand French.

6 I <u>can/can't</u> ride a bike.

2c 49 Listen again and repeat the correct sentence.

3a SPEAKING Work with a partner. Use the pictures to ask and answer questions with *can* or *can't*.

Can you sing?

Yes, I can. And you?

Yes, I can.

1 

sing

2 

dance

3 

play the piano

4 

ski

5 

speak Chinese

6 

paint

3b Now tell the class about your partner.

Alex can sing, but he can't dance.

Adverbs of manner

4 Look at the sentences and choose the correct alternative.

a People need to get information **quickly** and **easily**.

b They can get information **fast**, **clearly** and **concisely**.

c Plan **well**.

d Work **hard**.

1 Adverbs of manner say <u>how/how often</u> we do something.

2 Adverbs of manner <u>usually/don't usually</u> go with the verb ***to be***.

3 Adverbs of manner <u>normally/don't normally</u> finish in ***-ly***.

4 ***Fast***, ***well*** and ***hard*** are examples of <u>regular/irregular</u> adverbs of manner.

GRAMMAR REFERENCE ➤ PAGE 72

5 **Complete the table.**

Adjective	Adverb
bad	1 ....
calm	2 ....
3	carefully
clear	4 ....
5	easily
fast	6 ....
7	well
hard	8 ....
quick	9 ....
10	slowly

6 **Read the text. Find and correct seven mistakes with adjectives and adverbs.**

I study ICT at school. My ICT teacher speaks very fastly but he explains things good. I don't think ICT is very difficult. I understand everything quite easy, even when the teacher talks quickly. The only problem is that I often do bad in my exams. I don't know why, because I always study hardly. I read the questions carefuly too. Maybe the problem is that I don't write very clear. I think I need to be calm and write slowly next time.

7 SPEAKING **Work in a small group. Find someone who …**

1 sings well.
2 writes very clearly.
3 swims fast.
4 does exams calmly.
5 works hard on a hobby.
6 writes quickly on a computer or laptop.
7 walks to school easily.
8 eats slowly.

Do you sing well?

Yes, I do.

Do you write clearly?

The Internet

1 **Are you an Internet expert? Read the definitions (1–6) and choose the correct word from the box.**

blog • password • search engine
social network • virus • website

1 The letters or numbers that you put into a computer or website to be able to use it. It's important that only *you* know the letters or numbers.
2 A place on the Internet where you can get information about a particular subject. It has got an address that usually begins with http://www.
3 A computer program like Google or Yahoo that you use to look for information on the Internet.
4 A program that enters your computer and does bad things to the information inside it.
5 An online diary with a writer's ideas, opinions and experiences.
6 A place on the Internet where you can connect with other people by sending messages, comments, photos …

2 50 **Listen, check and repeat.**

3 SPEAKING **Work with a partner. Talk about your answers to these questions.**

1 What is your favourite website and why?
2 What do you think of social networks on the Internet?
3 Do you read or write any blogs? Give details.
4 What search engine do you usually use?

Preparing PRESENTATIONS

LIFE SKILLS OBJECTIVES

- To learn about a style of presentation called Pecha Kucha
- To look at common mistakes when preparing and giving presentations
- To prepare and give a mini-presentation about Pecha Kucha

KEY CONCEPTS

slide [n]: *A computer presentation has different 'pages', which are called slides.* **font [n]:** *Each word in this sentence is in a different font.* **font size [n]:** Each word in this sentence is in a different font size. **bullet point [n]:** *■ At the start of this sentence there is a bullet point.* **animation [n]:** *An animation is something that moves in a computer presentation.* **background [n]:** *The background is what you can see behind the words on a slide.*

1 SPEAKING **Work with a partner. Ask and answer the questions.**

1. How often do you give presentations at school?
2. Do you use a computer for presentations?
3. Apart from school, when, where and why do people give presentations?

2 READING **Read about Pecha Kucha below. Do you think it's a good idea? Why/Why not?**

3 Look at these four slides. Do you think they are good slides to use in a presentation? Why/Why not?

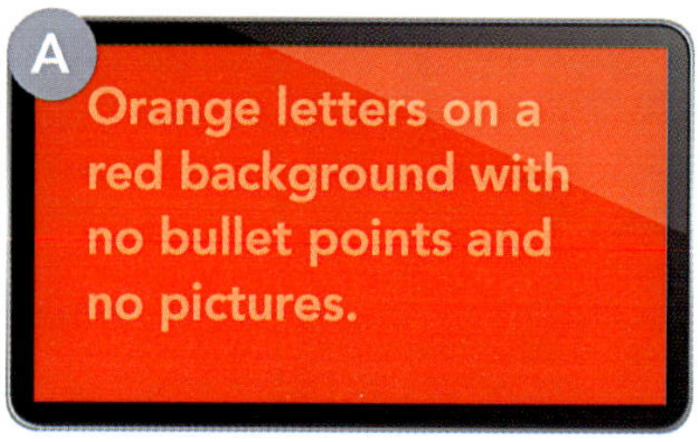

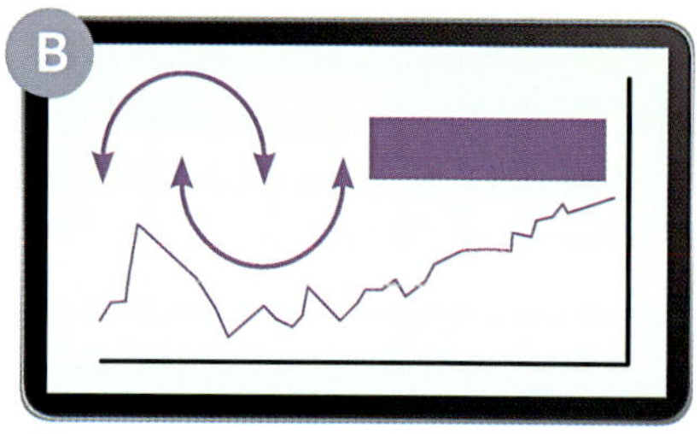

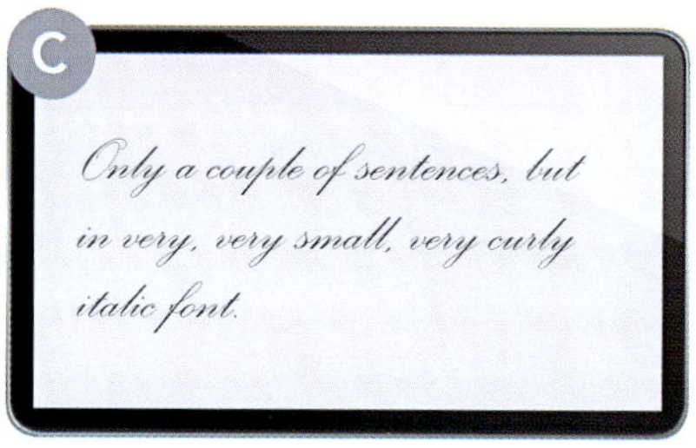

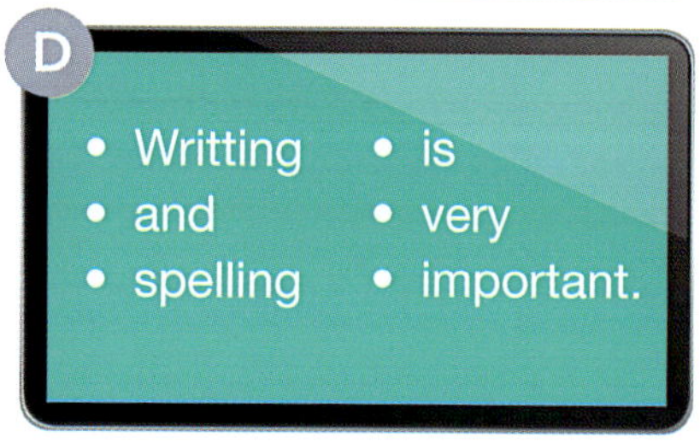

PECHA KUCHA PRESENTATIONS

Pecha Kucha 20 X 20 IMAGES SECONDS

Pecha Kucha is a Japanese word which means 'chit-chat', or a friendly conversation. It is also a type of presentation.

- For a Pecha Kucha presentation, you can only use a maximum of 20 slides.
- You can only talk about each slide for 20 seconds.
- You can't control the slides – they change automatically.
- The idea of Pecha Kucha is to stop people talking on and on and on …
- The idea is also to stop people having slides with hundreds of words and complicated visuals and animations.
- Pecha Kucha presentations must be creative and original because you can only have 20 times 20 seconds of presentation.

4 Read this text from a website giving help with presentations. Match each slide in 3 with the mistake or mistakes.

Home | About | Blog | Culture | Advice | Message board

8 PRESENTATION MISTAKES TO AVOID

SLIDE ....

Mistake 1: The number of words on a slide
When there are a lot of words on one slide, people can't read it. Write the key words, not every word you say.

Mistake 2: Colours
With very colourful backgrounds and fonts, it's impossible to read the text. Choose a dark background with light letters, or a light background with dark letters.

Mistake 3: No visuals
Pictures can make presentations interesting and easy to understand. With only text, a presentation can be boring and unattractive.

SLIDE ....

Mistake 4: The font you use
Some fonts are difficult to read, especially at a distance. Arial and Garamond are usually clear. Don't change fonts frequently for no reason.

Mistake 5: The font-size
A very small font size is difficult to read, especially from a distance. Depending on the font, around size 30 is good.

SLIDE ....

Mistake 6: Complicated and unnecessary visuals and animations
Arrows, boxes, circles and graphs can be useful. But when you use complicated visuals and animations, it can be difficult to understand. Keep it simple and clear.

SLIDE ....

Mistake 7: Spelling and grammar mistakes
These can create a bad impression.

Mistake 8: Too many/ No bullet points
Bullet points can make it easy to see the main points of your text. But when everything has a bullet point, it's difficult to know what is or isn't important.

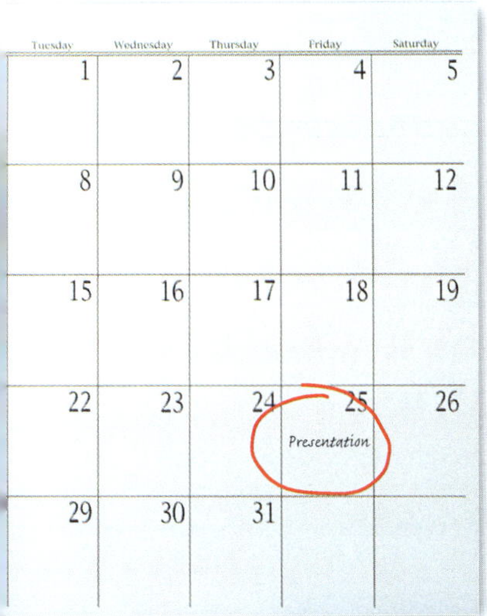

5 LISTENING ▶ 51 **A student is giving a presentation. Watch or listen. Are these statements True (T) or False (F)?**

1 He prepares the computer and other equipment before he starts his talk. T/F
2 He speaks slowly. T/F
3 He speaks clearly. T/F
4 He sometimes reads the exact words on the slides. T/F
5 He always looks at the audience. T/F
6 You can always see the presentation on the screen. T/F
7 He didn't practise the difficult words in his presentation. T/F

6 Work with a partner. Use the sentences in 5 to write a list of <u>positive</u> ideas about how to give a presentation.

It's important to prepare the computer and other equipment before the talk.

LIFE TASK

Prepare a mini-Pecha Kucha presentation to give to the class. Follow this plan:

1 *Decide what you want to talk about. It's a good idea if it's something that you really like, or are interested in, or know about.*
2 *Prepare ten slides. Remember not to make the mistakes in the text on this page!*
3 *Prepare some notes for each slide. But remember you've only got 20 seconds for each slide.*
4 *Work with a partner and practise giving the presentation.*
5 *Give your presentation to the class.*

1a Work with a partner and discuss the questions.

1 When do you use passwords?
2 Why are passwords important?

1b With your partner, create an imaginary good password and bad password. Decide what it is important to do or not to do to create a password.

2 LISTENING ▶ 52 **Listen to an expert talking about online passwords. Which of your ideas in 1b does she mention?**

3 ▶ 52 **Listen again. Are the sentences True (T) or False (F)?**

1 Jackie says that people like having a password that's easy to remember. T/F
2 '12345678' is in the top three passwords. T/F
3 Jackie says a long password is a good password. T/F
4 She says that commas, full stops and question marks are a bad idea in a password. T/F
5 She says it can be a good idea to use a word from a different language as a password. T/F
6 More than two thirds of teenage girls don't keep their passwords secret. T/F
7 Sometimes it can be necessary to write your password and send it in an email. T/F

4 SPEAKING **What about *you*?**

Work with a partner. With the information from the listening text …

1 evaluate your passwords in 1.
2 create a really good password together.

Grammar in context

The imperative

1 Look at the sentences and choose the correct alternative.

a **Don't use** real words!
b **Make** your password long.

1 We use/don't use the imperative to tell people what to do or what not to do.
2 Sentence a is affirmative/negative.
3 We make/don't make the affirmative imperative with the infinitive.
4 We use Not/Don't for the negative imperative.
5 We can/can't use exclamation marks (!) with the imperative.

GRAMMAR REFERENCE ➤ PAGE 72

2 Look at these ideas for security on the Internet. Choose the alternative that gives good advice.

1 Give/Don't give personal information to a person that you don't know.
2 Change/Don't change your password often.
3 Use/Don't use your password on public computers.
4 Make/Don't make 'abcdefg' your password.
5 Use/Don't use just one password for everything.
6 Log off/Don't log off when you finish using a public computer.
7 Have/Don't have long, complicated passwords like xCt?flw98Woo.

3 Match the words to make classroom instructions.

1 Look
2 Answer
3 Compare
4 Don't
5 Open
6 Turn

a to page 70.
b your book.
c answers with your partner.
d draw pictures in your book.
e as many questions as possible.
f at your book.

Flipped classroom: watch the grammar presentation video.

4 Use imperatives and the words given to write typical school rules.

1 be late — *Don't be late.*
2 bring your books ....
3 do your homework ....
4 shout ....
5 listen to the teacher ....
6 write on the desk ....
7 use your mobile phone without permission
....

5 SPEAKING Work with a partner. Make a list of good ideas to learn English fast.

Speak in English in class.
Watch films in English.

like, love, hate + gerund

6 Look at the sentences and answer the questions.

a We **love** surfing the net.
b People **like** using passwords that are easy to remember.
c Some teenagers **hate** keeping secrets.

1 What form of the verb do we use after verbs of liking – the infinitive or the *-ing* form?
2 In which sentence can we change the verb in **blue** for *can't stand*?

GRAMMAR REFERENCE ➤ PAGE 72

7 Write sentences with *love, like, don't like, hate/ can't stand* and the gerund.

1 Oliver/☺☺/listen to rock music.
Oliver loves listening to rock music.
2 Jess and Holly/☹☹/watch TV.
....
3 You/☹/chat online.
....
4 We/☺/play computer games.
....
5 She/☺☺/do sport.
....
6 They/☹/read.
....
7 Our friends/☹☹/listen to hip-hop.
....

8 SPEAKING Work with a partner. Ask your partner about the activities in 7. Look at the possible replies.

Do you like listening to rock music?

Yes, I do.

Yes, I do. I love it!

No, I don't.

No, I don't. I can't stand/hate it.

9 Read the text. Choose the best word (A, B or C) for each gap.

Do you like **(1)** .... the Net in your free time? I have some friends who don't enjoy it. In fact, they **(2)** .... stand using a computer after school! But I have other friends who love being online all weekend. **(3)** .... careful! Experts say that surfing the Net can become addictive. **(4)** .... sit in front of your computer for hours and hours. **(5)** .... sport or go out with friends. I **(6)** .... play the guitar quite **(7)** .... That's because I don't **(8)** .... spending all day with a computer.

	A	B	C
1	A surf	B surfing	C surfs
2	A can	B can't	C don't
3	A Are	B Be	C Being
4	A Do	B Don't	C Please
5	A Do	B Doing	C Don't
6	A can	B like	C want
7	A good	B hard	C well
8	A hate	B like	C love

✓ EXAM SUCCESS

In this type of exercise, there is a text with gaps. You fill the gaps in the text with one of three words. Is it important to look at the words just before the gap, the words just after the gap, or the words both before and after the gap? Why?

➤ EXAM SUCCESS page 152

Asking for and giving information

1 Look at this advertisement. What type of information is missing?

(a) surname

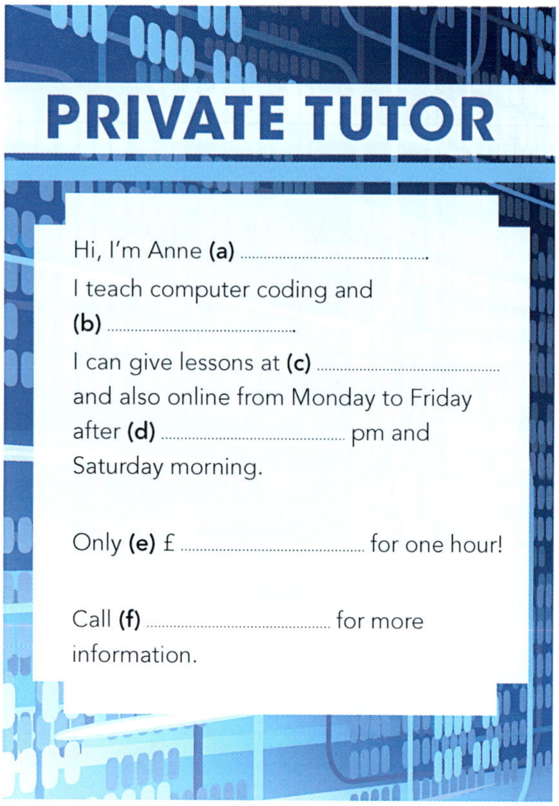

2 LISTENING 53 **A boy called William asks his friend Kay about the tutor in the advertisement. Complete the missing information in 1.**

3 Put the words in order to make questions from the dialogue. Then match each one with the missing information (a–f) in 1. For one of the pieces of information there are two questions.

1 she What teach does?
2 do you Sullivan How spell?
3 lessons give When can she?
4 home at your she Can give lessons?
5 lessons the cost How much do?
6 the name What's teacher's?
7 Have her telephone you got number?

4 Look at the information in the Speaking bank. Then find in 3 an example of a:

1 *Wh-* question
2 *Yes/No* question
3 question with *do/does*
4 question with *be*
5 question with *have*
6 question with *can*

SPEAKING BANK

Questions revision

- *Wh-* questions begin with a question word, e.g. *What, How, How much, How long, How often, Who* ... We answer *Wh-* questions with long answers.
- *Yes/No* questions have no question word. We answer *Yes/No* questions with short answers.
- We use *do/does* to make questions with main verbs like *teach, go, spell, cost* ...
- We do not need to use *do/does* with other auxiliary verbs like *be, have* or *can*.
- In questions, *do, does, is, are, have, has* and *can* come before the subject.

5 Work with a partner.

Student A: Your partner knows all about a science museum. Use these words to help you to prepare questions to ask about the museum.

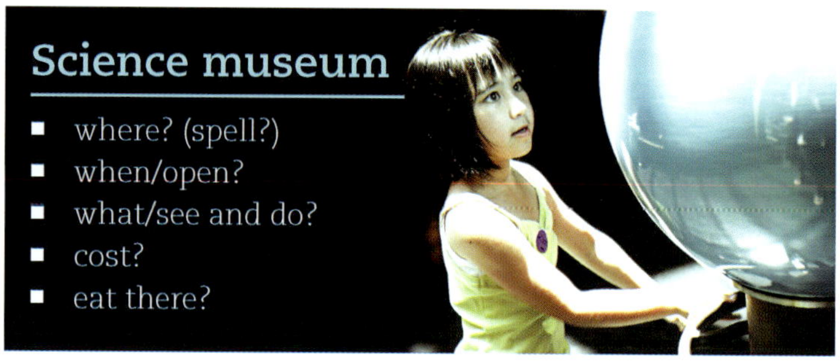

Student B: Your partner knows all about a new science fiction film. Use these words to help you to prepare questions to ask about the film.

PRACTICE MAKES PERFECT

6a SPEAKING **Work with a partner.**

Student A: Ask your partner your questions from 5.

Student B: Look at page 154 for information about the science museum. Use the information to answer your partner's questions.

6b Student B: Ask your partner your questions from 5.

Student A: Look at page 155 for information about a new science fiction film. Use the information to answer your partner's questions.

EXAM SUCCESS

In this type of exercise, is it important to listen to what your partner says? Why/Why not?

➤ EXAM SUCCESS page 152

A questionnaire

1 SPEAKING **Work with a partner. Discuss these questions.**

1 How often do you visit museums?
2 Which museum(s) do you like? Why?
3 Who do you usually visit museums with?

2 READING **Match the questions and answers.**

QUESTIONNAIRE:

ARE MUSEUMS BECOMING A THING OF THE PAST?

Help us with your opinions.

1 Is this your first visit to this museum? ....
2 What is your main reason for visiting the museum? ....
3 What do you think of the exhibits here? ....
4 How near is the museum to your house? ....
5 How often do you visit museums in general? ....
6 What other museums do you like visiting? ....
7 Do you usually visit museums alone, with friends/relatives, or with your school? ....
8 What is your general opinion of the museum and the services it offers? ....

Answers

a It's quite near. I can walk here in about ten minutes.
b I think they're really good. I like the exhibits that do things when you touch them.
c I like going to the history museum too.
d It's really good. You can see lots of interesting things and the 3D cinema is brilliant.
e I sometimes go with my school and I also go with my mum and dad.
f Three or four times a year.
g No, I think it's my third or fourth.
h I need information for a school project.

3a Look at the instructions in the Writing bank about how to write a good questionnaire.

WRITING BANK

Useful advice for writing questionnaires

- Give your questionnaire an interesting title.
- Make all your questions relevant to the questionnaire.
- If possible, put the questions in order. We usually start with general questions and then we ask specific things. The last question can ask for a general conclusion.
- Be very careful with grammatical mistakes in questions. Do you have the correct word order? Is the auxiliary verb *do* necessary?

3b Read this questionnaire written by a student. Does the student follow the advice in the Writing bank?

Ebooks – yes or no?

1 You like reading ebooks?
2 Have you an ebook?
3 What you think of reading in general?
4 You can read?
5 Which you prefer – ebooks or traditional books?
6 What does you like about traditional books?

4 Work with a partner and do the tasks.

1 Correct the mistakes in the questions in 3.
2 Take out any questions that are not relevant.
3 Add one or two relevant questions.
4 Think of an interesting title.

PRACTICE MAKES PERFECT

5a Write a questionnaire to find out what people in your class think about computers and/or the Internet. What do they like doing with computers or online? What don't they like? Use the information in the Writing bank to help you.

WRITING BANK ➤ PAGE 156

5b Give students your questionnaire to complete. Ask them to write their answers on a separate piece of paper.

5c Report back to the class. Tell them some interesting answers to the questions in your questionnaire.

Grammar reference

can/can't

FORM

Affirmative	I/You/He/She/We/They **can** read.
Negative	I/You/He/She/We/They **can't (cannot*)** sing.
Question form	**Can** I/you/he/she/we/they play the guitar?
Short answers	Yes, I/you/he/she/we/they **can**./ No, I/you/he/she/we/they **can't**.

* We write *cannot* as one word, not two.

USE

- We use *can* to talk about ability.
  She can use a computer.

Adverbs of manner

FORM

Regular adverbs

- We add **-ly** to the adjective:
  slow – slow**ly**, clear – clear**ly**, careful – careful**ly**
- We sometimes need to change the spelling of the original adjective:
  easy – easi**ly**, terrible – terrib**ly**

Irregular adverbs

good – well, fast – fast, hard – hard, early – early, late – late

USE

- We use adverbs of manner to describe how we do something. They go with verbs (but not the verb *to be*).

The imperative

FORM

Affirmative	**Go!** **Look** at this.
Negative	**Don't go!** **Don't look** at that.

- We make the imperative with the infinitive without *to*.
- The form of the imperative is the same in singular and plural.
- We can use exclamation marks (*!*) with the imperative.

USE

- We use the imperative to give instructions, orders or advice.

like, love, hate, etc. + gerund

FORM

I love playing football.
She likes playing computer games.
We don't like watching films.
They hate/can't stand swimming.

- After verbs of liking we use the *-ing* form of the verb.

USE

- *Can't stand* has a similar meaning to *hate*.

Vocabulary

Computers keyboard • monitor/screen • mouse • printer/scanner • screensaver • speaker • touchpad touch screen • USB cable and port • webcam

Using computers click on • copy • cut and paste • download • log on/off • print • save • send an email

The Internet blog • password • search engine • social network • virus • website

Other words and phrases ➤ page 145

Grammar revision

can/can't / 6 points

1 Use the prompts to write sentences with *can* and *can't*.

1 Ann/ski?

....

2 Nathan/✗/dance.

....

3 I/✓/speak English.

....

4 Liz and Kate/✗/understand German.

....

5a Q: Mike/play the guitar?

....

5b A: ✓

....

Adverbs of manner / 5 points

2 Choose the correct alternative.

1 I don't write very quick/quickly.
2 She works very hard/hardly at school.
3 My friend speaks Spanish quite fast/fastly.
4 Her explanations are very clear/clearly.
5 Please listen careful/carefully.

The imperative / 4 points

3 Write imperatives using the prompt sentences.

1 It's important to do your homework.

..........!

2 It's a very bad idea to walk in the road.

..........!

3 It isn't a good idea to copy in exams.

..........!

4 It's important to do your homework tonight.

..........!

like, love, hate, etc. + gerund / 6 points

4 Find and correct six mistakes in this dialogue.

Chloe: Do you like use your tablet?

Andy: Yes, I like. And I love read my ebook. What about you?

Chloe: I prefer traditional books. I like to going to bookshops. My dad is the same. He doesn't stand reading digital books. He really loves reading them.

Vocabulary revision

COMPUTERS / 7 points

1 Complete the last three letters in each word.

1 k e y b o ....
2 m o n i ....
3 t o u c h ....
4 USB c a ....
5 s p e a ....
6 t o u c h s c r ....
7 s c r e e n s a ....

USING COMPUTERS / 6 points

2 Choose the correct alternative.

1 When you copy/send an email, a message goes from your computer to another computer.
2 When you log off/on, you start using a computer or computer system by giving some information (e.g. your name).
3 When you download/print data, you transfer it from another computer or via the Internet to your computer.
4 When you click off/on something with your mouse, you make it work.
5 When you cut and paste/save something on a computer, you keep the information that you put into it.
6 When you cut and paste/log on to something, you copy or move words or pictures on a computer screen from one place to another.

THE INTERNET / 6 points

3 Put the letters in the correct order to make words connected with the Internet.

1 glob ....
2 suvri ....
3 bestwie ....
4 swordsap ....
5 hesacr igneen ....
6 lascio tenkrow ....

Total: / 40 points

6 Good buys

Vocabulary

Shops

1 **Look at the plan of the shopping centre. Match the shops with these words.**

bakery • bank • chemist's • clothes shop
jeweller's • newsagent's • post office • shoe shop
sports shop • supermarket

2 **54 Listen and repeat.**

3 LISTENING **55 Listen. Where in the shopping centre are these people?**

1 ....
2 ....
3 ....
4 ....
5 ....
6 ....

4 SPEAKING **Work with a partner. Ask your partner how often they go to the places in 1.**

How often do you go to the bakery?

I sometimes go to get bread on Saturday. And you?

Shopping

5 **Work with a partner. Match the photos with the words.**

cash • change • cheque • credit card • price
purse/wallet • sale • size

1

2

3

4

5

6

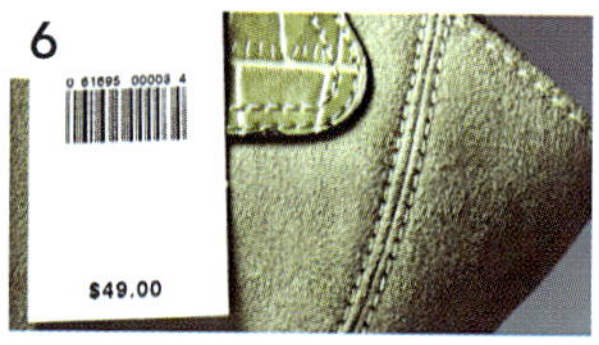

7

8

6a **Complete the dialogue with words in 5. Which person is the shop assistant? Which is the customer?**

A: Excuse me. What (1) .... is this T-shirt?
B: Let me see. It says M here.
A: Oh, yes. Can you tell me the (2) .... ?
B: Yes, it's £19.49.
A: Great. Can I pay by (3) .... card?
B: No, I'm sorry. We only accept (4) ....
A: OK. I think I've got some money in my (5) .... Yes. Here's £20.
B: Thanks. Here is 51p (6) ....

6b **56 Listen and check your answers.**

6c SPEAKING **Work with a partner. Practise the dialogue and invent a similar dialogue.**

1 READING **Read this text message conversation between Mason and Evan. They are shopping in the Greenwood Shopping Centre. Where exactly is** Mason **and where is** Evan **?**

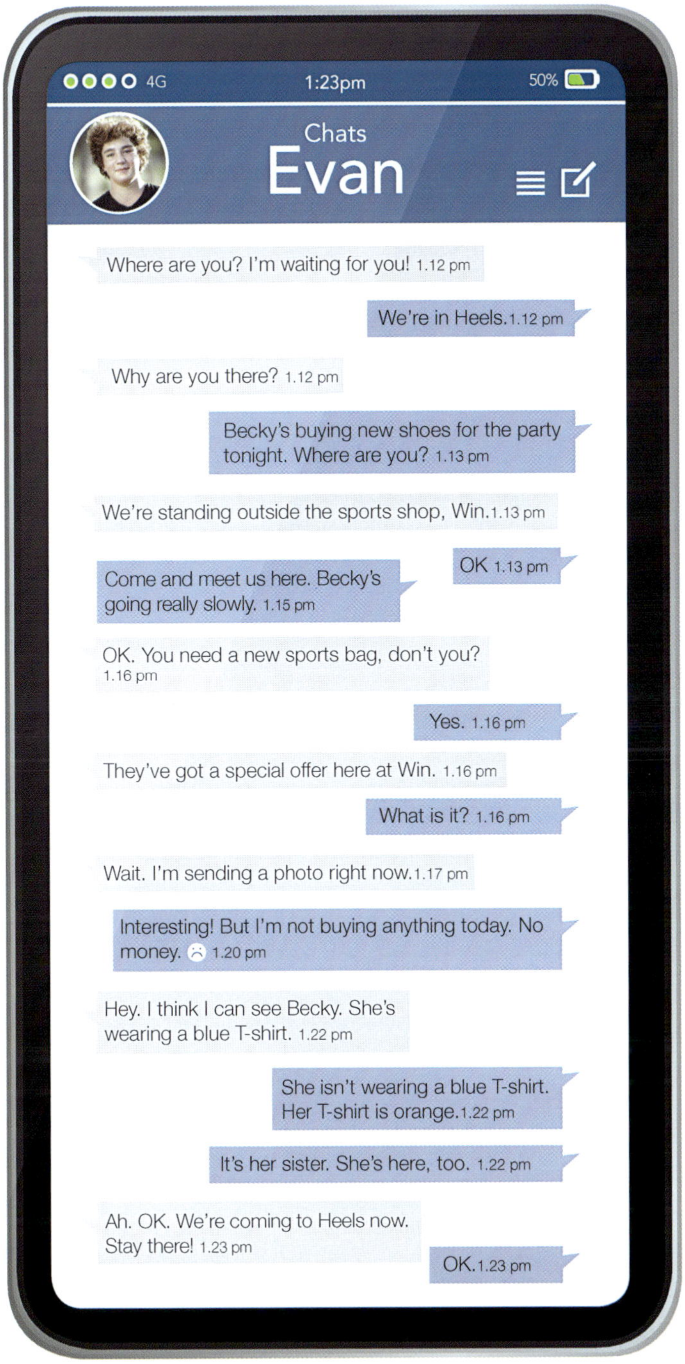

2 **Read the text message again and answer the questions.**

1. Where is Becky and what does she need?
2. What photo does Mason send to Evan and why?
3. Who does Mason see?
4. Where do Mason and Evan decide to meet in the end?

3 **Look at the notices at the bottom of the page. They are all from Greenwood Shopping Centre. Which is the notice that Mason sends to Evan?**

4 **Which notice (A–G) says this (1–5)?**

1. Some books here are at a special low price for just a very short period.
2. When you buy things in this shop, you can get an extra item for nothing.
3. If you're at school or university and you need to get something to read, this is a good time to do it.
4. Find what this person is looking for and you can get some money.
5. You need to use cash here.

✓ EXAM SUCCESS

In this type of exercise, is it important to read all the notices before you make your decision? Why/Why not?

➤ EXAM SUCCESS page 152

5 **CRITICAL THINKING**

Think! Then compare ideas with your class.

- According to the British newspaper *The Independent*, 33% of American teenagers receive and send 100 texts a day, about ten every hour that they are awake. What do you think of this statistic?

6 SPEAKING **What about *you*?**

How many texts do you send each day? Who do you send the most texts to? Do you send many picture messages?

A

PLEASE HELP!
LOST!
Green wallet
£50 for its safe return
Call 9856721

B

C

D

E

F

G

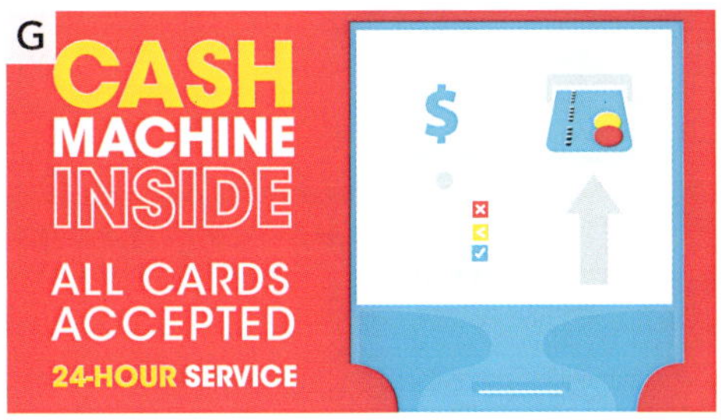

Grammar in context

Flipped classroom: watch the grammar presentation video.

Present continuous – affirmative and negative

1 Look at the sentences and answer the questions.

a I'm waiting for you.
b Becky's buying new shoes for the party.
c I'm not buying anything today.
d She isn't wearing a blue T-shirt.
e We're coming to Heels now.

1 Apart from the *-ing* form of the verb, what do we need to make the present continuous?
2 How do we make the negative form of the present continuous?
3 Do we use the present continuous to talk about routines and habits or to talk about things happening now?

GRAMMAR REFERENCE ➤ PAGE 84

2a Look at the examples and complete the table with the correct *-ing* forms.

List A	List B	List C
wait ➤ *waiting*	come ➤ *coming*	put ➤ *putting*
buy ➤ *buying*	make ➤ *making*	swim ➤ *swimming*
play ➤ *playing*	write ➤ *writing*	run ➤ *running*
wear ➤	dance ➤	chat ➤
cook ➤	take ➤	sit ➤
study ➤	have ➤	shop ➤
read ➤	save ➤	stop ➤

2b Match the spelling rules (1–3) with the correct list (A–C).

1 With verbs that end in consonant + *e*, take away *e* and add *-ing*.
2 For most verbs we just add *-ing*.
3 With verbs ending in one vowel and one consonant, we double the consonant and add *-ing*.

3a PRONUNCIATION ▶ 57 Listen to the example *-ing* words in the table in 2a. Where is the stress in each word? Mark the stress.

waiting *buying*

3b ▶ 57 Listen again. Repeat the words with the correct stress.

4 Complete the text messages with the correct form of *to be*.

4G 12:45pm 50%

Where are you?

I (1) .... standing inside the sports shop. And you?

I'm with Dan. We (2) .... waiting for you.

But Dan's at home! He (3) .... doing his homework right now.

He (4) .... doing his homework. He (5) .... standing here with me outside the post office. Hey, don't spend all your money!

Don't worry. I (6) .... buying anything. It's Jack and Wayne. They (7) .... buying trainers. OK. They (8) .... coming out.

We (9) .... walking to the sports shop now. Stay there!

OK. It's easy to see us. Jack and I (10) .... wearing orange T-shirts!

5 Put the verb in the correct form of the present continuous.

1 My sister .... (watch) TV at the moment.
2 Jason and Kyle .... (not talk) to the teacher right now.
3 My dad .... (make) the dinner.
4 I .... (do) an English exercise.
5 We .... (write) the answers.
6 I .... (not sit) in the library.
7 My parents .... (shop) right now.

6 Look at the photos below. What are the people doing? Complete the sentences using these verbs in the present continuous.

listen • play • read • run • talk • write

1 Isabella ....
2 Gavin and Lucas ....
3 Matt and Oliver ....
4 Leo ....
5 Stella ....
6 Alyssa ....

1

2

3

4

5

6

7a Write four sentences about the people in the photo. Make two sentences true and two false.

....

....

....

....

....

....

....

7b SPEAKING **Work in a small group. Close your books. Take it in turns to read out your sentences. Which sentences are true and which are false?**

A man and a woman are running.

They aren't running. They're walking.

Clothes

1 Find someone in the pictures on this page who is wearing the items in the box.

boots • coat • dress • jacket • jeans • jumper shirt • skirt • sweatshirt • T-shirt • top • trainers trousers

boots – Anna

2 58 **Listen and repeat.**

3 SPEAKING **Work with a partner. Close your books. Can you remember what the people are wearing?**

I think Simon is wearing an orange jumper.

No, I think it's a green sweatshirt.

4 SPEAKING **Work with a partner. Ask and answer the questions.**

1 How often do you wear the different clothes in 1?
2 What do you usually wear at school?
3 What clothes do you like wearing outside school and at the weekend?

Identifying SELLING TECHNIQUES

LIFE SKILLS OBJECTIVES

- To think about how special offers influence us
- To look at different techniques used in adverts
- To identify the ways adverts make us want to buy things

KEY CONCEPTS

sell [v]: *Newsagents in the UK sell newspapers and also sweets and chocolate, for example.* **product [n]:** *All the products in this shop are very high quality.* **discount [n]:** *10% discount on something that costs £50 is £5, so it now costs £45.*
sales/advertising technique [n]: *Shops use different techniques to make people buy things.*

1 Work with a partner. Ask and answer the questions. If the answer is *Yes*, give details.

Do you ever buy things ...
1 because there is a special offer? 2 that you never use/eat/wear? 3 that you want but that you don't really need?

2 READING **Read the texts about how shops and businesses use special offers to make us buy things. Match each offer (a–c) to the correct text (1–3).**

3 Read the texts again. Choose the correct alternative.

1 The problem with 'Buy One Get One Free' offers is that the offers ...
   a are not really true.
   b make you buy unnecessary things.
2 'Drip pricing' is when ...
   a the original price is good but the final price goes up and up little by little.
   b you can only buy a product with a credit card.
3 'Baiting' is when a shop says they have a great special offer but in reality the offer is ...
   a only for one or two products.
   b only for a very short period.

1 BUY ONE GET ONE FREE

A very common offer in supermarkets is 'Buy One Get One Free' (sometimes called BOGOF). These offers often make us buy things that we don't want or need. When people buy food with this type of offer, 30% throw away some of the food in the end.

2 drip pricing

You see a special offer online to buy tickets for a concert. The tickets are cheap. You start to buy the tickets, but then you see that the price doesn't include tax, so the price goes up. Then you see that the cheap tickets aren't very good. You pay extra for a good seat. You also pay extra if your parents pay by credit card. And extra if ... So, in the end, the tickets aren't cheap. This is called 'drip pricing'.

3 BAITING

You're walking past a clothes shop and you see a big sign. It says SALE: 50% OFF so you go inside. But really the sign outside says '<u>up to</u> 50% OFF'. ('Up to' is usually in small letters.) So 50% is the maximum you can save. There are probably only one or two things with 50% discount. The rest is just 10% or 5% or 0%. But now that you're inside the shop and see nice clothes, it's difficult to say *no*. This technique is called 'baiting'. We use bait to catch fish!

a

b

c

4 Work with a partner. Look again at the offers. What do you need to think about before you take the offer?

5 Work with a partner. Think of an advert or type of advert that uses …

a happy and exciting music.
b an expert, for example a doctor or dentist.
c a famous person.
d a happy family.

6 LISTENING ▶ 59 **Watch or listen to two students talking about the advertising techniques (a–d) in 5. Put the techniques in the order that they are mentioned.**

1 ………… 2 ………… 3 ………… 4 …………

7 ▶ 59 **Listen again. According to the students, which technique (a–d) …**

1 works because it makes you feel happy?
2 works for sports fans?
3 works because we believe the person in the advert?
4 often sells things like cars?
5 works because you want to be like the people in the advert?
6 often sells health and beauty products?

8 SPEAKING **Work with a partner. Discuss the questions.**

1 Do you like any adverts on TV? Which? Why?
2 Do you think adverts can be a good thing? If so, how and when?
3 Do you think adverts influence you? Why/Why not?
4 What techniques do you think are effective for teenagers and why?

LIFE TASK

Work in groups. Your task is to make an advert. Follow this plan:

1 *Think of a product that is popular with you and your friends.*
2 *Think of techniques and ideas that are popular with teenagers.*
3 *Create an advert for the product.*
   a) *Decide if your advert is for the TV, radio, a newspaper, online …*
   b) *Prepare some of these for your advert: a video, music, photos or pictures, a dialogue …*
4 *Show your advert to the class. Choose the best.*

Listening

✔ EXAM SUCCESS

This exercise is a multiple-choice listening activity. You have three or four choices and you choose the correct one. Read 1 to 6 below. What words do you think are important? Underline them. How can they help you?

➤ EXAM SUCCESS page 152

1 LISTENING 60 **Listen to a phone conversation between a boy called Luke and his mum and choose the correct answers.**

1 Luke's mum …
   a is at the sports shop.
   b is going to the sports shop.
   c is at the supermarket.
2 Luke wants new tennis balls because …
   a he hasn't got any.
   b he doesn't know where his old ones are.
   c he can't play well with the ones he has.
3 The sports shop on Park Road has got …
   a good tennis balls.
   b special offers.
   c cheap tennis balls.
4 Luke's mum needs to spend about …
   a £12 on tennis balls.
   b £20 on tennis balls.
   c £24 on tennis balls.
5 Luke's dad …
   a is having dinner.
   b is getting pizza.
   c loves pizza.
6 Today the sports shop closes at …
   a half past five.
   b six o'clock.
   c half past six.

2 60 **Listen to the conversation again. Complete and check your answers.**

3 SPEAKING **What about *you*?**

Who usually buys these things in your family?

1 Food
2 Your clothes
3 Things you need for school or sport

Grammar in context

Present continuous – questions and short answers

1 Look at the sentences (a–d) and choose the correct alternative (1–3).

a What **are** you do**ing**?
b What**'s** he buy**ing**?
c **Are** you do**ing** the shopping?
d Yes, I **am**./No, I**'m not**.

1 In present continuous questions, the verb *to be* comes *after/before* the subject.
2 When we have a question word (*what*, *who*, etc.), it *is/isn't* usually the first word in the question.
3 In short answers, we *only use the verb to be/repeat the -ing form of the verb*.

GRAMMAR REFERENCE ➤ PAGE 84

2a Complete the questions with the present continuous form of the verbs given.

1 What ………… Isabella ………… (wear)?
2 ………… Gavin and Lucas ………… (play) football?
3 What ………… Matt and Oliver ………… (do)?
4 ………… they ………… (wear) T-shirts?
5 ………… Leo ………… (read) an ebook?
6 Where ………… Stella ………… (listen) to music?
7 Where ………… Alyssa ………… (write)?

2b Look at the photos on page 76 and answer the questions in 2a.

3a Put the words in order to make questions.

1 English doing Are an you exercise?
2 mum now is What your doing?
3 doing teacher moment is What your at the?
4 you are Where sitting?
5 What friends your doing are?
6 you are talking now right Who to?
7 the moment people writing Are at?

3b SPEAKING **Work with a partner. Ask and answer the questions. Give true answers.**

4 **Look at the pictures. Make questions and answers using the words given.**

1

Q: Adam and Ben/wear jeans?

....

....

A. ....

2

Q: Becky/play the guitar?

....

....

A. ....

3

Q: What/Nancy/eat?

....

....

A. ....

4

Q: Dylan/buy bread?

....

....

A. ....

Present simple and present continuous

5 **Look at the sentences (a–d) and then match them to statements (1–4).**

a Are you doing the shopping?

b I always do the shopping on Wednesday.

c He's buying something for dinner.

d He always buys pizza.

Which sentences …

1 talk about things that are happening now?

2 talk about routines?

3 are in the present continuous?

4 are in the present simple?

GRAMMAR REFERENCE ➤ PAGE 84

6 **Read the text and choose the correct alternative.**

It's a big, big world. There are approximately 7.13 billion people in the world. So what (1) *are they doing/do they do* right now? Let's see what the experts say.

(2) *Are you watching/Do you watch* TV during the week? Right now, this very second, 320 million people (3) *are watching/watch* the TV.

I (4) *am brushing/brush* my hair every morning. At this very moment, 22 million people around the world (5) *are brushing/brush* their hair!

And right now what (6) *are one million people sending/do one million people send*? Text messages, of course.

People often (7) *are surfing/surf* the Net to find information. Right now, 5.5 million people around the world (8) *are surfing/surf* the Net!

How many people (9) *are playing/play* football at the moment? 350,000!

Of course, at night we always (10) *are sleeping/sleep*. In some parts of the world it's day and in others it's night. So, what (11) *are 2 billion people doing/do 2 billion people do* at the moment? They (12) *'re sleeping/sleep*.

7 SPEAKING **Work with a partner. Discuss the questions.**

1 What things are people doing now in your part of the world?

2 What do people usually do at 9 pm?

3 Find out what time it is in different parts of the world. What do you think people are doing there right now?

a

b

Describing pictures

1 SPEAKING **Work with a partner. Look at picture a and answer these questions.**

1 How many people can you see?
2 Where are they?
3 What are they doing?
4 What are they wearing?

2 Now look at picture b and find ten differences between this picture and picture a. Use the questions in 1 again to help you.

3 LISTENING ▶ 61 **Listen to two students doing exercise 2 and check your answers.**

4 ▶ 61 **Listen to the students in 3 again. Tick (✓) the words and expressions from the Speaking bank which they use.**

SPEAKING BANK

Useful expressions to describe and contrast pictures

- We can begin our comments with *I can see …*, *There is/There are …*
- We use *but* to talk about differences between pictures: *In picture a there's a …* **but** *in picture b there's a …*
- We use prepositions (*on, in front of, behind …*) to say where people and things are.
- We use the present continuous to say what people are doing (*He's listening to music. She's talking to the girl.*).
- We use expressions like *I think* or *maybe* when we are not 100% sure of what we can see.

PRACTICE MAKES PERFECT

5 SPEAKING **Work with a partner. Take it in turns to talk about the two pictures and the ten differences between them. Use the expressions in the Speaking bank to help you.**

a

b

A short note – 2

1 Work with a partner. Look at these instructions for a writing task. Look at the example and write some ideas for what to include in the note to your friend.

It's Saturday morning. You have a friend staying with you. You need to go out early, but later you want to meet your friend at the shopping centre for lunch. Write a note to leave for your friend.

Say:

- why you are going to the shopping centre this morning ➤ *Need to buy new trainers for PE*
- where and when you can meet in the shopping centre
- where and what you can eat
- what you can do together after lunch

2 READING Two students do the task in 1. Read their notes and answer the questions.

1 Are any ideas similar to your ideas in 1?
2 What do you think of each note?

A

Hi Annette,

I'm going to Greenwood ~~Shoping~~ Shopping Centre now. I need to buy a new pair of trainers because the trainers I wear in PE are really old. Meet me for lunch! We can meet at the sports shop at 12.30, for example. Then we can go to the new ~~Italien~~ Italian pizza place – my mum says they've got a special offer this week. After lunch, we can maybe go and see a film.

See you!

Wendy

B

Dear Miss Smith,

I go to Greenwood Shoping Centre now. I need to buy a new pair of trainers because the trainers I wear in PE are really old. meet me for lunch! we can meet at the sports shop at 12.30, for example. Then we can go to the new italian pizza place – my mum say theyve got an offer special this week. After lunch, we can maybe go and see a film.

see you!

Wendy

3 Look at the correction checklist in the Writing bank. Find an example of each mistake in one of the notes and correct it.

punctuation – theyve they've

WRITING BANK

Correction checklist

When you finish writing a text in English, it is important to check it before you hand it in. Check for mistakes with:

- punctuation
- capital letters
- spelling
- word order
- agreement between the subject and verb
- correct style (informal or formal)
- tenses
- handwriting and presentation

PRACTICE MAKES PERFECT

4a Look at the instructions. Write some ideas to include in your note.

You have a friend from the US staying with you. It's Sunday morning. You are going out somewhere together now. Your brother is still sleeping but you want to meet up with him later. Write a note to your brother.

Say:

- what you and your American friend are doing now
- where and when in your town/city you can meet up
- where you can spend the afternoon
- what you can do together

4b Use your ideas in 4a to write the note. When you finish, check your work using the correction checklist in the Writing bank.

WRITING BANK ➤ PAGE 156

Grammar reference

Present continuous

FORM

Affirmative	subject + am/are/is + verb+-ing *We're waiting.*
Negative	subject + am not/aren't/isn't + verb+-ing *She isn't coming.*
Question form	Am/Are/Is + subject + verb+-ing? *Are they buying shoes?*
Short answers	Yes, subject + am/are/is. No, subject + am not/aren't/isn't. *Yes, they are. No, we aren't.*

Spelling

We usually add -ing to the verb to form the present participle.

wait ➤ waiting *wear ➤ wearing* *read ➤ reading*

When verbs end in one or more consonant +e, we omit the e and add -ing.

come ➤ coming *take ➤ taking* *save ➤ saving*

When a verb has only one syllable and finishes with one vowel and one consonant (except w, x or y), we double the consonant and add -ing.

put ➤ putting *chat ➤ chatting* *shop ➤ shopping*

USE

We use the present continuous to talk about actions that are happening now.

I can't go out. I'm doing my homework.

Present simple and present continuous

USE

We use the present simple to talk about regular habits and routines, and things that are always or usually true. We use the present continuous to talk about things that are happening now.

*I **wear** (present simple) school uniform during the week. But it's the weekend, so today **I'm wearing** (present continuous) jeans and a T-shirt.*

Vocabulary

Shops bakery • bank • chemist's • clothes shop • jeweller's • newsagent's • post office • shoe shop sports shop • supermarket

Shopping cash • change • cheque • credit card • customer • price • purse/wallet • sale • shop assistant size

Clothes boots • coat • dress • jacket • jeans • jumper • shirt • skirt • sweatshirt • T-shirt • top • trainers trousers

Other words and phrases ➤ page 146

Grammar revision

Present continuous – affirmative and negative / 6 points

1 Use the prompts to write sentences in the present continuous.

1 I/write the answers. ....
2 She/not/shop. ....
3 We/not/chat online. ....
4 Helen/wait for you. ....
5 Kay and Tim/sit on the sofa. ....
6 You/not/listen to me. ....

Present continuous – questions and short answers / 7 points

2 Choose the correct alternative.

Jen: Hi, Ali. **(1)** *Are/Is* you studying?
Liz: No, I'm **(2)** *don't/not*.
Jen: What are you **(3)** *do/doing*?
Liz: I'm just **(4)** *siting/sitting* in my bedroom, listening to music.
Jen: I can hear your brother. Who **(5)** *does/is* he talking to?
Liz: To my mum.
Jen: **(6)** *They are/Are they* shouting?
Liz: No, they **(7)** *aren't/don't*.

Present simple and present continuous / 6 points

3 Are the sentences correct? If not, write them correctly.

1 Listen! Sarah plays the piano.
2 I am always doing my homework in my bedroom.
3 Quickly! The teacher waits for us.
4 Why are you running? Are you late?
5 Usually she is going to bed at 10 pm.
6 My dad takes me to school by car every morning.

Vocabulary revision

SHOPS / 7 points

1 Name the shops where you can buy these things.

1  b ....
2  ....
3  ....
4  ....
5  ....
6  ....
7  ....

SHOPPING / 7 points

2 Read the definitions and write the words.

1 Person in a shop who wants to buy something: c ....
2 Men put their money and carry it here: w ....
3 How much something costs: p ....
4 Small, Medium, Large, Extra large: s ....
5 Plastic object you use to pay with: c ....
6 'Real' money: c ....
7 Something costs £1.50, you pay £2. This is the money they give you back: c ....

CLOTHES / 7 points

3 Put the letters in the correct order to make words for clothes.

1 atco ....
2 trish ....
3 strik ....
4 rempju ....
5 sanje ....
6 kejcat ....
7 rosstrue ....

Total: / 40 points

Reading

➤ TIP FOR READING EXAMS

In activities where you match notices, remember …
Read all the notices before you make your decision.

➤ EXAM SUCCESS page 152

1 READING **Which notice (A–G) says this (1–5)?**

1 If you find this object, you can get some money.
2 Go there if you are in a group and some of you don't eat meat, but some of you do.
3 This is the place to call if your computer has got problems.
4 If you need to buy something to wear, this is a good place and time to go.
5 If you have problems because you don't know anything about computers, these people can help.

2 **Work with a partner. What is the main message in the other notices?**

A

B

C

D
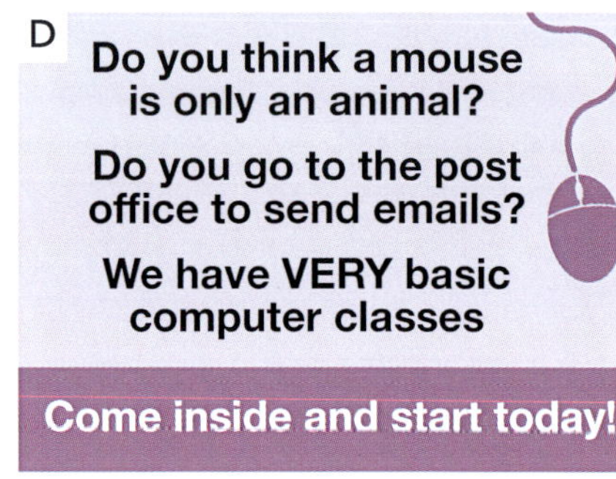

E

YOU DON'T EAT MEAT?

We only serve vegetarian food
Everything is healthy
And everything is DELICIOUS
We serve groups of all sizes

F

G

Use of English

➤ TIP FOR USE OF ENGLISH

In multiple-choice cloze activities, remember …
It's important to look at the words before and after each space to help you to decide the missing word.

➤ EXAM SUCCESS page 152

3 **Read the text. Choose the best word (A, B or C) for each space.**

I usually (1) .... a lot in my free time. I (2) .... got an electronic book, or ebook. My sister hates ebooks. She (3) .... stand them. Personally, I like traditional books and ebooks. At the moment, I (4) .... reading a book that has seven hundred pages. It isn't (5) .... to take it with me on the bus every morning! But there (6) .... something special about traditional books, too. The important thing is to read. I think I do (7) .... in my English exams because I read a lot. My teacher always says the same thing. '(8) .... stop reading!'

	A	B	C
1	A read	B reading	C reads
2	A have	B has	C don't
3	A can	B can't	C doesn't
4	A am	B are	C do
5	A easily	B easy	C well
6	A –	B are	C is
7	A right	B good	C well
8	A –	B Do	C Don't

Listening

➤ TIP FOR LISTENING EXAMS

In multiple-choice listening activities, remember …
Look for the important words in the sentences and choices. They can help you when you listen.

➤ EXAM SUCCESS page 152

4a Look at 1 to 5. Underline the important words.

1 Eve has a problem with …
   a her laptop because it's old.
   b a new laptop.
   c computers in general.
2 At the moment, Eve …
   a can't see anything on her screen.
   b can't write correctly with her keyboard.
   c hasn't got all the letters on her keyboard.
3 Joe …
   a can't do anything to help Eve.
   b helps Eve to write with her laptop.
   c has a brother who can help Eve.
4 At the moment Tom is probably …
   a working.
   b studying.
   c going home.
5 Tom's number is …
   a 5346612.
   b 5366412.
   c 5344612.

4b LISTENING ▶ 62 **Listen to two teenagers talking about a problem. Choose the correct answers in 4a.**

Speaking

➤ TIP FOR SPEAKING EXAMS

In speaking exams, remember …
It's important to listen to your partner. You need to know what they are asking or telling you so that you can continue the conversation.

➤ EXAM SUCCESS page 152

5 Work with a partner. Student A, your partner knows all about an interesting new shop. Use these words to help you to prepare questions.

New shop
- name?
- what/sell?
- where? (spell?)
- when/open?
- special offers?

Student B, your partner knows all about a new restaurant. Use these words to help you to prepare questions.

New restaurant
- name?
- type of food/serve?
- where? (spell?)
- when/open?
- special offers?

6a Student A: Ask your partner your questions from 5.

Student B: Look at page 154 for information about a new shop. Use the information to answer your partner's questions.

6b Student B: Ask your partner your questions from 5.

Student A: Look at page 155 for information about a new restaurant. Use the information to answer your partner's questions.

'CAN DO' PROGRESS CHECK UNITS 5–6 — CEF

1 How well can you do these things in English now? Give yourself a mark from 1 to 4.

1 = I can do it very well.	3 = I have some problems.
2 = I can do it quite well.	4 = I can't do it.

a I can talk about abilities using *can/can't* and adverbs of manner. ☐
b I can give basic instructions using the imperative. ☐
c I can understand spoken and written texts about computing. ☐
d I can ask for and give information about places, films, etc. ☐
e I can write a simple questionnaire. ☐
f I can talk about what is happening now using the present continuous. ☐
g I can understand simple written and spoken texts connected with shops and shopping. ☐
h I can name different clothes and say what people are wearing. ☐
i I can describe pictures. ☐
j I can correct mistakes in my written work. ☐

2 Now decide what you need to do to improve.

1 Look again at my book/notes.
2 Do more practice exercises. ➤ WORKBOOK Units 5–6
3 Ask for help.
4 Other: ……………………………………

7 Teamwork

Vocabulary

Sports

1 **Work with a partner. Match the photos with some of these words. Check that you know the other sports. Use your dictionary if necessary.**

baseball • basketball • cycling • football • golf
gymnastics • horse-riding • ice hockey • ice-skating
judo • rugby • skiing • swimming
tennis • volleyball

2a PRONUNCIATION **63 Look at A and B and listen to the pronunciation. How many syllables does each word have? Where is the stress?**

A ●• baseball

B ●•• basketball

2b **64 Listen to all the words in the box.**

1 Which are A (●•) and which are B (●••)?
2 Two words are not A or B. Which words?

2c **64 Listen again and repeat with the correct stress.**

3a **Look at this guide for how we use *play, do* and *go* with sports.**

1 We usually use *play* with sports that need a ball or something similar to a ball, e.g. *play baseball*
2 We usually use *go* with *-ing* words, e.g. *go cycling*
3 We usually use *do* with non-ball sports and words that don't end *-ing*, e.g. *do gymnastics*

3b **Now decide if each sport in 1 goes with *play, go* or *do*.**

4 SPEAKING **Work with a partner. Ask and answer the questions.**

1 Which of the sports do you like doing? When do you do them?
2 Which of the sports do you like watching? When do you watch them?

Sports competitions

5 **Work with a partner. Read the sentences. Find the words in the box in the sentences and check that you understand the meaning. Use your dictionary if necessary.**

champion • competition • cup • final • match
medal • player • prize • race • referee • team
winner

1 In a football team, there are eleven players.
2 When you are an Olympic champion, they give you a gold medal.
3 The final is the last match in a competition.
4 In a race, it is important to go fast.
5 The winners of a final or a race usually get a cup or a medal.
6 In a competition, different people or teams all want to win a prize, maybe a cup or a medal.
7 In football matches, the referee is the person who decides what is right or wrong.

6 **65 Listen and repeat the words.**

7a SPEAKING **Work with a partner. Talk about the photo. How many of the words in 5 can you use?**

7b LISTENING **66 Listen to two people talking about the same photo. Tick (✓) the words in 5 that they use.**

1 **Work with a partner. What can you see in the pictures? What do you think is the connection between each picture and football?**

2 READING **Read the texts. What exactly do the three photos below show? Were your ideas in 1 correct?**

1

2

3

THE MUSEUM OF FOOTBALL

1 Henry VIII (1491–1547) was the famous British king with six wives. We know that Henry was mad about sport. He was particularly good at horse-riding and at tennis. But he was a football player, too! In King Henry VIII's papers there was an order for a pair of football boots. This is unusual because in King Henry VIII's time football wasn't a sport for gentlemen. Traditionally, there was only one football match a year. It was usually violent and dangerous. Henry was very competitive. Because he was the king, he was probably always the winner!

2 The British school Eton was important in the invention of modern football. A game called the Field Game was popular there. It was quite similar to modern football. Eton was the first place in the world to write down football rules. The rules are not the same now, but they were important in the creation of today's football. For example, before the Eton rules of 1845 there weren't any referees. So school football was really the origin of modern, professional football.

3 During the First World War, in December 1914 the British and German armies were very near to each other in Ypres, Belgium. The fighting was terrible and there were many dead soldiers. But at Christmas, something incredible happened. Between the British and German soldiers, there was a space called No-man's Land. One of the soldiers had a ball. Suddenly there wasn't any fighting. There was a football match! For a while all the soldiers were friends. But the British and German generals weren't happy. Soon, there were orders from the generals to stop playing football and start fighting again.

3 **Read the text again. Are these sentences True (T) or False (F) or is the information Not Mentioned (NM)?**

1 In King Henry VIII's time football matches were very common. T/F/NM
2 King Henry VIII's boots were very beautiful. T/F/NM
3 King Henry VIII was interested in doing different sports, but winning wasn't important to him. T/F/NM
4 The rules of modern football are exactly the same as the rules of the Eton Field Game. T/F/NM
5 There were referees at Eton in 1845. T/F/NM
6 Thanks to football, the British and German soldiers were friends for a short time at Christmas in 1914. T/F/NM
7 The British soldiers were the winners of the football match. T/F/NM
8 The football match between the British and German Armies was the idea of the generals. T/F/NM

4 **CRITICAL THINKING**

Think! Then compare ideas with your class.

- What do you think about football today? What do you think are the good and bad effects it has on people?

5 **What do the underlined words in the text mean? Guess and then check in your dictionary.**

6 SPEAKING **What about *you*?**

1 Which is your favourite sport and why?
2 What do you know about that sport in history?

Past simple of *to be*

1 Look at the sentences and choose the correct alternative in 1–4.

a They **were** very strong.
b Football **wasn't** a sport for gentlemen.
c The generals **weren't** happy.
d Henry VIII **was** the king with six wives.
e **Was** Henry VIII a football player?
f Yes, he **was**.

1 We use **was** with I and *he, she, it/they*.
2 We use **were** with you, we and *he, she, it/they*.
3 The negative forms of **was not** and **were not** are *isn't, aren't/wasn't, weren't*.
4 To make questions we put **was** or **were** *after/before* the subject.

GRAMMAR REFERENCE ➤ PAGE 98

2a Look at the ticks (✓) and crosses (✗). Write complete sentences with *was, were, wasn't, weren't*.

1 I/interested in dinosaurs at primary school. ✗
2 Yesterday I/at school. ✓
3 My friend/with me yesterday afternoon. ✗
4 Last weekend I/really happy. ✓
5 My last English exam/difficult. ✓
6 My parents/at home yesterday evening. ✗
7 My friends and I/late for school this morning. ✓

2b SPEAKING Work with a partner. Use the prompts to talk about you. Give true answers.

I wasn't interested in dinosaurs at primary school.

I was!

3a Complete the sentences with *was* or *were*.

1 In 2012, the winner of the 100 metres Olympic gold medal .... Usain Bolt.
2 The first modern Olympic Games .... in 1896.
3 They .... in London.
4 Golf .... originally a Scottish sport.
5 The Formula 1 champion Ayrton Senna .... Brazilian.
6 Rugby .... originally a sport played at a British school called Rugby School.
7 The first football World Cup finals .... in Uruguay.

3b Work with a partner. All of the sentences in 3a are true, except one. Decide which one you think is false.

3c ▶ 67 Listen. Which one is false?

4a Complete the questions with *was* or *were*.

1 .... you good at English when you .... five years old?
2 Who .... your best friend at primary school?
3 What .... you interested in at the age of seven?
4 Where .... you last Saturday afternoon?
5 .... yesterday a good day for you?
6 When and what .... your last exam?
7 What .... your favourite film, album or book last year?

4b SPEAKING Work with a partner. Ask and answer the questions. Give true answers.

There was/There were

5 Look at the sentences and answer the questions.

a There was only one football match a year.
b There wasn't any fighting.
c There were orders from the generals.
d Before 1845, there weren't any referees.

1 Which forms in a–d are affirmative?
2 Which forms are negative?
3 Which forms are singular?
4 Which forms are plural?

GRAMMAR REFERENCE ➤ PAGE 98

6 Read the notes and complete the sentences with *there was, there wasn't, there were* or *there weren't*.

First NYC Marathon (1970) – 127 people running

2012 – no NYC marathon because of Superstorm Sandy

2013 NYC Marathon – over 50,000 runners

2013 – winner of men's race – Geoffrey Mutai (Kenya), winner of women's race Priscah Jeptoo (Kenya)

1 .... a marathon in New York City in 1970.
2 In 1970 .... 50,000 people running in the NYC marathon.
3 .... 127 runners in 1970.
4 .... a marathon in New York City in 2012.
5 .... a marathon in New York City in 2013.
6 .... over 50,000 runners in 2013.
7 In 2013 .... two winners from Kenya.
8 .... a British winner in the 2013 NYC marathon.

Sports people

1 Work with a partner. Match the photos with some of these words.

climber • cyclist • (Formula 1) driver • gymnast
(football/ice hockey/tennis) player
(horse/motorbike) rider • runner • skater • skier
swimmer

1

2

3

4

2 The words in 1 are for people. All of them except one come from verbs. Write the verbs. Which word does not come from a verb?

climb, cycle ...

3 Play a game. One student draws one of the words in 1. The rest of the class says what the word is.

4a SPEAKING **Work with a partner. Look at the people. What types of sports person are/were they?**

1

2

3

4

4b Can you name other famous sports people?

Evgeni Malkin is a famous ice hockey player.

Ayrton Senna was a great racing car driver.

Working in a TEAM

LIFE SKILLS OBJECTIVES

- To think about when and why we work in teams.
- To learn how to work well in a team.
- To work together on a team task and think about the experience.

KEY CONCEPTS

role [n]: *Everybody has an important role in a team.* **interrupt [v]:** *Please don't interrupt me when I'm talking.* **pay attention [phr]:** *Pay attention to what she's saying!* **make a contribution [phr]:** *She makes an important contribution with her ideas.*

1 Work individually. Think about your answers to these questions. Make notes if necessary.

1. How often do you do work in teams or groups at school?
2. What activities do you do in teams or groups at school?
3. What teams or groups are you a member of outside school?
4. Why are teams important and useful?

2 Work in groups of three.

Student A: Tell Student B your answers to the questions in 1. Talk for as long as you can.
Student B: Listen to your partner.
Student C: Turn to page 154.

3 READING **Read Mike's advice about working in a team and answer the questions.**

1. What does a good team player do?
2. What different things stop us from being a good team player?
3. How carefully did you listen in 2?
4. Do you think the advice is good? Why/Why not?

A good team player listens carefully to what other team members say. Sometimes when people talk to us we don't really listen. Maybe we don't pay attention because we are thinking of other things. Maybe we interrupt the other person again and again. Maybe we listen, but we only hear what we want to hear. We don't really try to understand the other person's opinion.
To work well in a team, you need to be a good listener. Listen first and speak second. Only interrupt if you want to check that you understand. And show that you are interested.

A good team player is reliable. Sometimes I am busy or tired. Then I don't want to go to training or a match. But to work well in a team, we all need to be responsible and work together. You have to help your team mates even if you are tired.
Also, it's important to arrive on time. I always try to tell someone when I am late for training. Then my team can start without me and not waste time!

A good team player is active and participates constructively in the team. Sometimes in a team we sit on the side and let other people do the work. Or we participate, but in a negative way. For example, some people just make negative comments about other people's ideas. Or they talk about other things. Or they are never serious.
To work well in a team, we need to contribute ideas. We need to be positive about other people's ideas and show respect to other team members. And it's important to think of solutions, not just problems.

4 **Now read Mike, Katie and Shona's advice about working in a team. Complete the sentences with one to three words in each space.**

1 In a team, it's bad to let other people ....

2 It's important to arrive ....

3 Don't make .... comments about other people's ideas.

4 We need to contribute ....

5 Tell someone if you are late – then your team won't .... time.

6 We need to show .... to other team members and think of ...., not problems.

5 **Work with a partner. Do you think the advice in 4 is good? Why/Why not?**

6 LISTENING 68 **Watch or listen. Match the speakers and what they think they bring to a team.**

Speaker 1 ....
Speaker 2 ....
Speaker 3 ....
Speaker 4 ....
Speaker 5 ....

a good at creating a positive atmosphere
b good at organising the team
c good at art and design
d good with computers and preparing presentations
e good at explaining things clearly

7 SPEAKING **Work with a partner. What do you think you bring to a team?**

LIFE TASK

Take part in a team task. Follow this plan:

1 Work in a team. Your task is to think of a vocabulary game or activity (a mime game, a crossword, a word search ...) to practise the sports vocabulary in this unit. Then you need to present the activity to the class and ask them to do it.

2 When you finish the task, give yourself a mark from 5 (yes, definitely) to 0 (not at all).

1 Our team worked well together.
2 I was a good listener.
3 I gave ideas to the team.
4 I brought something else to the team. (Say what.)
5 I was positive about other people's ideas.
6 I helped the group to take decisions.
7 I participated actively.

3 Work with your team. Discuss your answers in 2. Do you agree? Give your group a mark from 5 (we worked really well together) to 0 (we worked really badly together).

Listening

1 LISTENING 69 **Listen to Poppy talking about what sports and sports activities she did last week. When did she do the different sports? For questions 1–5, write a letter (a–g) next to each sport or activity. You will hear the conversation twice.**

1 basketball – match
2 basketball – training
3 judo
4 swimming
5 volleyball

a Monday
b Tuesday
c Wednesday
d Thursday
e Friday
f Saturday
g Sunday

✓ EXAM SUCCESS

Why is it important not to panic if you don't hear an answer the first time you listen?

➤ EXAM SUCCESS page 152

2 69 **Can you remember? Are these sentences about Poppy True (T) or False (F)? Listen again if necessary.**

1 This week, swimming at school wasn't on the normal day. T/F
2 Her basketball training is usually two hours. T/F
3 Poppy's volleyball team lost 3-0. T/F
4 Poppy is quite new to judo. T/F
5 Poppy never watches basketball on TV. T/F
6 Poppy's basketball team lost 56-60. T/F

3 SPEAKING **What about *you*?**

1 What sport do you do in a typical school week?
2 What new sport would you like to do?

Grammar in context

Past simple affirmative – regular verbs

1 **Look at the sentences and answer the questions.**

a They **changed** it this week.
b I **played** basketball.
c We **rested** on Thursday.
d I only **started** doing it four weeks ago.
e My friends and I **loved** it from the start.

1 What is the present form of the verbs in a–e?
2 How do we make the affirmative form of regular verbs in the past simple?

GRAMMAR REFERENCE ➤ PAGE 98

2a PRONUNCIATION 70 **Listen to the words in the three lists. Match each of these sounds to the correct list:**

a) /ɪd/ b) /d/ c) /t/

1	2	3
changed	liked	rested
played	worked	started
loved	watched	wanted
stayed	washed	decided
listened	stopped	needed

2b 70 **Listen to each list again and repeat the words.**

2c **Look at the list for the /ɪd/ sound. Which two letters come just before *-ed* in the words finishing with the /ɪd/ sound?**

3 **Complete the sentences with the past form of the verbs in the box. They are all regular.**

love • play • stay • walk • want • watch

1 Yesterday I .... to school.
2 Last night my friend and I .... a football match on TV.
3 The film was great. We .... it!
4 Bosnia and Herzegovina .... in the World Cup for the first time in 2014.
5 Last summer we .... in a beautiful hotel.
6 She .... to win the race but it was impossible.

Flipped classroom: watch the grammar presentation video.

Past simple affirmative – irregular verbs

4 Look at the sentences (a–j). They all contain irregular past forms. Match the past forms with the verbs (1–10).

a I **had** training.
b We **won** 3-0.
c We **went** to the pool.
d On Friday I **did** judo at school.
e On Saturday, my mum **bought** me a new pair of trainers.
f After that I **ate** with my mum.
g We **lost** 56-70.
h I **saw** a basketball match on TV.
i I **got up**.
j My mum **took** me to the shops.

1 buy
2 do
3 eat
4 get up
5 go
6 have
7 lose
8 see
9 take
10 win

GRAMMAR REFERENCE ➤ PAGE 98

5 Look at the pictures. They show what Oliver did last weekend. Write one sentence for each picture using some of the verbs in 4.

Saturday

1

His dad took him to the shops.

2

....

3

....

4

....

Sunday

5

....

6

....

7

....

8

....

6 Complete the text with the correct past form of the verbs in the box. Use each verb once. Some are regular and some irregular.

be • go • play • see • start
train • win • lose

Serena Williams (1) .... born in Michigan, in the US. She (2) .... to California at the age of four. She (3) .... playing tennis when she was very small. Her father (4) .... her great talent. She (5) .... every day to be a great player. She was 14 when she (6) .... her first professional match but sadly she (7) .... 2002 was a great year for Serena. She (8) .... the final at Wimbledon for the first time!

7a Write down two things that you did …

1 yesterday
Yesterday I did a history exam. I played football in the morning break.
2 last week
3 last year
4 when you were small

7b SPEAKING Work with a partner. Compare answers.

Yesterday I watched a TV programme about Egypt.

Me too!

7c Tell the class something interesting about your partner.

Asking for and giving opinions

1 SPEAKING **Work with a partner. What can you see in the photo?**

David Beckham

2 Match the questions and answers.

a What do you think about football players? Do you think they're good role models for young people?
b Do you like football?
c Excuse me. Can I ask you some questions?
d How do you feel about the salaries of top football players?

1 It's a lot of money. But I think when you're the top doctor or top artist you always make a lot of money. So I think it's normal.
2 I'm not mad about it, but I like watching it sometimes. I usually watch important matches like finals or matches between really good teams.
3 Yes, OK.
4 Well, it depends. Some are, but some aren't. Some are very young and they have a lot of money and they do stupid things. But, in my opinion, there are some who give a good example because they help others and do good things.

3 LISTENING 71 **Listen to the dialogue. Check your answers and put the conversation in order.**

Question:	Question: ....
Answer:	Answer: ....
Question:	Question: ....
Answer:	Answer: ....

4 Look at the Speaking bank and complete the expressions. Look at the dialogue again if necessary.

SPEAKING BANK

Useful expressions to ask for and give opinions

Asking for opinions

- Do you ....?
- What do you .... about ...?
- How do you .... about ...?

Giving opinions

- I think/don't think ...
- In my ....,
- Well, it ....
- I'm (not) .... about ...
- It's brilliant/great/OK/not bad/awful/terrible.
- I love/like/don't mind ...
- I don't like/hate/can't stand ...

5 SPEAKING **Work with a partner. Student A, ask the questions in 2 in order. Student B, give *your* opinion. Then change roles.**

PRACTICE MAKES PERFECT

6a Individually, think of three questions to find out people's opinions of something that you are interested in – a sport or other free-time activity (music, computer games, films, etc.)

Begin your questions:

1 Do you like ...?
2 What do you think about ...?
3 How do you feel about ...?

6b SPEAKING **Interview other students with your questions. Then answer their questions. Use the expressions in the Speaking bank to help you give your opinions.**

Developing writing

A story

1 **Work with a partner. Look at the title of the story and the pictures. Try to put the pictures in order. What do you think happens in this story?**

1

2

3

4

5

2 READING **Read the story and check your ideas in 1.**

A very special racket

Madelyn loved tennis, but she wasn't very good at it. Every Sunday she had a match, but she always lost. One Sunday she lost her racket and so she decided to buy a new one. They were all very expensive. Then she saw an old, second-hand racket. She picked it up and suddenly had a good feeling. She bought it.

In Madelyn's next match, she was fast and strong. She won the match easily. Then she won her next five matches! In the end, she won the final and became the Under-15 champion. After the match, an old woman came and asked to see her racket. 'I know this racket,' she said. 'It was mine. I was the world champion forty years ago!'

3 **Put the events in the story in order. Read the story again if necessary.**

1 .... 3 .... 5 ....
2 .... 4 .... 6 ....

a Madelyn won her first match.
b Madelyn bought a second-hand racket.
c Madelyn became the champion.
d Madelyn found out something interesting about her racket.
e Madelyn lost all her matches.
f Madelyn lost her racket.

4 **Look at the words and expressions in the Writing bank. Which appear in the story? Check that you understand all the words.**

WRITING BANK

Useful words in stories

- Words and expressions of time, e.g. *One day, Then, Next, Suddenly, After (the final), After that, In the end …*
- Basic linkers, e.g. *and, because, but, and so*

PRACTICE MAKES PERFECT

5a **Work with a partner. Think of ideas for a story where somebody buys a second-hand object, for example a pair of trainers, a pair of football boots, skis, skates, a bike … Make notes with your ideas for each part of the story.**

1 Start/Introduction of the character(s)
2 Middle/Main events
3 End

5b **Individually, use your notes to write your story. Include words from the Writing bank and the information in the Exam success box.**

WRITING BANK ➤ PAGE 157

✔ EXAM SUCCESS

Look at the story on this page. What tense are the verbs in? Do the verbs change suddenly between the present and the past?

➤ EXAM SUCCESS page 152

Grammar reference

Past simple of to be

FORM

Affirmative	I/He/She/It **was** at a tennis match yesterday. You/We/They **were** at a tennis match yesterday.
Negative	I/He/She/It **wasn't (was not)** at a football match yesterday. You/We/They **weren't (were not)** at a football match yesterday.
Question form	**Was** I/he/she/it at a race yesterday? **Were** you/we/they at a race yesterday?
Short answers	Yes, I/he/she/it **was**. No, I/he/she/it **wasn't**. Yes, you/we/they **were**. No, you/we/they **weren't**.

There was/There were

FORM

Affirmative singular Affirmative plural	**There was** a winner from Brazil last year. **There were** two British teams in the final.
Negative singular Negative plural	**There wasn't** a winner from Brazil last year. **There weren't** two British teams in the final.

Past simple – affirmative

FORM

Affirmative	I/You/He/She/It/We/They **walked** to school. I/You/He/She/It/We/They **went** by bus.

Spelling

- Spelling of regular past simple forms.
  Most verbs: add **-ed**.
  walk – walked, want – wanted, need – needed.
  Verbs that end in **-e**: add **-d**.
  decide – decided, phone – phoned, arrive – arrived.
  Verbs that end in a consonant + *y*: take away **-y** and add **-ied**.
  study – studied, cry – cried, try – tried.
  Verbs that end in one vowel + one consonant: double the consonant and add **-ed**.
  stop – stopped, chat – chatted
- Many common verbs are irregular. See the list of irregular verbs on page 158.

USE

- We use the past simple to describe finished actions or situations in the past.
  I watched a film last night.
- With the past simple we often use time expressions like *yesterday, last night/ week/month/year.*

Vocabulary

Sports baseball • basketball • cycling • football • golf • gymnastics • horse-riding • ice hockey • ice-skating judo • rugby • skiing • swimming • tennis • volleyball

Sports competitions champion • competition • cup • final • match • medal • player • prize • race • referee team • winner

Sports people climber • cyclist • (Formula 1) driver • gymnast • (football/ice hockey/tennis) player (horse/motorbike) rider • runner • skater • skier • swimmer

Other words and phrases ➤ page 147

Grammar revision

Past of to be / 7 points

1 Complete the dialogue with *was, were, wasn't* or *weren't*.

Jon: (1) .... Steffi Graf and Martina Hingis famous gymnasts?

Sophie: No, they (2) .... They (3) .... famous tennis players.

Jon: Where (4) .... Steffi Graff from?

Sophie: She (5) .... German. But Martina Hingis (6) .... from Germany, she (7) .... from Switzerland.

There was/There were / 4 points

2 Look at the answers to this exercise. Are they correct? If not, write them correctly.

1 There/a good film on TV last night.
There is a good film on TV last night.

2 There/not/ten people in the team last year.
There wasn't ten people in the team last year.

3 There/not/a prize for the winner last Saturday.
There wasn't a prize for the winner last Saturday.

4 There/a problem at school last week.
There were a problem at school last week.

Past simple – affirmative / 9 points

3 Change these sentences from present simple to past simple.

1 I get up at 7.30 am.
2 She does sport every day.
3 They go to our school.
4 We run in the morning.
5 He walks to school.
6 They've got training on Friday.
7 You buy magazines.
8 We see her at the weekend.
9 I want orange juice.

Vocabulary revision

SPORTS / 7 points

1 Look at the objects and name the sports.

1  ....

2  ....

3  .... - ....

4  ....

5 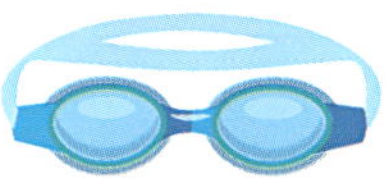 ....

6 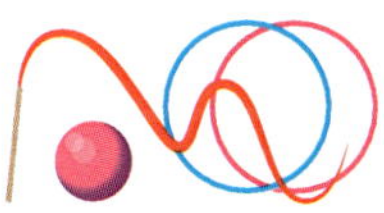 ....

7  ....

SPORTS COMPETITIONS / 6 points

2 Complete the sentences with the correct words.

1 The r .... is in control of a football match.
2 In a r ...., you need to go very quickly.
3 Real Madrid and Barcelona are two famous football t ....
4 The last match in a competition is the f ....
5 Sebastian Vettel was the Formula 1 c .... from 2010 to 2013.
6 The p .... in this competition is a cup.

SPORTS PEOPLE / 7 points

3 Write the correct word for the person who does each sport in 1.

1 *tennis player*
2 ....
3 ....
4 ....
5 ....
6 ....
7 ....

8 Great job!

Vocabulary

Jobs

1 Work with a partner. Match the photos with these words.

builder • bus driver • businessman/woman • chef
engineer • hairdresser • mechanic • nurse • shop assistant
waiter/waitress

1

2

3

4

5

6

7

8

9

10

2 72 Listen, check and repeat.

3 SPEAKING Work with a partner. Ask and answer the questions.

1 Which of the jobs in 1 would you like? Why?
2 Which of the jobs wouldn't you like? Why not?

I think I'd like to be a chef.

Personal qualities

4 Match the words in the box with the examples.

calm • cheerful • clever • creative
friendly • hard-working • kind
responsible

1 We study for hours and hours every day.
2 She can understand very difficult ideas very easily.
3 Andrea likes talking to people.
4 Dan always helps other people and gives them what he can.
5 Jon is a happy, positive person.
6 My brother has lots of good ideas and is good at art and music.
7 When you ask Helen to do something, you can relax because you know that she always does it.
8 Kay is always quiet and relaxed, even in very difficult situations.

5 LISTENING 73 Listen to somebody asking about a job. What job is it? Which three personal qualities in 4 are necessary for the job?

Job: ....

Personal qualities: (1) ....

(2) .... (3) ....

6 SPEAKING Work in a small group. Talk about the different jobs in 1 and what personal qualities you think are necessary for them.

What about businessmen and women?

I think you need to be responsible.

1 Work with a partner. Look back at exercise 6 on page 100. In your opinion, what were the important personal qualities of a chef or a nurse?

2 READING Read the text. What personal qualities do they mention for a chef and a nurse? Are they similar to your ideas?

HOME ABOUT LEARNING PARENTS SUPPORT CONTACT US SEARCH

VALLEY HIGH GOES JOB SHADOWING!

In June some of our students had the opportunity to do a job shadow, working next to an adult professional for a day. Two students tell us about their experiences.

Jade Smith, Year 9

I love cooking in my free time so I went to a restaurant for my job shadow. I worked with the head chef, Mr Perry. Before the job shadow, I didn't really know what a chef did. For example, Mr Perry didn't only prepare food. He also wrote a new menu, spoke to the restaurant director, explained the new menu to the waiters, and lots of other things. He didn't have time to sit down all day! I saw that professional chefs need to be creative. But they also need to work fast and stay calm when the restaurant is busy. It was a great experience. Now I know that I want to do this when I leave school.

Mandy Swan, Year 9

I always wanted to be a doctor, so I decided to do the job shadow at a hospital. They didn't let me watch a doctor, but I was with a nurse for the day. She was brilliant. There were some really difficult moments, but the nurses didn't stop for a second. They were all very kind and cheerful. I didn't find it easy. Doctors and nurses need to be calm and strong, emotionally and physically. Now I think it isn't the right job for me. So, in the end, the job shadow really helped me.

3 Read the text again. Is this information about Jade (J), Mandy (M) or both (B)?

1 They saw people being happy and positive. J/M/B
2 They saw the importance of having new ideas and making new things. J/M/B
3 In the future, they want to do the job in their job shadow. J/M/B
4 They think that their job shadow was useful. J/M/B
5 The job shadow was interesting because they learned new things about the job. J/M/B
6 They saw that it's important to continue working in difficult situations. J/M/B
7 They decided on their job shadow because of a hobby. J/M/B

✓ EXAM SUCCESS

In this type of exercise, is it always important to check for the answer in both texts? Why/Why not?

➤ EXAM SUCCESS page 153

4 **CRITICAL THINKING**

Think! Then compare ideas with your class.

- Do you think it is a good idea to do a job shadow? Why/Why not?

5 What do the underlined words in the text mean? Guess and then check in your dictionary.

6 SPEAKING What about *you*?

1 Would you like to be a chef, doctor or nurse? Why/Why not?
2 Imagine you can do a job shadow. Who would you like to work with for a day?

Grammar in context

Past simple – negative

1 Look at the sentences. Are statements 1–3 True (T) or False (F)?

a I **didn't know** what a chef did.
b I **went** to a restaurant for my job shadow.
c He **didn't have** time to sit down all day.
d The nurses **didn't stop** for a second.
e The job shadow really **helped** me.

1 Sentences a, c and e are negative. T/F
2 We use **didn't** to make the past negative. T/F
3 After **didn't** we need the infinitive of the verb without *to*. T/F

GRAMMAR REFERENCE ➤ PAGE 110

2 Make the sentences negative.

1 Shakespeare wrote comics.
Shakespeare didn't write comics.

2 Beethoven played the electric guitar.

3 Queen Elizabeth I ate burgers.

4 Cleopatra wore jeans.

5 The Ancient Romans had cars.

6 Leonardo Da Vinci used a computer.

3a Look at this picture of a factory in 1900. Find eight mistakes in the picture.

3b Write sentences about each mistake using the past simple negative.

drink • have • listen to • ~~travel~~ • use • watch • wear (x2)

In 1900 they didn't travel by plane.

4a Write true sentences using the past affirmative or negative form of the verbs given.

1 I .... (win) a prize last year.
2 We .... (have) an English lesson last Monday.
3 My family .... (eat) in a restaurant last weekend.
4 I .... (buy) a present for my teacher last Saturday.
5 I .... (wear) jeans at the weekend.
6 My parents .... (get up) before 7 am this morning.
7 The US president .... (come) to my house last night.
8 I .... (see) a good film last week.

4b SPEAKING Work with a partner. Read out your true sentences in 4a. How many of your sentences are the same?

5 **Complete the text with the past simple of the verbs given.**

Success **(1)** .... (not come) easily for Brad Pitt. He **(2)** .... (study) at university but he **(3)** .... (not finish) his course. He **(4)** .... (go) to Los Angeles to study acting. He **(5)** .... (not have) much money. They **(6)** .... (not give) him very good acting jobs at first. So he **(7)** .... (work) as a driver and for a Mexican restaurant, dressing up as a chicken! That **(8)** .... (not stop) him. Now he's a world-famous actor and an important businessman.

6a **Write five true affirmative sentences about things you did yesterday.**

1 I played basketball.
2 I went to my friend's house.

6b **Now write true negative sentences for each sentence in 6a.**

1 I didn't play ice hockey.
2 I didn't go to my grandparents' house.

6c SPEAKING **Work with a partner. Read your negative sentences only. Can they guess the original affirmative sentence?**

I didn't play ice hockey.

I think you played football.

No. I played basketball.

Adjectives to describe jobs

1 **Work with a partner. Look at the words in the box. Match each word with its opposite. Use a dictionary if necessary.**

badly-paid • full-time • indoor • outdoor • part-time skilled • unskilled • well-paid

2 74 **Listen and repeat.**

3 **Use the words in 1 to complete the sentences.**

1 Jan has a .... job. He works for half the day.
2 Pete's job is .... so his parents give him extra money each month.
3 Jenna works about seven or eight hours a day, five days a week. It's a .... job.
4 Rick has an .... job. He's a builder.
5 Alex has a .... job. He studied for four years to do it.
6 I sit in an office all day. It isn't very healthy. Sometimes I think I'd like an .... job.

4 SPEAKING **Work with a partner. Look at the photos. Which words can you use for each of the jobs in the photos?**

A

B

C

I think the job in A is badly-paid.

Getting *work experience*

LIFE SKILLS OBJECTIVES

- To learn about work experience.
- To read advice about applying for work experience.
- To consider your own interests and personal qualities for a job.

KEY CONCEPTS

apply for [v], application [n]: *When you want a job, you need to apply for it, to tell them you want the job.* **company [n]:** *Apple and Microsoft are very big, international companies.*
experience [n]: *This is my first day at work. I have no other experience.*
attitude [n]: *She likes her job. She has a positive attitude to it.*
personal qualities [n pl]: *Being a good listener is one of the personal qualities needed to be a doctor.*

1a READING **Read the text 'Work experience in the UK' and answer the questions.**

1 What is the minimum age for work experience in the UK?
2 Why do people do work experience?
3 Where can you do work experience?
4 How can work experience help you?

1b Work with a partner. What is your opinion of work experience? Would you like to do it? Why/Why not?

2 Look at the advice from a work experience website below. Match the titles and sections.

A Know yourself B Have you got the right attitude? C Be honest D Don't panic! E Why this job?

| Work Experience > Help with your work experience application Search SIGN IN

Work experience in the UK

Students in the UK have got the opportunity of doing 'Work experience' from the age of 14. For two weeks they don't go to school, they go to work. The idea is to discover the real world of work. Students can apply for work in banks, supermarkets, hospitals, restaurants, hotels ... anywhere! Work experience can help you to see if you like a job, and if you are good at it. You can also get experience of writing an application or a CV, and experience of interviews too.

Help with your work experience application

This is probably your first application for work. It's important to spend time preparing it because it can help you to get the job you want. Here are some things to think about when you're preparing an application or getting ready for an interview.

1 ☐ Are you ready to work hard? In the world of work, you need to be ready to do everything you can to help your company or organisation. And you need to show this in your application.

2 ☐ Nobody is perfect, but everyone has got different skills and abilities. What are yours? Think about your skills before you write your application or go for an interview. Which of your personal qualities and interests make you ideal for the job?

3 ☐ Applying for work isn't easy. But remember that the people who are interviewing you want you to do well. Try to relax. Tell them what you can do and what you can bring.

4 ☐ Are you applying for a job in a supermarket or a bank? Which one? How did you decide? You need to tell the company or organisation that you really want to work for them, and not for somebody else. Give them good reasons why you are interested in them.

5 ☐ Don't say that you're good at something if you aren't. Don't say you're interested in something if it isn't true. In the end, it doesn't help. Just be yourself.

3 Read the text again. Which section of the text (1–5) gives this advice? One piece of advice does not appear in any section. Which one?

1 Show them what you are good at.
2 Tell the truth.
3 Stay calm.
4 Be good at everything.
5 Show them that you want to work a lot.
6 Show them that you think they are special.

4 In the text it says you need to show that you are really interested in the company or job that you are applying for. How interested are you in these types of work? Give each one a mark out of 5 (0 = not interested, 5 = extremely interested).

1 Administrative work (e.g. businessman/woman) ......
2 Caring work (e.g. teacher, doctor) ......
3 Construction work (e.g. builder, painter) ......
4 Creative work (e.g. artist, writer) ......
5 Service work (e.g. shop assistant, waiter) ......
6 Technical and scientific work (e.g. engineer, mechanic) ......

5 LISTENING ▶ 75 Four teenagers are talking about work experience they are applying for. Watch or listen. Match each speaker with one of the jobs.

Speaker 1 (Liam) ......
Speaker 2 (Amber) ......
Speaker 3 (Max) ......
Speaker 4 (Phoebe) ......

a mechanic/engineer
b teacher
c ICT worker
d doctor

6 ▶ 75 Look at the interests and personal qualities. Match each one to a speaker. Watch/Listen again if necessary.

1 I love computers. ......
2 I like helping people. (Two speakers) ....
3 I like science. ......
4 I enjoy doing creative things. ......
5 I'm good at maths. ......
6 I enjoy working in a team. ......
7 I love cars. ......
8 I'm good at listening to people. ......

7 SPEAKING Work with a partner. Talk about which of the sentences in 6 are true for you.

LIFE TASK

Follow this plan:

1 *Make a list of your personal qualities. Look at the words on page 100 for ideas.*
2 *Make a list of your interests. They can be hobbies or things that you like at school.*
3 *Imagine that you can do two weeks of work experience. Choose a job from the list below. Use your lists to help you decide.*
4 *Write a personal statement saying why you are applying for this job. Include the personal qualities and interests in your list that you think are relevant. Follow the other advice in the text on page 104.*

Job list

actor/actress, artist, businessman/woman, chef, doctor, engineer, hairdresser, ICT worker, mechanic, musician, shop assistant, sportsperson, teacher, waiter/waitress

Listing

1 Work with a partner. Look at these things. They each have a connection with the billionaire businessman Sir Richard Branson. What do you think the connection is?

records

trains

space travel

mobile phones

planes

magazines

2 Look at the sentences about Sir Richard Branson. Check your ideas in 1. What order do you think they happened in? Guess.

A He created a mobile company.
B He opened a record shop.
C He started a company to fly people into space.
D He started a record company.
E He began his own airline, flying to the US and other places.
F He started a magazine for students.
G He bought a train company.

3 LISTENING ▶ 76 **Listen. Put the events in 2 in the correct order.**

1 .... 3 .... 5 .... 7 ....
2 .... 4 .... 6 ....

4 ▶ 76 **Choose the correct alternative. Listen again if necessary.**

1 Sir Richard Branson _was/wasn't_ a successful student at school.
2 _Students/University professors_ wrote the magazine *Student*.
3 He began his _record company/record shop_ in 1972.
4 *Virgin Airlines* is about _20/30_ years old.
5 Branson began his mobile company in _1997/1999_.
6 Sir Richard Branson would probably _like/not like_ to go into space.
7 *Virgin Galactic* is a company for _professional astronauts/normal people_.
8 Tickets to travel in space cost _$25,000/$250,000_.

5 SPEAKING **What about *you*?**

1 Do you know any other famous business-people? How did they become famous?
2 Would you like to start your own business? What type of business?
3 Would you like to fly into space? Why/Why not?

Grammar in context

Past simple – questions and short answers

1 Look at the sentences and answer the questions (1–3).

a What type of business **did** he **start**?
b How much **do** the tickets **cost**?
c Why **did** he **create** that company?
d **Did** he **continue** with the magazine?
e Yes, he **did**./No, he **didn't**.

1 Which question is in the present simple?
2 What do we do to change a question from the present simple to the past simple?
3 Do we repeat the main verb (e.g. start, cost, continue) in short answers?

GRAMMAR REFERENCE ➤ PAGE 110

2a Complete the questions with the correct form of the verbs given.

FAMOUS PEOPLE QUIZ

1 Which famous company .... Bill Gates .... (create)?

2 What job .... Ronald Reagan .... (do) before he became President of the US?

3 How .... Matt Groening .... (become) a millionaire?

4 Which famous shoes .... Bill Bowerman .... (invent)?

5 What sport .... Michael Jordan .... (play)?

6 Which clothes .... Levi-Strauss .... (make) for the first time in the 19th Century?

2b Work with a partner. Write down your answers to the questions.

2c LISTENING ▶ 77 **Listen. How many correct answers have you and your partner got?**

3 Choose the correct alternative in the dialogue.

Jo: There's a funny story here about some train drivers in Stockholm, Sweden.

Ryan: Why? What (1) *did/do* they do?

Jo: The men wore skirts to work.

Ryan: (2) *When/Why* did they do that?

Jo: Because the train company didn't let them wear short trousers.

Ryan: When did this (3) *happen/happened*?

Jo: In June. It was 35°C in the trains. The drivers weren't happy wearing long trousers.

Ryan: (4) *Did/What* the train company let them wear skirts?

Jo: Yes, they (5) *did/let*. The company rules didn't say anything about skirts.

Ryan: (6) *Did/Do* they wear skirts for a long time?

Jo: No, they (7) *did/didn't*. The company changed their mind and let them wear shorts!

4 Write questions for the underlined part of the answer.

1 James Dashner wrote The Maze Runner.
What did James Dashner write?
2 Claude Monet painted his garden.
3 Jennifer Lawrence won an Oscar in 2013.
4 Apple made their first watch in 2015.
5 Gustave Eiffel designed the Eiffel Tower.
6 Mark Zuckerberg created Facebook.
7 Jimi Hendrix played the guitar.

5a Put the words in order to make questions.

1 What you watch did night on TV last?
2 did Why study last you night?
3 weekend What last you did do?
4 you did school finish primary When?
5 you eat last What night did?
6 your best How you did friend meet?
7 What night last time go you did to bed?

5b Match the answers to the questions in 5a.

a I went to the cinema. ....
b At half past ten. ....
c I had chicken. ....
d Because I've got an exam today. ....
e When I was eleven. ....
f I met her at a summer school. ....
g We watched a reality show. ....

5c SPEAKING Work with a partner. Ask and answer the questions in 5a. Give true answers.

How did you meet your best friend?

We met at primary school.

6a Write complete questions.

1 you/go to school yesterday?
Did you go to school yesterday?
2 you/pass your last English exam?
3 your parents/go shopping last weekend?
4 you/have a pet when you were seven?
5 you/have a big breakfast this morning?
6 your teachers/give you a lot of homework yesterday?
7 your class/go on an excursion last year?

6b Now write true short answers.

Personal questions – 2

1 Look at these questions. They are typical questions in an oral exam. Think about your answers.

1 Where do you study?

....

2 What are your favourite subjects?

....

3 What do you do in your free time?

....

4 What did you do last weekend?

....

5 Tell me about your plans for the future.

....

2 LISTENING 78 **Listen to a boy answering the questions. Do you think he answers them well? Why/Why not?**

....

....

....

3 LISTENING 79 **Listen to a girl answering the same questions. Do you think she answers them well? Why/Why not? What do you notice about her answer to the last question?**

....

....

....

✓ EXAM SUCCESS

Does the second student answer questions 1 to 4 with very short answers? And is her answer to question 5 short or long? What do you think is an important thing to remember in any speaking exam?

➤ EXAM SUCCESS page 153

4 79 **When we speak, we often use words or sounds that give us time to think without stopping the conversation. Listen to the second student again. Tick (✓) the words or expressions in the Speaking bank which she uses.**

SPEAKING BANK

Useful words and expressions to give us thinking time

- Err …
- Well …
- That's a good question.
- The thing is …
- I'm not (really/totally/completely) sure.
- Let me see …
- You know …
- I think …
- I imagine …

5 SPEAKING **Work with a partner. Take it in turns to ask and answer the questions in 1. Remember to answer the 'Tell me about …' question with an extended response.**

PRACTICE MAKES PERFECT

6a Individually, write down three personal questions and one 'Tell me about …' question to ask your partner.
You can ask about:

- School – subjects they like/dislike, homework, exams …
- Free time – hobbies, sport, holidays …
- The past – yesterday, last weekend, their last holiday …
- Family and friends

....

....

....

....

6b SPEAKING **Ask your partner your questions. Then answer their questions. Use the expressions in the Speaking bank to give you time to think.**

An informal email: giving news

1 READING **Read the two emails. Who is in the photo – Natalie or Grace?**

A

Hi Grace,

How are you? I hope you're well.

I've got some great news! My brother Jake found a job last week! You know he decided to have time off before he goes to university. So he wanted to get a part-time job to get some work experience. On Wednesday that new sports shop in the shopping centre gave him an interview and he got the job! He starts on Monday.

Apart from that, last week was quite good. I had a biology exam on Monday and I think I did well. On Wednesday I had a volleyball match and we won. We're second in the league now.

How about you? How was your week? Write back soon and let me know.

Love

Natalie

B

Hi Natalie,

Good to hear from you. That's great news about Jake! That job is perfect for him – he loves sport. Say hi to him from me and give him my congratulations.

I was really busy last week. Did I tell you that it was my dad's birthday? He took us for a great meal on Friday night.

Do you remember Chloe from the sports club? I met her at the restaurant. She has a part-time job there as a waitress. Anyway, we decided to meet up again next weekend. Do you want to come, too?

That's all for now. Write back soon.

Best wishes

Grace

2 Read the emails again. Who …

1 had a birthday last week? ....
2 found a job? ....
3 did well in an exam? ....
4 met an old friend? ....
5 is already working part-time? ....
6 played sport? ....
7 had an interview last week? ....

3 Look at the expressions in the Writing bank. Who uses each one – Grace (G) or Natalie (N)? Check that you understand what each expression means.

WRITING BANK

Useful expressions in 'news' emails

- How are you? G/N
- I hope you're well. G/N
- Good/Great to hear from you. G/N
- I've got some great news! G/N
- That's great news about … G/N
- Did I tell you that/about …? G/N
- How/What about you/your (week/weekend)? G/N
- How was your (week/weekend)? G/N
- Say hi to … from me. G/N
- Give (him/her) my (love/congratulations). G/N
- That's all for now. G/N

4 Make notes with good news and good things that happened to you, your family or friend(s) last week. Invent the information if necessary. Look at the ideas.

- Somebody found a job.
- Somebody found something.
- Somebody won something.
- You met somebody special.
- Somebody celebrated something.
- Somebody went to a special place.

PRACTICE MAKES PERFECT

5a Use your notes in 4 to write an email to a friend giving your news. Use Natalie's email as a model and include expressions from the Writing bank.

WRITING BANK ➤ PAGE 156

5b Exchange emails with a partner. Write a reply to your partner's email. Use Grace's email as a model.

Grammar reference

Past simple – negative

FORM

Negative	I/You/He/She/It/We/They **didn't (did not)** + verb *I didn't work in a restaurant.* *He didn't like the job.* *They didn't go to work yesterday.*

- After ***did/didn't*** we use the infinitive form of the verb without *to*.

USE

- We use the past simple negative to talk about things that didn't happen in the past.

Past simple – questions and short answers

FORM

Question form	**Did** I/you/he/she/it/we/they + verb? *Did you work in a restaurant?* *Did he like the job?* *Did they go to work yesterday?*
Short answers	Yes, I/you/he/she/it/we/they **did**. No, I/you/he/she/it/we/they **didn't**. *Yes, I did.* *No, he didn't.* *Yes, they did.*

- After ***did/didn't*** and the subject we use the infinitive form of the verb without *to*.
- In short answers, we do not repeat the main verb.

USE

- We use past simple questions to ask about things that happened in the past.

Vocabulary

Jobs builder • bus driver • businessman/woman • chef • engineer • hairdresser • mechanic • nurse shop assistant • waiter/waitress

Personal qualities calm • cheerful • clever • creative • friendly • hard-working • kind • responsible

Adjectives to describe jobs badly-paid • full-time • indoor • outdoor • part-time • skilled • unskilled well-paid

Other words and phrases ➤ page 147

Grammar revision

Past simple – negative

/ 7 points

1 Look at the sentences. Are they correct? If not, write them correctly.

1 My mum doesn't work in an office when she was young.
2 My dad didn't went to work yesterday.
3 My grandfather didn't study when he was 17.
4 In 1900 people didn't have laptops.
5 She didn't likes her old job but she likes her new one.
6 Today people didn't usually work seven days a week.
7 My friend didnt know all the answers.

Past simple – question forms

/ 5 points

2 Write questions in the past simple.

1 Where/you/watch the film last night?
2 Who/they/go out with last weekend?
3 Why/your friend/study last Saturday?
4 What time/you/get up this morning?
5 When/your first class/start this morning?

Past simple – question forms and short answers

/ 8 points

3 Look at the information about what the people did yesterday. Use the prompts to write yes/no questions and short answers.

1 Lee/walk to school?
Q: ....
A: ....

2 Kate and Amy/work?
Q: ....
A: ....

3 Max and Luke/watch a film?
Q: ....
A: ....

4 Lily/go shopping?
Q: ....
A: ....

Vocabulary revision

JOBS

/ 7 points

1 Look at the objects and name the jobs.

1  ....
2 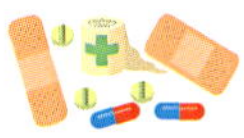 ....
3  ....
4  ....
5  ....
6  ....
7  ....

PERSONAL QUALITIES

/ 7 points

2 Write the adjectives.

This person …

1 helps other people and gives them things: k ....
2 is happy and positive: c ....
3 can understand new ideas very quickly: c ....
4 stays relaxed in difficult situations: c ....
5 has a lot of imagination and new ideas: c ....
6 studies or works a lot: h .... - ....
7 talks to other people easily and is good to them: f ....

ADJECTIVES TO DESCRIBE JOBS

/ 6 points

3 Match the correct halves of the words to make adjectives describing jobs. You can use the words in column B more than once.

Column A			Column B	
1) full-	3) out	5) un	door	skilled
2) in	4) part-	6) well-	paid	time

Total: / 40 points

✓ Gateway to exams: Units 7–8

Reading

1 **Work with a partner. In your opinion, what are the good and bad things about being a young sports star?**

2 READING **Read the text. Do they talk about any of your ideas in 1?**

3 **Read the text. Is the information about Dina Asher-Smith (DA), Rebecca Tunney (RT) or both (B)?**

> **➤ TIP FOR READING EXAMS**
>
> In activities where you match people and information, remember …
>
> Check for the answers in both/all the texts. The information may be about both/all the people.
>
> ➤ EXAM SUCCESS page 153

STARTING YOUNG

DINA ASHER-SMITH

Dina Asher-Smith was born in 1995. When she was young, she did well in lots of different sports, including hockey, dancing and running long distances. But, when she was just eight, her coach* saw that she was really good at running short distances. So now she runs in 200 metre races. In the Moscow World Championships, she won a bronze medal as part of the British 4 x 100 metre relay team. She was only 17 years and 247 days old, a record! She also met the world champion, Usain Bolt. But after she met sports stars like Bolt, she went back home to do the normal things a 17 year old does, like study maths and English and do her homework.

REBECCA TUNNEY

Rebecca Tunney is a British gymnast. When she was eleven, she moved from Manchester to Liverpool. She needed to be close to the gym where she trains. Now she can walk from her school to the gym in just ten minutes. She lives with her coach's family. At 15, Rebecca was already in the Olympic team. In the Olympic Games in London they finished 6th and she was 13th in the individual final. Of course, Rebecca works hard, in the gym and at school. At school, she does maths, English, biology … and PE of course. In PE, she does gymnastics. She doesn't have much time for friends or a social life, but she knows that to go to the Olympics, this is what she needs to do.

* *coach = person who helps you to train in your sport*

Adapted material taken from www.iaaf.org. Originally written by Emily Moss.

1 They study normal school subjects. DA/RT/B
2 They have an Olympic or World Championship medal. DA/RT/B
3 They competed in the London Olympics. DA/RT/B
4 They do their sport at school. DA/RT/B
5 They were good at a variety of sports when they were small. DA/RT/B
6 They compete individually and in teams. DA/RT/B
7 They live with their family. DA/RT/B
8 Their coach helped them to decide what sport to do. DA/RT/B

Listening

> **➤ TIP FOR LISTENING EXAMS**
>
> In listening exams, remember …
>
> Don't panic if you don't hear an answer the first time you listen. You usually hear the text more than once.
>
> ➤ EXAM SUCCESS page 152

4 LISTENING ▶ 80 **Yesterday was Alex's first day at work. He worked as an actor in a studio and filmed an advert. Listen and answer the questions.**

1 Who was in the advert with Alex?
2 What did Alex wear in the advert?
3 What did Alex learn about acting?

5 ▶ 80 **Listen again. What did Alex do at each time? For questions 1–5, write a letter (a–h) next to each time. Listen twice if necessary.**

1 10.30 am
2 2.30 pm
3 3 pm
4 3.30 pm
5 4.30 pm

a get dressed
b go for a walk
c go to the hairdresser
d have lunch
e make the advert
f sign autographs for fans
g meet the director
h wait

6 SPEAKING **What about *you*?**

1 Do you think acting is usually an exciting job or not? Why?
2 Would you like to be an actor/actress? Why/Why not?

Writing

➤ TIP FOR WRITING EXAMS

In writing exams where you write a story, remember …
Think carefully about the tense(s) that you use. Don't change from the past to the present if it is not necessary.

➤ EXAM SUCCESS page 152

7 SPEAKING **Work with a partner. Look at the pictures. What can you see?**

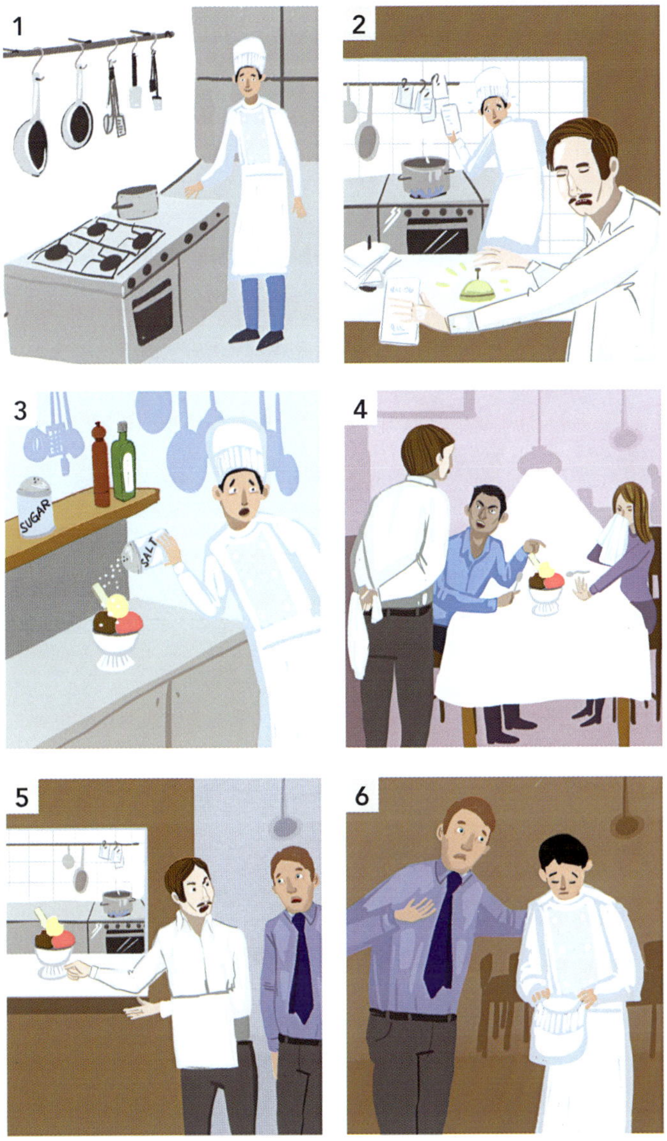

8a Look at the start of the story.

Last week Ryan started his first job. The job was as a chef at a very important restaurant. On the first day …

8b Continue the story. Use the past tense and some of the words from the boxes.

after that • in the end • next • then

and • because • but • so

8c When you finish, check your story. How many words from 8b did you use?

Speaking

➤ TIP FOR SPEAKING EXAMS

In speaking exams, remember …
The important thing in a speaking exam is to speak! Give extended responses. Don't just answer *yes* or *no*.

➤ EXAM SUCCESS page 153

9 Look at these questions. Think about your answers. Remember that you need to give an extended response to the questions 'Tell me about …'

1 Where are you from?
2 Tell me about your family.
3 Do you like sport? Why/Why not?
4 What music do you like?
5 Tell me about your plans for next weekend.

10 Work with a partner. Take it in turns to ask and answer the questions in 9.

'CAN DO' PROGRESS CHECK UNITS 7–8 — CEF

1 How well can you do these things in English now? Give yourself a mark from 1 to 4.

1 = I can do it very well.
2 = I can do it quite well.
3 = I have some problems.
4 = I can't do it.

a I can talk about the past using the past simple affirmative. ☐
b I can name different sports and sports people. ☐
c I can understand basic written and spoken texts about sports. ☐
d I can ask for and give my opinion on basic topics. ☐
e I can write a simple story. ☐
f I can ask questions about the past. ☐
g I can name different jobs and the personal qualities needed for them. ☐
h I can understand simple written and spoken texts about jobs. ☐
i I can give longer, extended responses to personal questions. ☐
j I can write an email giving news. ☐

2 Now decide what you need to do next to improve.

1 Look again at my book/notes.
2 Do more practice exercises.
➤ WORKBOOK Unit 7–8
3 Ask for help.
4 Other: ....

9 Mother nature

Vocabulary

Animals and insects

1 **Work with a partner. For each letter of the alphabet, can you think of an animal or insect? If you can't think of a word, omit the letter and continue.**

A – ?, B – bear, C – cat …

2 **Match the words in the box to the photos.**

antelope • beetle • cheetah • frog • kangaroo
penguin • rhinoceros/rhino • whale

1

2

3

4

5

6

7

8

3 81 **Listen and repeat.**

Parts of the body

4 **Put the words in order to make parts of the face.**

1	are	4	umoth
2	yee	5	seon
3	hari	6	hetet

5 **Look at the photo. This animal is an aye-aye. Work with a partner. Talk about the aye-aye using the words in the box and in 4. Use a dictionary to help you if necessary.**

arm • finger • foot (pl. feet) • hand
head • horn • leg • neck • stomach
tail • toe • wing

It hasn't got wings.

But it's got big ears.

6 LISTENING 82 **Listen to the descriptions. Which three animals or insects in 2 do they describe?**

7a **Think of three animals or insects. Prepare a description of them using the parts of the body in 5.**

7b SPEAKING **Work in a small group. Describe your animals or insects. Can other people in the group identify them?**

1 **Work with a partner. Look at the pictures and the title of the text. What do you think the text is about?**

2 READING **You have two minutes to read the text and check your ideas in 1. Were you right?**

✓ EXAM SUCCESS

Why is it useful to give yourself a time limit the first time that you read a text?

➤ EXAM SUCCESS page 153

3 **Read the text again and choose the best answers.**

1 Cheetahs …
- a like going fast.
- b need to go fast.
- c are always fast.

2 Pronghorn antelopes are …
- a slow in comparison with humans.
- b fast in comparison with cheetahs.
- c able to run fast for a long time.

3 Cheetahs …
- a eat pronghorn antelopes.
- b and pronghorn antelopes run for different reasons.
- c and pronghorn antelopes live in the same region.

4 Rhinoceros beetles …
- a use their horns to escape danger.
- b can lift more kilos than African elephants.
- c are not very strong or powerful.

5 The Southern cricket frog can jump …
- a about 180 centimetres.
- b the same distance as kangaroos.
- c higher than humans.

4 **CRITICAL THINKING**

Think! Then compare ideas with your class.

- Do you think this text can help people to respect animals more? Why/Why not?

5 **What do the underlined words in the text mean? Guess and then check in your dictionary.**

6 SPEAKING **What about *you*?**

1 Which piece of information was most surprising?

2 Do you know any other surprising facts about animals or insects?

THE ANIMAL OLYMPICS

In the Olympic Games, athletes compete to see who is faster, stronger, better than the rest. Humans do this for sport. But in the natural world animals and insects do it to stay alive.

Usain Bolt once ran at 44.72 kph. But the cheetah is faster than any human. A cheetah can run at around 112 kph. In Africa, cheetahs run fast to catch food. But they can only run at this speed for 250 metres.

The 'pronghorn antelope', from North America, is slower than the cheetah. But it can run at 50 to 60 kph for about 6 km. Cheetahs run fast to catch animals like the pronghorn antelope. But pronghorn antelopes run fast to escape hunters like the cheetah!

African elephants are much stronger than humans. That's because they're bigger and heavier than us. They can lift 272 kilos!

Rhinoceros beetles are much smaller and lighter than elephants. But, with their large horns, they can lift 850 times their own body weight. That makes them much more powerful than the elephant, which can only lift a quarter of its weight. These beetles don't use their horns to attack. They use them to make holes, to escape danger.

Some whales can dive 1,600 metres under water and stay there for two hours. Emperor penguins can dive nearly 540 metres under water. Some kangaroos can jump a distance of nine metres. Southern cricket frogs are only 3 cm long but they can jump more than 60 times their body length. That's like us jumping up a building with 38 floors!

Flipped classroom: watch the grammar presentation video.

Comparative adjectives

1a Look at the sentences. The words in blue are comparative adjectives. Match each comparative adjective with a normal adjective (1–7).

a The cheetah is faster than any human.
b Rhinoceros beetles are smaller than elephants.
c African elephants are stronger than humans.
d They're bigger and heavier than us.
e They are more powerful than the elephant.
f We watch to see who is better than the rest.

1 big
2 fast
3 good
4 heavy
5 powerful
6 small
7 strong

1b What word comes after the comparative adjectives?

GRAMMAR REFERENCE ➤ PAGE 124

2a Look at the table. Put the adjectives and comparative adjectives from 1a in the correct section (1–5).

Adjective	Comparative adjective	Rule
(1) hard	harder	One-syllable adjectives – add *-er*.
(2) fat, thin	fatter, thinner	One-syllable adjectives ending in one vowel and one consonant – double the consonant and add *-er*.
(3) easy, silly	easier, sillier	Two-syllable adjectives ending in *-y* – omit *-y* and add *-ier*.
(4) beautiful, interesting	more beautiful, more interesting	Adjectives with two syllables or more – put *more* before the adjective.
(5) bad, far	worse, farther, further	Irregular

2b Where do these adjectives go in the table? What is the comparative form of each adjective?

1 creative *4 – more creative*
2 kind ....
3 friendly ....
4 dangerous ....
5 old ....
6 fit ....
7 quick ....
8 short ....

3 Each sentence contains a mistake. Write the sentences again correctly.

1 African elephants are more strong than humans.
2 Humans are more intelligent that other mammals.
3 Dogs are often friendlyer than cats.
4 Cheetahs are thiner than rhinos.
5 I think beetles are badder than frogs.
6 Rhinos are more bigger than antelopes.
7 I think animals are amazinger than humans.

4 Complete the text with the comparative form of the adjectives given.

When you think of danger in the water, you usually think of sharks and killer whales. Piranhas are (a) .... (small) than sharks, but sometimes they are (b) .... (dangerous), especially when they are in groups. Piranhas live in South American rivers. From April to September, the weather is (c) .... (dry) than in the rest of the year. Conditions for the piranhas are (d) .... (bad) than usual because there isn't much food in the rivers. So the fish are (e) .... (hungry) than usual … and (f) .... (aggressive). You need to be (g) .... (careful) than ever during this period. If you really need to go into a river in the dry season, it's (h) .... (good) to go in at night than in the day. Piranhas hunt in the day and sleep at night.

5a Work in groups of three. Look at the photos. You have five minutes to write as many sentences as possible comparing the different animals. You can use the comparative form of the adjectives in the box, or of any other adjectives you like.

big • dangerous • fast • friendly good • heavy • intelligent • slow small • strong

1

2

3

4

5

6

Snakes are more dangerous than dogs.

5b Count your sentences. Who has more? The winning group can read out their sentences. Are your sentences similar?

6a Make sentences comparing the two things or people, giving your own true opinion. You can use any comparative adjectives, but you cannot use the same adjective twice.

1 basketball/football
2 dogs/cats
3 English/maths
4 burgers/salads
5 books/films

6b SPEAKING Work with a partner. Compare your sentences.

I think basketball is faster than football.

Maybe. But I think it's worse than football.

Geographical features

1 Work with a partner. Match the photos with some of these words.

beach • desert • forest • island • lake • mountain ocean/sea • river • waterfall

1

2

3

4

5

6

2 83 Listen and repeat.

3 Work in a small group. What are these famous geographical features? Who knows them all? Check the answers on page 154.

? ? Geography quiz! ? ?

1 the Mediterranean *a sea*
2 Titicaca
3 K2
4 Sherwood
5 Iguazu Falls
6 the Mississippi
7 Mallorca
8 the Kalahari
9 Copacabana

4a Individually, think of a different example of each geographical feature in your country or another country.

4b SPEAKING Work with a partner. Say your examples. Can your partner say what type of geographical feature it is?

The Thames.

It's a river.

Reducing POLLUTION

LIFE SKILLS OBJECTIVES

- To learn about pollution caused by plastic.
- To think about how we can reduce pollution caused by plastic.
- To make an action plan to reduce pollution from plastic.

KEY CONCEPTS

garbage (Am Eng), rubbish (GB Eng) [n]: *Lots of garbage/rubbish can cause problems for the environment.* **biodegradable [adj]:** *This plastic is biodegradable – it disappears naturally.* **toxic [adj]:** *This product is toxic – it can kill humans and animals.* **environment [n]:** *The environment is the world around us. We need to protect it.* **recycle [v]:** *When you recycle paper, you can make new paper products from old paper.*

1 Work with a partner. What can you see in the photos?

2 Do you think these statements are True (T) or False (F)? Guess.

1. 90% of the rubbish in oceans is plastic. T/F
2. Over a million birds and animals die each year because of plastic in the sea. T/F
3. 50% of the plastic in the sea comes from ships. T/F
4. Plastic in the sea disappears after about ten years. T/F
5. Plastic in the sea can be a problem for humans too. T/F
6. Plastic is only really a problem in the Pacific Ocean, not in other seas or oceans. T/F

3 READING **Read the text and check your answers in 2. If a statement is false, say why.**

The Great Pacific Garbage Patch

What is it?

There is a place in the Pacific Ocean with large amounts of rubbish. The sea is calm there and the rubbish doesn't move. The problem comes from plastic, because a lot of plastic is not biodegradable. Some say the area is bigger than Texas. Others say it's smaller.

Why is it important?

Experts think that 90% of the rubbish in oceans is plastic. Scientists collected 750,000 pieces of plastic in just one square kilometre of The Great Pacific Garbage Patch.

Plastic kills more than a million seabirds and 100,000 marine mammals every year.

4 **Read the text again. Why do these numbers and places appear?**

1 17
2 750,000
3 Texas
4 90%
5 hundreds
6 20%

5 SPEAKING **Work with a partner. Discuss these questions.**

1 What do you think about the rubbish in the Pacific Ocean?
2 What do you think we can do to help?
3 Do you think there are other materials that are better for the environment than plastic?

6 LISTENING 84 **Watch or listen to a podcast made by a student. How does she answer the questions in 5?**

7a 84 **Work with a partner. Can you remember Charlotte's five ideas to stop using so much plastic? Make a list. Watch or listen again if necessary.**

1 Don't take plastic bags in supermarkets.

7b **Can you add any other ideas of your own?**

....

....

....

....

LIFE TASK

Work in a group. Follow this plan:

1 *Decide the top five things you can do to stop using so much plastic. Think of the ideas given in 7a and your ideas in 7b. Investigate other ideas on the Internet.*
2 *Make a poster to explain and illustrate your top five ideas.*
3 *Exhibit your posters.*
4 *Do the things on your poster. After a month, evaluate the difference you are making to the environment by following your plan.*

Many types of plastic objects appear inside the stomachs of dead seabirds. The birds eat the objects because they think they are food.

Scientists think that about 20% of the plastic in the oceans comes from ships or platforms in the sea. But the other 80% comes from the land.

Most plastic is not biodegradable. It stays in the sea for hundreds of years. It gets smaller and smaller but it doesn't disappear.

Small fish sometimes eat toxic plastic. Larger fish eat the small fish, and then we eat those fish. That means the toxic chemicals pass into humans.

Plastic doesn't just kill small fish, and it isn't just a problem in the Pacific. It can even kill big whales. In 2013, near the south of Spain a whale died after eating 17 kilos of plastic. Scientists found more than fifty different plastic objects inside the whale's stomach.

Listening

1 Work with a partner. Look at the photo and answer the questions.

1 Is this man young or old?
2 Do you think he's at the North Pole or on Mount Everest? Why?
3 What do you think he's doing in the photo?

2 Look at these sentences about the man in the photo, Sir Ranulph Fiennes. What words or types of words do you think are missing?

Sir Ranulph Fiennes climbed Everest when he was (1) .... years old. The Transglobe Expedition started in the year (2) .... and finished in (3) .... The expedition first went from the UK to the (4) .... Then it went to the (5) .... and finished back in the UK. Sir Ranulph (6) .... across Antarctica. In 2003 he ran (7) .... marathons on (8) .... different continents in just (9) .... days. He made £6.5 (10) .... to help a cancer charity. He's written approximately (11) .... books. He nearly became the actor in a (12) .... film!

3 LISTENING 85 **Listen and complete the sentences with one or two words, or a number.**

✔ EXAM SUCCESS

Is it a good idea to write four or five words in each space? Why/Why not? Do you think it is important to spell the words correctly?

➤ EXAM SUCCESS page 153

4 SPEAKING **What about *you*?**

Which of Sir Ranulph Fiennes' adventures do you think was the most difficult? Why?

Grammar in context

Superlative adjectives

1a Look at the sentences. The words in blue are superlative adjectives. Match each superlative adjective with a normal adjective (1–7).

a Sir Ranulph Fiennes is the greatest explorer in the world.
b Everest is the highest mountain in the world.
c The biggest and the most difficult adventure was the Transglobe Expedition.
d The worst marathon was in Singapore.
e That is one of the best things about these adventures.
f It isn't the easiest thing in the world to do!

1 bad
2 big
3 difficult
4 easy
5 good
6 great
7 high

1b What word comes before the superlative adjectives?

1c Look at sentences a, b and f. Do we use the preposition *in* or *of* with the superlative?

GRAMMAR REFERENCE ➤ PAGE 124

2a Look at the table. Put the adjectives and superlative adjectives from 1a in the correct section (1–5).

Adjective	Superlative adjective	Rule
(1) hard, fast	the hardest, the fastest	One-syllable adjectives – add -*est*.
(2) fat, thin	the fattest, the thinnest	One-syllable adjectives ending in one vowel and one consonant – double the consonant and add -*est*.
(3) happy, silly	the happiest, the silliest	Two-syllable adjectives ending in -*y* - omit -*y* and add -*iest*.
(4) beautiful, dangerous	the most beautiful, the most dangerous	Adjectives with two syllables or more – put *the most* before the adjective.
(5) far	the farthest, the furthest	Irregular.

2b Where do these adjectives go in the table? What is the superlative form of each adjective?

1 heavy *3 – the heaviest*
2 short ....
3 interesting ....
4 funny ....
5 small ....
6 hot ....

3a Choose the correct alternative.

1 Watching TV is the _better/best_ thing to do in your free time.
2 English is _more/most_ interesting than history.
3 I am the _worse/worst_ singer in the world.
4 This is the _more/most_ beautiful place in my country.
5 Speaking English is _easier/easiest_ than writing English.
6 I think Jennifer Lawrence is the best actress _in/of_ the world.
7 The _bigger/biggest_ problem in the world right now is protecting the environment.

3b SPEAKING Work with a partner. What do you think of the statements in 3a?

I don't think that watching TV is the best thing to do in your free time.

Me neither. I think the best thing is being with friends.

4a Complete the sentences with the superlative form of the adjectives given. Then decide the place. When you finish, check your answers on page 154.

1 .... is the .... (large) hot desert and probably the .... (famous) desert in the world.
2 .... is the .... (populated) country in the world.
3 .... is the .... (long) river in the world.
4 .... is the .... (high) waterfall in the world.
5 .... is the .... (deep) freshwater lake in the world.
6 The .... Islands are probably the .... (good) islands for unusual species. Charles Darwin went there to study them.
7 The .... (hot) place in the world is .... Valley in the US. It's also one of the .... (dry).

4b 86 Listen and check your answers.

Present perfect with ever and never

5 Look at the sentences and choose the correct alternative.

a **Has** he ever **climbed** Everest?
b Yes, he **has**./No, he **hasn't**.
c He**'s** never **worked** as an actor.
d He**'s climbed** Everest two or three times.

1 With the present perfect we _say/don't say_ the exact time when something happened in the past.
2 We make the present perfect with the present simple of _be/have_ and the past participle of the main verb.
3 ***Ever*** means at _any/no_ time in your life.
4 ***Never*** means at _any/no_ time in your life.

GRAMMAR REFERENCE ➤ PAGE 124

6 Match the verbs and the past participles.

been • climbed • jumped • run • seen • swum • walked

1 see
2 walk
3 be
4 run
5 climb
6 jump
7 swim

7a Put the verbs in the correct form of the present perfect.

1 .... you ever .... (swim) in a river?
2 .... you ever .... (walk) in a forest at night?
3 .... your father ever .... (climb) a mountain?
4 .... you ever .... (see) the Pacific Ocean?
5 .... your best friend ever .... (run) a marathon?
6 .... you ever .... (be) on an island?

7b SPEAKING Work with a partner. Ask and answer the questions.

Have you ever swum in a river?

Yes, I have.

Agreeing and disagreeing

1 SPEAKING **Work with a partner. What is your opinion of the animals in the photos?**

1

2

3

4

5

6

I like dogs, but I don't like cats much.

I prefer cats.

2a SPEAKING **Mrs Henderson is an older lady who lives alone. She wants a pet. Discuss which pets in 1 you think are good or bad for an older lady.**

2b LISTENING 87 **Listen to two people, Evelyn and Miles, talking about the different animals in 1. Which do they think are the two best and the two worst pets for Mrs Henderson? Are their ideas similar to yours?**

3 Look at the expressions in the Speaking bank. Use different expressions to give your true opinion of the things that Evelyn and Miles say below (1–8).

SPEAKING BANK

Useful expressions for agreeing and disagreeing

Agreeing
- I agree.
- I agree with (you/that).
- That's true.
- (Yes,) I think you're right.

Disagreeing
- I don't agree/disagree.
- I don't agree with (you/that).
- That's true, but …
- I agree, but …
- It depends.

1 Miles: It's easier to look after a parrot than to look after a dog.
I agree with Miles.
2 Miles: I think a goldfish is a good idea.
3 Miles: I think a snake is a terrible idea!
4 Evelyn: A goldfish is better than a turtle.
5 Evelyn: Dogs are friendlier than cats.
6 Miles: I think the worst are the snake and the turtle.
7 Evelyn: The two best are probably the cat and the goldfish.
8 Miles: Cats and goldfish don't go well together!

4 SPEAKING **Work with a partner. Look at these different statements. With your partner, say if you agree or disagree with them. Give reasons.**

1 'Dogs are very intelligent.'
2 'Animals are stupid.'
3 'Zoos are bad for animals.'
4 'It's wrong to do experiments on animals.'
5 'Animals can't really communicate.'

PRACTICE MAKES PERFECT

5a Look at the animals. Think of reasons why each one is useful to humans. Make notes.

1

2

3

4

5

5b SPEAKING **Work in a small group. Talk about the animals and put them in order from the most useful to the least useful. Use the expressions in the Speaking bank to agree and disagree with other opinions.**

A blog post

1 SPEAKING **Work with a partner. What type of places do you think are good for school excursions?**

2 READING **Read Beth's blog and answer the questions. Do not worry about the order of the paragraphs at the moment.**

1 Where did she go on her school excursion?
2 Did she like it? Why/Why not?
3 What did she do on the excursion?

Beth's Blog

Home About me Blog Contact me Follow me

A visit to a British rainforest!

May 9th

A We had a special guide. She told us all about the rainforest. Then we went on the 'aerial walkway'. You walk above the rainforest and you look down on all the trees. Here are some photos. Go and see it one day!

B The rainforest is at an amazing place called the Eden Project in the South of England. It has different domes. One has got a rainforest, the biggest indoor rainforest in the world! I've seen some unusual places, but this is one of the most incredible.

C Yesterday was a really great day! We usually have biology on Thursday. At the moment we're studying tropical rainforests. So yesterday our biology teacher took us to see one!

Like Comment

3a **Put the three paragraphs in Beth's blog in the correct order.**

1 .... 2 .... 3 ....

3b **Which paragraph ...**

1 gives important information about the place she visited? ....
2 introduces what she wants to talk about in the blog? ....
3 explains what she did in more detail? ....

4a **What different tenses can you find in the blog?**

'We had a special guide'. Past simple.

4b **Read the information in the Writing bank. Check that you have an example sentence from the blog for each tense.**

WRITING BANK

Using present and past tenses

We use the:

- **present simple** to talk about routines, and things that are generally true.
- **present continuous** to talk about things that are happening now.
- **past simple** to talk about things that happened at a specific time in the past.
- **present perfect** to talk about things that happened at an unspecified moment in the past.

5 **Think about a day when you went somewhere interesting, for example on a school excursion. It could be a zoo, a safari park, a nature reserve ... Make notes about it. Use these questions to help you.**

1 When was it?
2 Who were you with?
3 Where did you go?
4 What was the place like?
5 Why was it interesting?
6 What did you do there?

PRACTICE MAKES PERFECT

6 **Use your notes in 5 to write a blog post about your day out. Use Beth's blog as a model. Think carefully about the tenses you use and why. Use the information in the Writing bank to help you.**

WRITING BANK ➤ PAGE 157

Grammar reference

Comparative adjectives

FORM

	Adjective	Comparative
One syllable: add *-er*	small strong	smaller stronger
One syllable ending in one vowel and one consonant: double the consonant and add *-er*	big fat	bigger fatter
Two syllables ending in *-y*: omit the *-y* and add *-ier*	easy heavy	easier heavier
Two or more syllables: add *more* before the adjective	dangerous interesting	more dangerous more interesting
Irregular	bad good far	worse better farther/further

USE

- We use comparative adjectives to compare two people, places or things.
  Elephants are bigger than cheetahs.
- We use *than* in sentences that compare two people, places or things.
  *Your dog is smaller **than** mine.*

Superlative adjectives

FORM

	Adjective	Superlative
One syllable: add *-est*	small strong	the smallest the strongest
One syllable ending in one vowel and one consonant: double the consonant and add *-est*	big fat	the biggest the fattest
Two syllables ending in *-y*: omit the *-y* and add *-iest*	easy heavy	the easiest the heaviest
Two or more syllables: add *the most* before the adjective	dangerous interesting	the most dangerous the most interesting
Irregular	bad good far	the worst the best the farthest/furthest

USE

- We use superlative adjectives to compare more than two people, places or things.
- We use *the* before the superlative form of the adjective and we often use *in*.
  *It's **the** most beautiful animal **in** the world.*

Present perfect with *ever* and *never*

FORM

Affirmative	subject + have/has + past participle *She has swum in the Pacific.*
Negative	subject + haven't/hasn't + past participle *We haven't seen a waterfall.*
Question form	have/has + subject + past participle *Have you been on an island?*
Short answers	Yes, subject + has/have. No, subject + hasn't/haven't *Yes, I have. No, they haven't.*

USE

- We use the *present perfect* to talk about experiences in the past, without saying the exact time.
- We can use *ever* in questions with the present perfect. It means 'at any time in your life'. It comes just before the participle.
  Have you ever run a marathon?
- We can use *never* in negative sentences in the present perfect. It means 'at no time in your life'. *Never* comes just after the first verb.
  I've never run a marathon.

Vocabulary

Animals and insects antelope • beetle • cheetah • frog • kangaroo • penguin • rhinoceros/rhino • whale

Parts of the body arm • finger • foot (pl. feet) • hand • head • horn • leg • neck • stomach • tail • toe • wing

Geographical features beach • desert • forest • island • lake • mountain • ocean/sea • river • waterfall

Other words and phrases ➤ page 149

Grammar revision

Comparative adjectives

/ 7 points

1 Look at the information and the adjective given. Write a true sentence using the comparative form of the adjective.

1 Brad – 15 years old, Sam – 13 years old (old)

....

2 Brazil – 8,510,000 km², Argentina – 2,780,000 km² (big)

....

3 chocolate $2, caviar = $200 (expensive)

....

4 fruit – healthy, chips – not healthy (good for you)

....

5 Andrea – 1m 63, Lily – 1m 65 (short)

....

6 Robin – 4 in last maths exam, Luke – 10 in last maths exam (bad at maths)

....

7 mosquitoes - kill approx. 655,000 people a year, sharks – kill approx. 6 people a year (dangerous)

....

Superlative adjectives

/ 7 points

2 Use the information to write true sentences using the superlative form of the adjectives given.

	height	weight	speed	danger
hippo	1.5 m	1,600 kilos	30 kph	***
tarantula	a few centimetres	85 grams	16 kph	*
cheetah	90 cm	70 kilos	112 kph	**

1 heavy: ....

2 small: ....

3 danger: ....

4 big: ....

5 slow: ....

6 fast: ....

7 tall: ....

Present perfect with *ever* and *never*

/ 6 points

3 Complete the dialogue.

Max: (1) .... you ever ridden a horse?

Leo: No, I (2) .... I've (3) .... ridden a horse.

Max: Has your brother (4) .... ridden a horse?

Leo: No, he (5) .... But he has (6) .... a marathon.

Vocabulary revision

ANIMALS AND INSECTS

/ 6 points

1 Name the animals or insects.

1 

....

2 

....

3 

....

4 

....

5 

....

6 

....

PARTS OF THE BODY

/ 7 points

2 Name the parts of the body.

1 

2 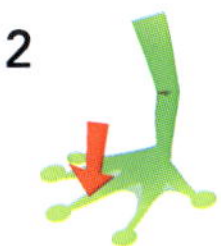

3 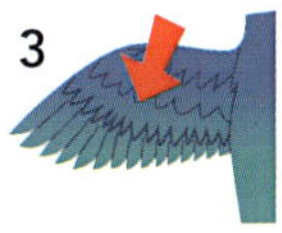

4 

....

5 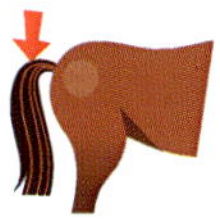

6 

7 

....

GEOGRAPHICAL FEATURES

/ 7 points

3 Put the letters in order.

1 lafterwal
2 treeds
3 habec
4 vierr
5 tinanumo
6 sandil
7 frotes

Total: / 40 points

10 Holiday planner

Vocabulary

The weather

1 Work with a partner. Use the phrases to talk about the photos. Use your dictionary if necessary.

It's cloudy • It's cold • It's hot • It's raining
It's snowing • It's stormy • It's sunny
It's warm • It's windy

1

2

3

4

2 ▶ 88 Listen and repeat.

3 SPEAKING Where you live, what is the weather like …

1 today?
2 in the summer?
3 in the winter?
4 in the autumn?
5 in the spring?

Today it's sunny and dry.

Yes, but it isn't very warm.

Things to take on holiday

4 Match the pictures with the words.

gloves • guidebook • passport • suitcase • sunglasses
sunscreen • swimsuit/swimming trunks • umbrella

5 ▶ 89 Listen, check and repeat.

6 What objects in the suitcase do we use when …

1 it's raining?
2 it's cold?
3 it's sunny and warm?
4 we're at the beach?
5 we're visiting a new city?

7 LISTENING ▶ 90 Listen. A boy and his mother are preparing the boy's suitcase. Which objects in 4 does the boy take? Where is he going?

1a Work with a partner. Talk about the photos. They show things that people sometimes do in the holidays. Make a list of other things you can do.

1b Which of the things in your list do you do, or would you like to do, in the holidays?

2 READING Read the text. Do they mention any of the activities in your list? Which?

Home | Students | Video | **News** | Resources | Archive | Message Board | Subscribe

ARE LONG SCHOOL HOLIDAYS BAD FOR YOU?

The school holidays are nearly here in the UK. But some experts say that the holidays need to be shorter. They say that students forget everything they learn and that they don't do anything useful. What do you think? Are the holidays long? Is that a good or bad thing?

Here in Portugal we're already on holiday. The summer holidays are long here, usually between ten and twelve weeks. It's too hot and sunny to be in a classroom. I think long holidays are great. On Friday my family and I are going to drive to the beach and stay there for a few weeks. In August I'm going to study English at a summer camp. So I'm going to relax and do something useful.

*by **Miguel** on 17th July at 5.15 pm*

I'm here in the UK. Our summer holidays aren't that long. They're usually about six weeks. Personally I'm not going to have much time to sit around and watch TV. In the afternoons I'm going to help my dad at work. He's a mechanic. I love cars and the holidays give me a great chance to learn things that I don't learn at school.

*by **Dylan** on 17th July at 5.45 pm*

I'm from Finland. Our holidays are between two and three months long. But our exam results are usually the best in Europe. So I don't think long holidays are bad or that they stop you from learning. In the winter it's very cold here. So in the summer, when the days are warmer and longer, I'm going to go cycling and swimming every day. I'm going to relax and get fit at the same time.

*by **Riika** on 17th July at 6.20 pm*

3 Read the text again and answer the questions. Write one or two sentences for each answer.

1 Why do some experts think long holidays are bad?
2 Why are the summer holidays long in Portugal?
3 What are Miguel's plans for the holidays?
4 How long are the summer holidays in the UK?
5 What does Dylan think about working in the summer and why?
6 What argument does Riika give in favour of long holidays?
7 What are Riika's plans for the summer and why?

4 CRITICAL THINKING

Think! Then compare ideas with your class.

- Do you think the holidays are long in your country? Do you think that is a good or bad thing? Why?

5 What do the underlined words in the text mean? Guess and then check in your dictionary.

6 SPEAKING What about *you*?

Which of the holiday plans do you prefer? Why?

Grammar in context

Flipped classroom: watch the grammar presentation video.

be going to

1 Look at the sentences and answer the question.

a On Friday, we're going to drive to the beach.

b I'm not going to have time to watch TV.

c Are you going to study English in the summer?

We use be going to to talk about future plans and intentions. After be going to we use the infinitive.
How do we make the negative and questions forms of be going to?

GRAMMAR REFERENCE ➤ PAGE 136

2a Choose the correct alternative.

Julia: What (a) <u>are/do</u> you going to do tonight?
Chris: I (b) <u>–/'m</u> going to study.
Julia: Are you (c) <u>go/going</u> to study maths?
Chris: No, I'm (d) <u>not/not going</u>. I'm going to (e) <u>study/studying</u> English.

2b 91 Listen and check.

2c 91 Listen and repeat.

3a Write questions about your partner's next holidays. Use *be going to*.

1 you/stay at home?
2 your parents/be on holiday, too?
3 you/study English?
4 you/sleep a lot?
5 you/learn something new?
6 you/visit your grandparents?
7 you/meet your friends?

3b SPEAKING Work with a partner. Ask and answer the questions.

4 Look at Tyler's plans for next weekend. Write sentences about Tyler using the correct form (affirmative or negative) of *be going to*.

1 He's going to do his English homework.

PLANS FOR THE WEEKEND	
1	do English homework ✓
2	visit Molly in hospital [✗ – she's out now!]
3	buy a present for Mum [✗ – next week!]
4	go out with Max and Leo ✓
5	play tennis with Tom ✓
6	go to the cinema with Toby [✗ – no money!]
7	send Uncle Al an email ✓

5a Look at the picture. What do you think the people in the picture are going to do?

Pete is going to surf.

5b SPEAKING Memory test! Work with a partner. Student A, close your book. Student B, ask your partner questions about the picture.

What's Liam going to do?

I think he's going to jump in the water.

Prepositions of time

6 Match the sentences with the rules.

a **On** Friday, we're going to drive to the beach.
b Posted by Miguel **on** July 17th.
c Posted by Dylan **at** 5.45 pm.
d **In** the afternoons, I'm going to work.
e **In** August I'm going to study English.
f I'm going to go out **at** the weekend.
g **In** the winter, it's cold.
h **In** 2015 I went to Spain.
i It's cold, especially **at** night.

1 We use **on** with days. *Sentence* ....
2 We use **at** with times. *Sentence* ....
3 We use **in** with months. *Sentence* ....
4 We use **on** with dates. *Sentence* ....
5 We use **in** with parts of the day. *Sentence* ....
6 We use **at** with *night* and *the weekend*. *Sentences* ....
7 We use **in** with years. *Sentence* ....
8 We use **in** with seasons. *Sentence* ....

GRAMMAR REFERENCE ➤ PAGE 136

7a Complete the questions with the correct preposition.

1 What are you going to do .... the weekend?
2 Where are you going to go .... the summer?
3 What are you going to do .... the evening?
4 What are you going to do .... August?
5 Are you going to go to school .... Sunday?
6 How old are you going to be .... 2030?
7 Where are you going to be .... 11.30 pm tonight?
8 Where do you think you're going to be .... 1st January?

7b SPEAKING Work with a partner. Ask and answer the questions.

Vocabulary

Types of transport

1 Work with a partner. Match the pictures with some of these words.

boat • bus • car • helicopter • motorbike • plane
taxi • train • tram • underground

a

b
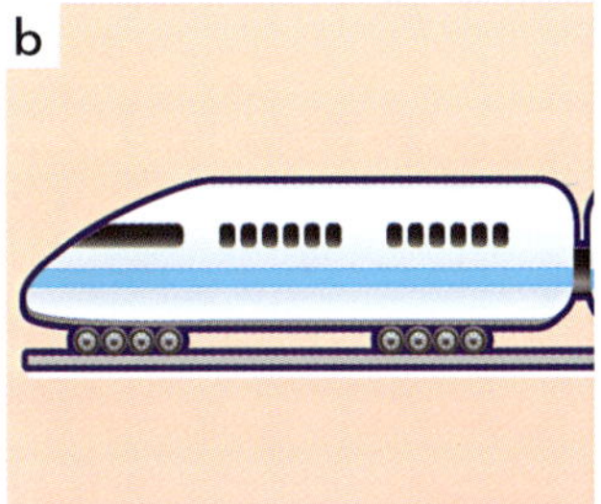
c
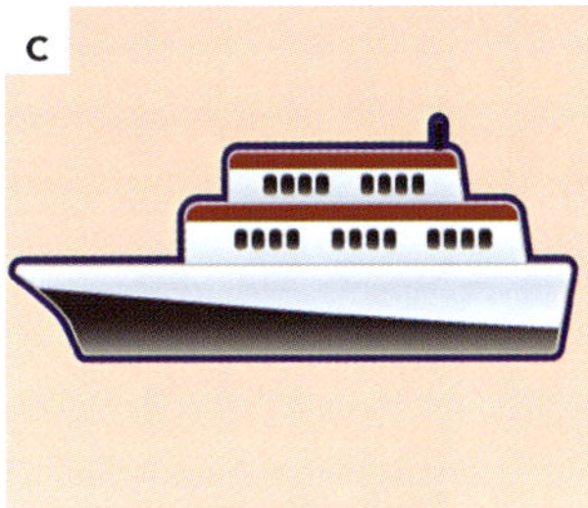
d

e

f

g

h

2 92 Listen and repeat.

3 SPEAKING Work in a small group. Decide which type of transport in 1 you think is …

1 the fastest.
2 the slowest.
3 the best for short distances.
4 the best for long distances.
5 the best for the environment.
6 the worst for the environment.
7 the most exciting.

Learning through literature

LIFE SKILLS OBJECTIVES

- To read a poem about a different country and culture.
- To analyse the possible message(s) in a poem.
- To learn about the UK by reading literature.

KEY CONCEPTS

poem, poet, poetry [n]: *This page has a poem written by the poet Benjamin Zephaniah. It's an example of modern poetry.* **verse [n]:** *The poem on this page has five verses.* **message [n]:** *What is the message of the poem? What is it saying about the world?* **express [v]:** *The writer is expressing his feelings about an important topic.*

1 **Work with a partner. Look at the photos of India. What do you know about India and Indian people? Make a list with your ideas.**

2 READING **Read this poem about India written by a British poet called Benjamin Zephaniah. Does it mention any of your ideas in 1?**

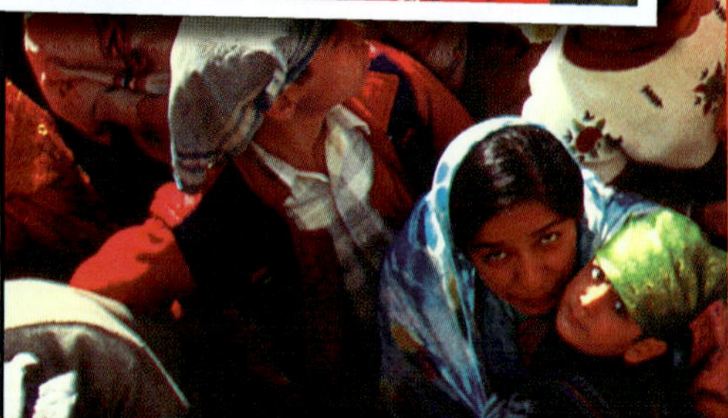

Variety is the SPICE

1 Millions travel upon their bikes
And millions travel in their cars
And millions dream of being like
Those super Bollywood film stars,
They dance Hindi, Hip-hop and Jazz
So people don't believe the hype,
Because there is no such thing as
An average Indian stereotype.

2 They are so rich, they are so poor
And millions are so in-between
Some want for nothing, some want more
And some are quick and very keen,
Some of them wear their hair so short
Some of the girls wear flowered frocks,
In this nation of many sorts
You'll find Sadhus* with long dreadlocks**.

3 Some of them live in villages
Some of them live in high-rise flats,
Some of them have big businesses
Some just do bits of this and that,
Sometimes I know that I've been wrong
But now I know that
I am right,
Because I know
that there's no
one Average
Indian stereotype.

4 Many are wise, many are smart
Many just simply want to be,
Many are light, many are dark
And many of them are just like me,
Many live on cold mountain tops,
Many live in the heat below,
Many have no spare time to stop,
Many have no spare time to go.

5 Some of them pray, some of them don't
Some of them sing, some of them won't,
Some of them serve, some of them cook
Some like to read rhymes in a book,
I may not be smart, wise and great
But this time I know I am right,
Make sure that you make no mistake
There is no Indian stereotype.

**Sadhus – Hindus who focus on spiritual practice*
***dreadlocks – long hair associated with Rastafarians*

3a Read the poem again. Find the verse where the poet talks about these different things in India:

1 music
2 types of transport
3 how much money people have
4 where people live (two answers)
5 hairstyles

3b For each of the things in 3a, does the poem give just one example or more than one example? Which example(s) does it give?

1 more than one – Hindi, Hip-hop, Jazz

4 Work with a partner. Do you agree with these opinions? Why/Why not?

1 'We're all from different places but we aren't very different in the basic things.'
2 'Life is interesting because we're all different.'
3 'Stereotypes aren't true. For example, you can't say that all British people drink tea.'
4 'Each person in the world is different and unique.'

5 LISTENING 93 **Four students are talking about the poem on page 130. Watch or listen. Which speaker expresses each opinion in 4?**

Speaker 1 ....
Speaker 2 ....
Speaker 3 ....
Speaker 4 ....

6 93 SPEAKING **Work with a partner. Discuss the questions. Watch or listen again if necessary.**

1a What does the title of the poem mean?
1b Do you think it's a good title for the poem? Why/Why not?
2a What line does speaker 4 think is the most important and why?
2b Do you agree that the line is important? Why/Why not?

LIFE TASK

Work in a group. Follow this plan:

1 *Read another poem by Benjamin Zephaniah called 'The British'. It is written as a recipe.*
2 *Look up any new words in your dictionary.*
3 *Each person in the group should investigate some of the people that appear in the poem. Who were they and what is their connection to Britain? When you finish, come together and talk about what you discovered.*

Picts Celts Romans Norman French Angles Saxons Vikings

4 *What have you learned about Britain by reading this poem? Discuss in your group.*
5 *Do you think the poem has got a message? If so, what is it?*

The British

Take some Picts, Celts and Silures
And let them settle,
Then overrun them with Roman conquerors.

Remove the Romans after approximately 400 years
Add lots of Norman French to some
Angles, Saxons, Jutes and Vikings, then stir vigorously.

Mix some hot Chileans, cool Jamaicans, Dominicans,
Trinidadians and Bajans with some Ethiopians, Chinese,
Vietnamese and Sudanese.

Then take a blend of Somalians, Sri Lankans, Nigerians
And Pakistanis,
Combine with some Guyanese
And turn up the heat.

Sprinkle some fresh Indians, Malaysians, Bosnians,
Iraqis and Bangladeshis together with some
Afghans, Spanish, Turkish, Kurdish, Japanese
And Palestinians
Then add to the melting pot.

Leave the ingredients to simmer.

As they mix and blend allow their languages to flourish
Binding them together with English.

Allow time to be cool.

Add some unity, understanding, and respect for the future,
Serve with justice
And enjoy.

Note: *All the ingredients are equally important. Treating one ingredient better than another will leave a bitter unpleasant taste.*

Warning: *An unequal spread of justice will damage the people and cause pain. Give justice and equality to all.*

Listening

1 SPEAKING **Work with a partner. Ask and answer the questions.**

1 Have you ever been to London? If so, what did you think of it? If not, would you like to go one day? Why/Why not?
2 Which types of transport do you think are the best to travel around London? Why?

2 LISTENING 94 **Miguel is a Spanish student. He's talking to his English teacher about visiting London. Which types of transport do they talk about?**

3 94 **Listen again and choose the correct answers.**

1 Miguel's teacher thinks …
   a the bus service in London is bad.
   b there aren't many bus stops in London.
   c buses are good if your journey is not very long.
2 The price of a ticket in the underground …
   a can change if your journey is long or short.
   b is always the same.
   c depends on the day you travel.
3 'Peak time' on the Tube is …
   a in the morning, when people are going to work.
   b cheaper than normal times.
   c a special time in the morning when there aren't any trains.
4 A 'fine' is …
   a the money you pay for a ticket on the underground.
   b a special card that you can use on the underground.
   c the money you pay for doing something wrong.
5 Miguel's teacher thinks that …
   a people don't usually ride bikes in London.
   b cycling isn't a great idea for people new to the city.
   c cycling makes the traffic worse near the centre of London.

Grammar in context

must, have to

1 **Look at the sentences and choose the correct alternative.**

a I **don't have to** go to classes in the morning.
b You **mustn't** travel without a ticket!
c They **have to** pay a big fine.
d You **must** be careful cycling in London.

1 We use **have to** and **must** for things that *are/aren't* necessary or obligatory.
2 We use **don't have to** for things that *are/aren't* necessary or obligatory (but we can do them if we want).
3 We use **mustn't** for things that we *can/can't* do because we *have/don't have* permission.

GRAMMAR REFERENCE ➤ PAGE 136

2 **Choose the correct alternative.**

1 Pilots *have to/don't have to/mustn't* wear a uniform.
2 You *have to/don't have to/mustn't* move your legs on a bike.
3 You *have to/mustn't/don't have to* pay to travel by taxi.
4 You *must/don't have to/mustn't* smoke in a plane.
5 You *must/mustn't/don't have to* pass a test to be able to drive a car.
6 You *have to/don't have to/must* go by car when you live near to your school.
7 Bus drivers *have to/must/mustn't* use their mobile phones when they're driving.

3 **Complete the sentences with the correct form, affirmative or negative, of *have to* or *must*. Make all your sentences true.**

1 I .... get up before 8 am during the week.
2 My father .... get up before 7.30 am during the week.
3 We .... wear a uniform at school.
4 We .... come to school at the weekend.
5 We .... stand up when the teacher comes into class.
6 We .... copy in exams.
7 I .... make the dinner at home in the evening.
8 I .... go to bed before 1 am during the week.

should, shouldn't

4 Look at the sentences and choose the correct alternative.

a You **should** use the Tube for longer distances.

b You **shouldn't** travel before 9.30 am.

1 We use **should** for things that we think *are/aren't* a good idea.

2 We use **shouldn't** for things that we think *are/aren't* a good idea.

GRAMMAR REFERENCE ➤ PAGE 136

5 Look at the situations. Complete the sentences with *should* or *shouldn't*.

1

You .... put your feet on the seat.

2

You .... wait for people to get out first.

3

You .... leave your rubbish.

4

You .... give your seat to older people.

5

You .... play loud music.

6

You .... eat smelly food.

6a An English-speaking student has arrived at your school. Complete the sentences with useful information for life at your school, in your city and in your country.

1 You have to …
2 You don't have to …
3 You must …
4 You mustn't …
5 You should …
6 You shouldn't …

6b SPEAKING Work in a group. Compare your sentences. Do you all agree that the information is useful? If not, say why.

7 Complete the text. Write one word in each gap.

Next week , **(a)** .... Wednesday, I'm going **(b)** .... take a test on my motorbike. The day before, **(c)** .... the morning, I had my last practice lesson. I didn't do my test last year because I **(d)** .... only 16 years old. In the UK you **(e)** .... be 17 to ride a motorbike. So now I can take it. **(f)** .... the test going to be difficult? I don't think so. You have **(g)** .... take a theory test first. I did that **(h)** .... 21st May and I passed it easily!

✔ EXAM SUCCESS

In this type of activity, how do you know what word goes in each gap?

➤ EXAM SUCCESS page 153

Invitations

1 SPEAKING **Work with a partner. Look at these three different places and activities. Which do you like? Why?**

1

2

3

2 LISTENING 95 **Listen to two dialogues where people make invitations. Complete the table.**

	What is the invitation for?	Does the person accept the invitation (✓) or not (✗)?
Dialogue 1	1	2 ....
Dialogue 2	3 .... 5	4 .... 6 ....

3 95 **Listen again and complete the expressions.**

1 Are you .... on Saturday?
2 I'm .... Why?
3 .... you like to come?
4 That'd be ....
5 .... you .... anything on Saturday?
6 I don't think .... Why?
7 .... you fancy coming?
8 Sorry, I'm .... mad about ....
9 Do you .... to meet after the match?
10 Yeah, good .... !

4 Put the completed expressions in 3 in the correct place in the Speaking bank.

SPEAKING BANK

Useful expressions for invitations.

Asking about somebody's plans
- (a) ....
- (b) ....

Making an invitation
- (c) ....
- (d) ....
- (e) ....

Accepting an invitation
- (f) ....
- (g) ....

Rejecting an invitation
- Sorry, I can't.
- Sorry, I'm busy.
- (h) ....

5a PRONUNCIATION 96 **Listen to the invitations again. What do you notice about the speaker's voice?**

5b 96 **Listen and repeat. Pay attention to your intonation.**

PRACTICE MAKES PERFECT

6a SPEAKING **Work with a partner. Use the diagram to prepare a dialogue.**

Student A

Say hello to your friend.

Ask about your plans for Sunday.

Make an invitation somewhere.

Make a second invitation.

Finish the conversation.

Student B

Say hello.

Say that you're not sure.

Say no to the invitation, but explain why.

Accept the invitation and say thanks.

6b Practise the dialogue. Then change roles. Pay attention to intonation.

An article

1 SPEAKING **Work with a partner. Look at this photo of a family on holiday and answer the questions.**

1 Where do you think they are?
2 What do you think they are doing and seeing on this holiday?
3 Would you like to go on this holiday? Why/Why not?

2 READING **Read this article. What do you think of Tanya's holiday?**

MY BEST HOLIDAY EVER!

TANYA REID

My best holiday was two years ago. I went to Kenya for a safari holiday. I went with my mum and dad, my sister, my uncle and aunt and my two cousins. It was an amazing experience!

We flew to Kenya. We were in the plane for more than nine hours! But, when we arrived, a taxi took us to our hotel. The hotel was beautiful and the food was excellent!

We went in August so the weather was warm and sunny. We went out in a safari bus and we saw some incredible animals. For example, we saw cheetahs, hippos, and zebras. We also saw a real Maasai village. It was very interesting. I took hundreds of photos! The best moment was visiting Lake Nakuru. It's called the pink lake because there are thousands of flamingos there.

My holiday in Kenya was brilliant. Everybody should see the country. I'm going to go back one day!

3 **Complete the first column in the table below with Tanya's answers.**

MY BEST HOLIDAY EVER		
	TANYA	ME
1 When did you go?		
2 Where did you go?		
3 Who did you go with?		
4 How did you travel there?		
5 What was the weather like?		
6 What did you do and see?		
7 Who would you recommend the holiday to?		

4a **Look at the information in the Writing bank. How many of these adjectives appear in Tanya's text?**

WRITING BANK

Describing positive experiences

- These adjectives can help us to write interesting descriptions of positive experiences: *amazing, beautiful, brilliant, excellent, exciting, great, ideal, incredible, interesting, perfect, spectacular*

4b **Rewrite these sentences using a different adjective instead of *good*. Use a different adjective in each sentence.**

1 My last holiday was good.
2 I did some really good things.
3 I saw some good places.
4 The food was good.
5 I took some good photos.

5 **Think about your best holiday ever. You can invent an ideal holiday if you prefer. Complete the second column in the table with your notes and ideas.**

PRACTICE MAKES PERFECT

6a **Look at the task.**

A travel magazine wants to know about your holidays. Write them an article about your best holiday ever.

WRITING BANK ➤ PAGE 157

6b **Use your notes in 5 to write your article. Use Tanya's text as a model and the adjectives in the Writing bank to help you to write an interesting article.**

✓ EXAM SUCCESS

When you are writing in exam conditions, what should you do if you are not sure that something is correct?

➤ EXAM SUCCESS page 153

Grammar reference

be going to

FORM

Affirmative	I/You/He/She/We/They + **am/are/is** + **going to** + verb *I'm going to surf.*
Negative	I/You/He/She/We/They + **am not/aren't/isn't** + **going to** + verb *She isn't going to swim.*
Question form	**Am/Are/Is** + I/you/he/she/we/they + **going to** + verb? *Are we going to watch TV?*
Short answers	Yes, I/you/he/she/we/they + **am/are/is**. No, I/you/he/she/we/they + **am not/aren't/isn't**.

USE

- We use **be going to** to talk about plans and intentions for the future.
  We're going to fly to the US in the holidays.
  I'm going to study English in Canada.

Prepositions of time

We use:

in with parts of the day (in the morning, afternoon)
with months (e.g. in September, December)
with years (e.g. in 1999, 2011)
with seasons (e.g. in the summer, winter)

on with days (e.g. on Monday, Sunday)
with dates (e.g. on 20th January, 6th November)

at with times (e.g. at six o'clock, ten to eleven)
with night and the weekend

have to, don't have to

FORM

Affirmative	I/You/We/They **have to** buy a ticket. He/She **has to** have a passport to travel.
Negative	I/You/We/they **don't have to** be 18 to use public transport. He/She **doesn't have to** do much homework.

USE

- We use **have to** to talk about things which are obligatory or necessary.
  I have to wear a uniform at school.
- We use **don't have to** to talk about things which are not obligatory or necessary.
  I don't have to wear a uniform at home.

must, mustn't

FORM

Affirmative	I/You/He/She/We/They **must** pass a test to drive.
Negative	I/You/He/She/We/They **mustn't** use mobile phones.

USE

- We use **must** to talk about things that are necessary or obligatory.
  You must pay the correct price.
- We use **mustn't** to talk about things we can't do because we don't have permission.
  You mustn't talk in the library.

should, shouldn't

FORM

Affirmative	You **should** use public transport.
Negative	You **shouldn't** put your feet up.

USE

- We use **should** to talk about things that it is a good idea to do.
  You should help your parents at home.
- We use **shouldn't** to talk about things that are not a good idea.
  You shouldn't talk on your mobile phone in the cinema.

Vocabulary

The weather cloudy • cold • hot • raining • snowing • stormy • sunny • warm • windy

Things to take on holiday gloves • guidebook • passport • suitcase • sunglasses • sunscreen swimsuit/swimming trunks • umbrella

Types of transport boat • bus • car • helicopter • motorbike • plane • taxi • train • tram • underground

Other words and phrases ➤ page 150

Grammar revision

be going to — / 6 points

1 Look at Lisa's plans. Complete the questions and write answers using the correct form of *be going to*.

Fri – *visit her grandparents*

Sat – *play tennis*

Sun – *go with Luke to visit Matt in hospital*

1a What .... Lisa .... (do) on Friday?
1b She ....
2a .... they .... (play) basketball on Saturday?
2b No, ...
3a What .... Lisa and Luke .... (do) on Sunday?
3b They ....

Prepositions of time — / 7 points

2 Choose the correct alternative.

1 He's going to arrive _at/on_ one o'clock.
2 The holidays start _in/on_ June.
3 Bats don't sleep _at/in_ night.
4 We have PE _at/in_ the afternoon.
5 We're going to see the film _in/on_ Monday.
6 We have holidays _in/on_ the summer.
7 What's going to happen _in/on_ 27th July?

should, must, have to — / 7 points

3 Are the sentences correct and/or logical? If not, write them correctly.

1 You musn't use mobile phones in exams.
2 You don't have to copy in exams.
3 You shouldn't go out in the rain without an umbrella.
4 You must wear sunglasses when it's sunny.
5 You have to have a passport to visit the US.
6 You have to shout in hospitals.
7 Our teacher mustn't wear a uniform.

Vocabulary revision

THE WEATHER — / 7 points

1 Look at the symbols. What is the weather?

1 
It's ....

2 
It's ....

3 
It's ....

4 
It's ....

5 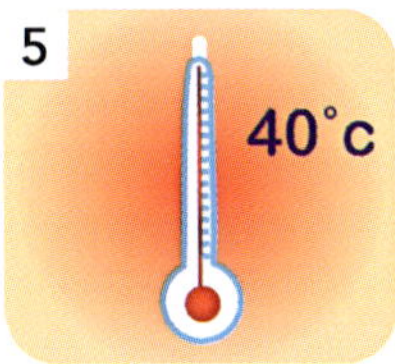

It's ....

6
It's ....

7 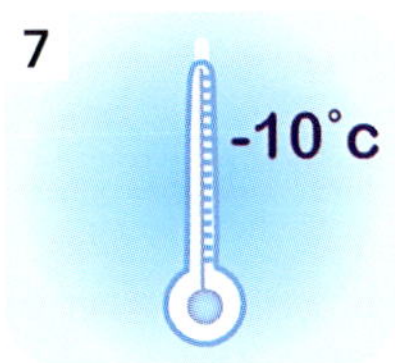

It's ....

THINGS TO TAKE ON HOLIDAY — / 6 points

2 Make words for things we take on holiday.

1	sun	a	suit
2	guide	b	book
3	suit	c	case
4	pass	d	screen
5	swim	e	glasses
6	sun	f	port

TYPES OF TRANSPORT — / 7 points

3 Complete the words to make different types of transport.

1 b o ....
2 h e l ....
3 u n d e r ....
4 p l ....
5 m o t o ....
6 t a ......
7 t r ......

Total: / 40 points

Reading

> **➤ TIP FOR READING EXAMS**
>
> In reading exams, remember …
>
> It is useful to give yourself a time limit the first time you read a text. This helps you to get a quick, general idea of the complete text.
>
> ➤ EXAM SUCCESS page 153

1 **Work with a partner. Look at the pictures and the title of the text. What do you think the text is about?**

2 READING **You have two minutes to read the text and check your predictions.**

THE DEEPEST PLACE ON EARTH

The Mariana Trench is in the Pacific Ocean and it is almost 11,000 metres deep. To give you an idea of its size, Mount Everest is 'only' 8,848 metres high. Over 5,600 have climbed Everest, twelve people have walked on the moon, but so far only four people have been to the bottom of the Mariana Trench.

One of those people is the Canadian James Cameron, one of Hollywood's most famous film directors. In 2012 he travelled inside a specially-made submarine and became the first person since 1960 to get back alive from the bottom of the Mariana Trench. He filmed the trip with 3D cameras.

Cameron wanted to spend six hours under water, but he was only there for three hours. Because of a technical problem, he didn't do one part of the mission. He wanted to take fish and rocks back up to the surface, but it wasn't possible.

The journey down was about 90 minutes, but only an hour to come back up. Cameron had a problem with the small submarine because he's 1.9 metres tall! He needed to do yoga to help him to get inside the submarine. Because of the pressure of the water, the submarine is over six centimetres smaller at the bottom of the ocean. Another uncomfortable thing was the temperature. At first, the temperature inside the sub was around 38°C, but at the bottom it was only 2°C. It was like starting his journey on a sunny day in a rainforest and ending it at night in the North Pole!

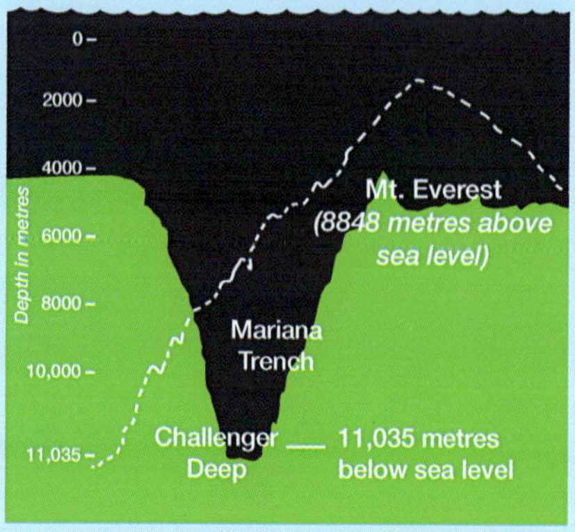

3 **Read the text again and choose the correct answer, a, b or c.**

1 The Mariana Trench is famous because …
   - a it is the same size as Mount Everest.
   - b it is extremely deep.
   - c nobody has been there before.

2 From the text, we know that James Cameron …
   - a is not from the US.
   - b was born in Hollywood.
   - c has made a lot of films underwater.

3 James Cameron's adventure …
   - a was perfect because everything worked well.
   - b had only one objective – to make a film.
   - c was special because it is more unusual to go there than to go to the moon.

4 When the submarine went down, everything became …
   - a warmer but darker.
   - b colder but brighter.
   - c colder and darker.

4 SPEAKING **What about *you*? Would you like to go on an adventure like this? Why/Why not?**

Listening

> **➤ TIP FOR LISTENING EXAMS**
>
> In activities where you have to listen and complete the sentences, remember …
>
> Usually we only need to write one or two words or a number in each space. It is important to spell those words correctly.
>
> ➤ EXAM SUCCESS page 153

5 **You are going to hear two people talk about Thomas Cook. Before you listen, look at the sentences. What words or types of words are missing?**

- Thomas Cook was born in Great Britain in **(1)** ………………… .
- In 1841 he organised an excursion for about 500 people, taking them 18 kilometres by **(2)** ………………… .
- The price of the excursion to Liverpool included transport, food and **(3)** ………………… .
- His trips to Egypt were very popular because people wanted to visit **(4)** ………………… .
- In his shop in London he sold **(5)** ………………… and suitcases.
- In **(6)** ………………… his 'round the world tour' cost £83,000 and took **(7)** ………………… days.

6 LISTENING ▶ 97 **Listen and complete the sentences with one or two words, or a number, in each space.**

7 SPEAKING **What about *you*?**

Would you like to go on a 'round the world tour'? Why/Why not?

Use of English

➤ TIP FOR USE OF ENGLISH

In open cloze activities, remember …
Read the text carefully. The answer depends on the words that come before and after each gap.

➤ EXAM SUCCESS page 153

8 Read the text quickly. Which two animals from the Amazon rainforest appear in the text?

(a) .... you ever been to the Amazon rainforest? My dad is a scientist. He and his friend (b) .... going to go there to work (c) .... June. He says it's the biggest and (d) .... amazing jungle in the world! But you have (e) .... be very careful there, because there are some dangerous animals. Take the jaguar, for example. It's the biggest cat (f) .... South America. Did you know that jaguars can swim and climb trees? And there are other animals and insects that are more dangerous (g) .... jaguars. There's the anaconda, the world's biggest snake. Anacondas can be seven metres or more. My dad hates snakes! I don't know how he's going to sleep (h) .... night!

9 Read the text carefully. Complete it by writing one word in each gap.

Writing

➤ TIP FOR WRITING EXAMS

In writing exams, remember …
When you are writing in an exam, only write what you know is correct. If you aren't sure that something is correct, change it.

➤ EXAM SUCCESS page 153

10 Create your own title for an article and make notes.

My	best funniest most exciting worst most unusual	day weekend excursion holiday meal	ever!

1 When was it?
2 Where was it?
3 How did you get there?
4 Who was with you?
5 What happened?
6 Why was it special/bad?

11 Write your article. Use a variety of adjectives and think carefully about the tenses you need.

'CAN DO' PROGRESS CHECK UNITS 9–10 — CEF

1 How well can you do these things in English now? Give yourself a mark from 1 to 4.

1 = I can do it very well.
2 = I can do it quite well.
3 = I have some problems.
4 = I can't do it.

a I can compare animals, people and things using comparative and superlative adjectives. ☐
b I can talk about experiences in the past using the present perfect with *ever/never*. ☐
c I can name different animals and parts of the body. ☐
d I can use expressions to agree or disagree with others. ☐
e I can write a simple blog post. ☐
f I can talk about the future using *be going to*. ☐
g I can talk about things that are necessary, not necessary or a good idea using *should, have to* and *must*. ☐
h I can understand spoken and written texts about holidays and transport. ☐
i I can make and reply to invitations. ☐
j I can write a short article about a holiday. ☐

2 Now decide what you need to do next to improve.

1 Look again at my book/notes.
2 Do more practice exercises. ➤ WORKBOOK Units 9-10
3 Ask for help.
4 Other: ....

(adj) = adjective
(adv) = adverb
(conj) = conjunction
(det) = determiner
(n/n pl) = noun/noun plural
(phr) = phrase
(prep) = preposition
(pron) = pronoun
(v) = verb

The most common and useful words in English are marked according to the Macmillan Dictionary 'star rating'. This is so you can easily recognise the vocabulary you need to know especially well.

★★★ = very common words ★★ = common words ★ = fairly common words

If there is no star next to the word, this means that it is not very common.

In the Macmillan Dictionary, (r) is used to indicate American English pronunciation, for example *board* /bɔː(r)d/. In British English, this use of (r) tends to occur only at the end of a word which is followed by a word starting with a vowel sound, for example *far away* /fɑːr ə'weɪ/.

Starter Unit

The classroom

bag (n) ★★★ /bæg/
board (n) ★★★ /bɔː(r)d/
board rubber (n) /'bɔː(r)d ˌrʌbə(r)/
book (n) ★★★ /bʊk/
chair (n) ★★★ /tʃeə(r)/
computer (n) ★★★ /kəm'pjuːtə(r)/
desk (n) ★★★ /desk/
dictionary (n) ★★ /'dɪkʃən(ə)ri/
door (n) ★★★ /dɔː(r)/
pen (n) ★★ /pen/
pencil (n) ★★ /'pens(ə)l/
poster (n) ★★ /'pəʊstə(r)/
rubber (n) ★★ /'rʌbə(r)/
ruler (n) ★★ /'ruːlə(r)/
window (n) ★★★ /'wɪndəʊ/

Colours

black (adj) ★★★ /blæk/
blue (adj) ★★★ /bluː/
brown (adj) ★★★ /braʊn/
green (adj) ★★★ /griːn/
grey (adj) ★★★ /greɪ/
orange (adj) ★★ /'ɒrɪndʒ/
pink (adj) ★★ /pɪŋk/
purple (adj) ★ /'pɜː(r)p(ə)l/
red (adj) ★★★ /red/
white (adj) ★★★ /waɪt/
yellow (adj) ★★★ /'jeləʊ/

Numbers - cardinal

one (number) ★★★ /wʌn/
two (number) ★★★ /tuː/
three (number) /θriː/
four (number) /fɔː(r)/
five (number) /faɪv/
six (number) /sɪks/
seven (number) /'sev(ə)n/
eight (number) /eɪt/
nine (number) /naɪn/
ten (number) /ten/
eleven (number) /ɪ'lev(ə)n/
twelve (number) /twelv/
thirteen (number) /ˌθɜː(r)'tiːn/
fourteen (number) /ˌfɔː(r)'tiːn/
fifteen (number) /ˌfɪf'tiːn/
sixteen (number) /ˌsɪks'tiːn/
seventeen (number) /ˌsev(ə)n'tiːn/
eighteen (number) /ˌeɪ'tiːn/
nineteen (number) /ˌnaɪn'tiːn/
twenty (number) /'twenti/
twenty-one (number) /'twenti ˌwʌn/
thirty (number) /'θɜː(r)ti/
forty (number) /'fɔː(r)ti/
fifty (number) /'fɪfti/

Numbers - ordinal

first (number) ★★★ /fɜː(r)st/
second (number) ★★★ /'sekənd/
third (number) /θɜː(r)d/
fourth (number) /fɔː(r)θ/
fifth (number) /fɪfθ/
sixth (number) /sɪksθ/
seventh (number) /'sev(ə)nθ/
eighth (number) /eɪtθ/
ninth (number) /naɪnθ/
tenth (number) /tenθ/
eleventh (number) /ɪ'lev(ə)nθ/
twelfth (number) /twelfθ/
thirteenth (number) /ˌθɜː(r)'tiːnθ/
fourteenth (number) /ˌfɔː(r)'tiːnθ/
fifteenth (number) /ˌfɪf'tiːnθ/
sixteenth (number) /ˌsɪks'tiːnθ/
seventeenth (number) /ˌsev(ə)n'tiːnθ/
eighteenth (number) /ˌeɪ'tiːnθ/
nineteenth (number) /ˌnaɪn'tiːnθ/
twentieth (number) /'twentiəθ/
twenty-first (number) /'twenti ˌfɜː(r)st/
thirtieth (number) /'θɜː(r)tiəθ/
fortieth (number) /'fɔː(r)tiəθ/
fiftieth (number) /'fɪftiəθ/

Days

Monday (n) ★★★ /'mʌndeɪ/
Tuesday (n) ★★★ /'tjuːzdeɪ/
Wednesday (n) ★★★ /'wenzdeɪ/
Thursday (n) ★★★ /'θɜː(r)zdeɪ/
Friday (n) ★★★ /'fraɪdeɪ/
Saturday (n) ★★★ /'sætə(r)deɪ/
Sunday (n) ★★★ /'sʌndeɪ/

Months

January (n) ★★★ /'dʒænjuəri/
February (n) ★★★ /'februəri/
March (n) ★★★ /mɑː(r)tʃ/
April (n) ★★★ /'eɪprəl/

May (n) ★★★ /meɪ/
June (n) ★★★ /dʒuːn/
July (n) ★★★ /dʒʊ'laɪ/
August (n) ★★★ /'ɔːgəst/
September (n) ★★★ /sep'tembə(r)/
October (n) ★★★ /ɒk'təʊbə(r)/
November (n) ★★★ /nəʊ'vembə(r)/
December (n) ★★★ /dɪ'sembə(r)/

Classroom expressions and instructions

answer (v) ★★★ /'ɑːnsə(r)/
ask (v) ★★★ /ɑːsk/
check (v) ★★★ /tʃek/
choose (v) ★★★ /tʃuːz/
complete (v) ★★★ /kəm'pliːt/
group (n) ★★★ /gruːp/
listen (v) ★★★ /'lɪs(ə)n/
look (v) ★★★ /lʊk/
partner (n) ★★★ /'pɑː(r)tnə(r)/
read (v) ★★★ /riːd/
repeat (v) ★★★ /rɪ'piːt/
say (v) ★★★ /seɪ/
text (n) ★★★ /tekst/
work (v) ★★★ /wɜː(r)k/
write (v) ★★★ /raɪt/

Grammar words

adjective (n) ★ /'ædʒɪktɪv/
adverb (n) ★ /'ædvɜː(r)b/
alternative (n) ★★★ /ɔːl'tɜː(r)nətɪv/
correct (adj) ★★★ /kə'rekt/
noun (n) ★ /naʊn/
plural (adj) ★ /'plʊərəl/
singular (adj) ★ /'sɪŋgjʊlə(r)/
table (n) ★★★ /'teɪb(ə)l/
verb (n) ★ /vɜː(r)b/

Unit 1

Countries

Australia (n) /ɒ'streɪliə/
Brazil (n) /brə'zɪl/
China (n) /'tʃaɪnə/
Egypt (n) /'iːdʒɪpt/
Mexico (n) /'meksɪkəʊ/
Russia (n) /'rʌʃə/
Spain (n) /speɪn/
the UK (n) /ðə ˌjuː 'keɪ/
the US (n) /ðə ˌjuː 'es/
Turkey (n) /'tɜː(r)ki/

Nationalities

American (adj) /ə'merɪkən/
Australian (adj) /ɒ'streɪliən/
Brazilian (adj) /brə'zɪliən/
British (adj) /'brɪtɪʃ/
Chinese (adj) /ˌtʃaɪ'niːz/
Egyptian (adj) /ɪ'dʒɪpʃ(ə)n/
Mexican (adj) /'meksɪkən/
Russian (adj) /'rʌʃ(ə)n/
Spanish (adj) /'spænɪʃ/
Turkish (adj) /'tɜː(r)kɪʃ/

The family

aunt (n) ★★★ /ɑːnt/
brother (n) ★★★ /'brʌðə(r)/
cousin (n) ★★ /'kʌz(ə)n/
father (n) ★★★ /'fɑːðə(r)/
grandfather (n) ★★ /'græn(d)ˌfɑːðə(r)/
grandmother (n) ★★ /'græn(d)ˌmʌðə(r)/
grandparents (n pl) ★ /'græn(d)ˌpeərənts/
husband (n) ★★ /'hʌzbənd/
mother (n) ★★★ /'mʌðə(r)/
nephew (n) ★ /'nefjuː/
niece (n) ★ /niːs/
parent (n) ★★★ /'peərənt/
sister (n) ★★★ /'sɪstə(r)/
uncle (n) ★★ /'ʌŋk(ə)l/
wife (n) ★★★ /waɪf/

Other words and phrases

about (prep) ★★★ /ə'baʊt/
action (n) ★★★ /'ækʃ(ə)n/
actor (n) ★★★ /'æktə(r)/
actress (n) ★ /'æktrəs/
age (n) ★★★ /eɪdʒ/
average (adj & n) ★★★ /'æv(ə)rɪdʒ/
baby (n) ★★★ /'beɪbi/
band (n) ★★★ /bænd/
be born (v) /biː 'bɔː(r)n/
best (adj) ★★★ /best/
bike (n) ★★ /baɪk/
birthday (n) ★★ /'bɜː(r)θdeɪ/
century (n) ★★★ /'sentʃəri/
cinema (n) ★★ /'sɪnəmə/
city (n) ★★★ /'sɪti/
club (n) ★★★ /klʌb/
coast (n) ★★★ /kəʊst/
diagram (n) ★★ /'daɪəgræm/
east (n & adj) ★★★ /iːst/
email address (n) /'iːmeɪl əˌdres/
English-speaking (adj) /'ɪŋglɪʃ ˌspiːkɪŋ/
ethnic (adj) ★★ /'eθnɪk/
expensive (adj) ★★★ /ɪk'spensɪv/
fan (n) ★★ /fæn/
favourite (adj) ★★ /'feɪv(ə)rət/
female (adj) ★★★ /'fiːmeɪl/
film (n) ★★★ /fɪlm/
flat (n) ★★★ /flæt/
football (n) ★★★ /'fʊtˌbɔːl/
friend (n) ★★★ /frend/
happy (adj) ★★★ /'hæpi/
hobby (n) ★ /'hɒbi/
ice cream (n) ★ /ˌaɪs 'kriːm/
interested in (phr) /'ɪntrəstɪd ɪn/
kid (n) ★★★ /kɪd/
male (adj) ★★★ /meɪl/
map (n) ★★★ /mæp/
member (n) ★★★ /'membə(r)/
million (number) ★★ /'mɪljən/

mobile phone (n) ★★ /ˌməʊbaɪl ˈfəʊn/
near (adj) ★★★ /nɪə(r)/
outside (adj) ★★★ /ˈaʊtˌsaɪd/
over (prep) ★★★ /ˈəʊvə(r)/
palace (n) ★★ /ˈpæləs/
people (n) ★★★ /ˈpiːp(ə)l/
per cent (n) ★★★ /pə(r) ˈsent/
perfect (adj) ★★★ /ˈpɜː(r)fɪkt/
pet (n) ★★ /pet/
photo (n) ★★ /ˈfəʊtəʊ/
photograph (n) ★★★ /ˈfəʊtəˌgrɑːf/
player (n) ★★★ /ˈpleɪə(r)/
point (n) ★★★ /pɔɪnt/
population (n) ★★★ /ˌpɒpjʊˈleɪʃ(ə)n/
present (n) ★★★ /ˈprez(ə)nt/
same (adj) ★★★ /seɪm/
singer (n) ★★ /ˈsɪŋə(r)/
special (adj) ★★★ /ˈspeʃ(ə)l/
sport (n) ★★★ /spɔː(r)t/
square kilometre (n) /ˌskweə(r) ˈkɪləˌmiːtə(r)/
statistic (n) /stəˈtɪstɪk/
superhero (n) /ˈsuːpə(r)ˌhɪərəʊ/
swimming (n) ★ /ˈswɪmɪŋ/
tennis (n) ★★ /ˈtenɪs/
thing (n) ★★★ /θɪŋ/
thousand (number) ★★ /ˈθaʊz(ə)nd/
type (n) ★★★ /taɪp/
under (prep) ★★★ /ˈʌndə(r)/
vanilla (adj) /vəˈnɪlə/
west (n & adj) ★★★ /★ /west/

Unit 2

School subjects

art (n) ★★★ /ɑː(r)t/
English (n) /ˈɪŋglɪʃ/
French (n) /frentʃ/
geography (n) ★★ /dʒiːˈɒgrəfi/
history (n) ★★★ /ˈhɪst(ə)ri/
ICT (Information and Communication Technology) (n) /ˌaɪ siː ˈtiː/
maths (n) ★ /mæθs/
music (n) ★★★ /ˈmjuːzɪk/
PE (Physical Education) (n) /ˌpiː ˈiː/
science (n) ★★★ /ˈsaɪəns/

Everyday objects

calculator (n) ★ /ˈkælkjʊˌleɪtə(r)/
folder (n) ★ /ˈfəʊldə(r)/
laptop (n) /ˈlæpˌtɒp/
marker pen (n) /ˈmɑː(r)kə(r) ˌpen/
mobile phone (n) ★★ /ˌməʊbaɪl ˈfəʊn/
MP3 player (n) /ˌem piː ˈθriː ˈpleɪə(r)/
pencil case (n) /ˈpens(ə)l ˌkeɪs/
snack (n) ★ /snæk/
tablet (n) ★★ /ˈtæblət/
trainers (n pl) ★ /ˈtreɪnə(r)z/

Describing faces

ear (n) ★★★ /ɪə(r)/
eye (n) ★★★ /aɪ/
hair (n) ★★★ /heə(r)/
mouth (n) ★★★ /maʊθ/
nose (n) ★★★ /nəʊz/
teeth (n) ★★★ /tiːθ/

Adjectives

big (adj) ★★★ /bɪg/
blue (adj) ★★★ /bluː/
brown (adj) ★★★ /braʊn/
curly (adj) ★ /ˈkɜː(r)li/
dark (adj) ★★★ /dɑː(r)k/
fair (adj) ★★★ /feə(r)/
green (adj) ★★★ /griːn/
grey (adj) ★★★ /greɪ/
long (adj) ★★★ /lɒŋ/
red (adj) ★★★ /red/
short (adj) ★★★ /ʃɔː(r)t/
small (adj) ★★★ /smɔːl/
straight (adj) ★★ /streɪt/
tall (adj) ★★★ /tɔːl/

Other words and phrases

actually (adv) ★★★ /ˈæktʃuəli/
apple (n) ★★ /ˈæp(ə)l/
artist (n) ★★★ /ˈɑː(r)tɪst/
better (adj) ★★★ /ˈbetə(r)/
brilliant (adj) ★★★ /ˈbrɪljənt/
bring (v) ★★★ /brɪŋ/
busy (adj) ★★★ /ˈbɪzi/
careful (adj) ★★★ /ˈkeə(r)f(ə)l/
chocolate (n) ★★ /ˈtʃɒklət/
clear (adj) ★★★ /klɪə(r)/
company (n) ★★★ /ˈkʌmp(ə)ni/
concentrate (v) ★★★ /ˈkɒns(ə)nˌtreɪt/
copy (n) ★★★ /ˈkɒpi/
disturb (v) ★★ /dɪˈstɜː(r)b/
easy (adj) ★★★ /ˈiːzi/
e-pal (n) /ˈiː ˌpæl/
evening (n) ★★★ /ˈiːvnɪŋ/
expensive (adj) ★★★ /ɪkˈspensɪv/
experience (n) ★★★ /ɪkˈspɪəriəns/
fair (adj) ★★★ /feə(r)/
fresh air (n) /ˌfreʃ ˈeə(r)/
handsome (adj) ★★ /ˈhæns(ə)m/
headteacher (n) ★ /ˌhedˈtiːtʃə(r)/
hospital (n) ★★★ /ˈhɒspɪt(ə)l/
hungry (adj) ★★ /ˈhʌŋgri/
ideal (adj) ★★★ /aɪˈdɪəl/
inventor (n) ★ /ɪnˈventə(r)/
light (n) ★★★ /laɪt/
logical (adj) ★★ /ˈlɒdʒɪk(ə)l/
manage your time (phr) /ˌmænɪdʒ jɔː(r) ˈtaɪm/
necessary (adj) ★★★ /ˈnesəs(ə)ri/
new (adj) ★★★ /njuː/
night (n) ★★★ /naɪt/

office (n) ★★★ /'ɒfɪs/
organise (v) ★★★ /'ɔː(r)gənaɪz/
organised (adj) ★ /'ɔː(r)gənaɪzd/
personal (adj) ★★★ /'pɜː(r)s(ə)nəl/
personal coach (n) /ˌpɜː(r)s(ə)nəl 'kəʊtʃ/
popular (adj) ★★★ /'pɒpjʊlə(r)/
practical (adj) ★★★ /'præktɪk(ə)l/
private (adj) ★★★ /'praɪvət/
problem (n) ★★★ /'prɒbləm/
project (n) ★★★ /'prɒdʒekt/
quickly (adv) ★★★ /'kwɪkli/
quiet (adj) ★★★ /'kwaɪət/
reading lamp (n) /'riːdɪŋ ˌlæmp/
rest period (n) /'rest ˌpɪəriəd/
rule (n) ★★★ /ruːl/
school timetable (n) /ˌskuːl 'taɪmteɪb(ə)l/
section (n) ★★★ /'sekʃ(ə)n/
shelf (n) ★★ /ʃelf/
simple (adj) ★★★ /'sɪmp(ə)l/
smartphone (n) /'smɑː(r)tˌfəʊn/
study planner (n) /'stʌdi ˌplænə(r)/
technology (n) ★★★ /tek'nɒlədʒi/
text (n) ★★★ /tekst/
time management (n) /'taɪm ˌmænɪdʒmənt/
topic (n) ★★★ /'tɒpɪk/
turn off (v phr) /ˌtɜː(r)n 'ɒf/
unusual (adj) ★★★ /ʌn'juːʒʊəl/
useful (adj) ★★★ /'juːsf(ə)l/

Gateway to exams: Units 1–2

altitude (n) ★ /'æltɪˌtjuːd/
Antarctica (n) /æn'tɑː(r)ktɪkə/
approximately (adv) ★★ /ə'prɒksɪmətli/
cold (adj) ★★★ /kəʊld/
journey (n) ★★★ /'dʒɜː(r)ni/
primary school (n) /'praɪməri ˌskuːl/
superhero film (n) /'suːpə(r)ˌhɪərəʊ ˌfɪlm/
tablet (n) ★★ /'tæblət/
village (n) ★★★ /'vɪlɪdʒ/

Unit 3

Everyday activities

do homework (phr) /ˌduː 'həʊmˌwɜː(r)k/
finish school (phr) /ˌfɪnɪʃ 'skuːl/
get up (v phr) /ˌget 'ʌp/
go home (phr) /ˌgəʊ 'həʊm/
go to bed (phr) /ˌgəʊ tə 'bed/
go to school (phr) /ˌgəʊ tə 'skuːl/
have a shower (phr) /ˌhæv ə 'ʃaʊə(r)/
have breakfast (phr) /ˌhæv 'brekfəst/
have dinner (phr) /ˌhæv 'dɪnə(r)/
have lunch (phr) /ˌhæv 'lʌntʃ/
start school (phr) /ˌstɑː(r)t 'skuːl/

Free-time activities

chat online (phr) /ˌtʃæt ɒn'laɪn/
do sport (phr) /ˌduː 'spɔː(r)t/
draw (v) ★★★ /drɔː/
go out with friends (phr) /gəʊ ˌaʊt wɪð 'frendz/
listen to music (phr) /ˌlɪs(ə)n tə 'mjuːzɪk/
paint (v) ★★★ /peɪnt/
play computer games (phr) /ˌpleɪ kəm'pjuːtə(r) ˌgeɪmz/
play the guitar (phr) /ˌpleɪ ðə gɪ'tɑː(r)/
play the piano (phr) /ˌpleɪ ðə pi'ænəʊ/
read (v) ★★★ /riːd/
surf the Internet (phr) /ˌsɜː(r)f ðiː 'ɪntə(r)ˌnet/
watch films (phr) /ˌwɒtʃ 'fɪlmz/
watch TV (phr) /ˌwɒtʃ tiː 'viː/

Places in a town

cinema (n) ★★ /'sɪnəmə/
library (n) ★★★ /'laɪbrəri/
museum (n) ★★★ /mjuː'ziːəm/
park (n) ★★★ /pɑː(r)k/
restaurant (n) ★★★ /'rest(ə)rɒnt/
shopping centre (n) /'ʃɒpɪŋ ˌsentə(r)/
sports centre (n) /'spɔː(r)tz ˌsentə(r)/
swimming pool (n) /'swɪmɪŋ ˌpuːl/

Other words and phrases

advert (n) ★ /'ædvɜː(r)t/
advertisement (n) ★★ /əd'vɜː(r)tɪsmənt/
always (adv) ★★★ /'ɔːlweɪz/
amazing (adj) ★★ /ə'meɪzɪŋ/
and (conj) ★★★ /ænd/
apart from (prep phr) /ə'pɑː(r)t frɒm/
because (conj) ★★★ /bɪ'kɒz/
blog (n) /blɒg/
body (n) ★★★ /'bɒdi/
book club (n) /'bʊk ˌklʌb/
brain (n) ★★★ /breɪn/
but (conj) ★★★ /bʌt/
collection (n) ★★★ /kə'lekʃ(ə)n/
competition (n) ★★★ /ˌkɒmpə'tɪʃ(ə)n/
cool (adj) ★★★ /kuːl/
corner (n) ★★★ /'kɔː(r)nə(r)/
creative (adj) ★★ /kri'eɪtɪv/
credit card (n) ★★ /'kredɪt ˌkɑː(r)d/
cry (v) ★★★ /kraɪ/
designer (n) ★★ /dɪ'zaɪnə(r)/
during (prep) ★★★ /'djʊərɪŋ/
enter (v) ★★★ /'entə(r)/
every (adj) ★★★ /'evri/
festival (n) ★★★ /'festɪv(ə)l/
flower (n) ★★★ /'flaʊə(r)/
footballer (n) /'fʊtˌbɔːlə(r)/
forget (v) ★★★ /fə(r)'get/
go past (v phr) /ˌgəʊ 'pɑːst/
go straight on (phr) /ˌgəʊ streɪt 'ɒn/
group (n) ★★★ /gruːp/
immediately (adv) ★★★ /ɪ'miːdiətli/
impossible (adj) ★★★ /ɪm'pɒsəb(ə)l/
in charge of (phr) /ɪn 'tʃɑː(r)dʒ ɒv/
in common (phr) /ɪn 'kɒmən/
influence (v) ★★★ /'ɪnfluəns/
inside (adj) ★★★ /ˌɪn'saɪd/
interesting (adj) ★★★ /'ɪntrəstɪŋ/

left (n) ★★ /left/
lunchtime (n) ★ /ˈlʌntʃˌtaɪm/
majority (n) ★★★ /məˈdʒɒrəti/
meet (v) ★★★ /miːt/
meeting (n) ★★★ /ˈmiːtɪŋ/
message (n) ★★★ /ˈmesɪdʒ/
miss (v) ★★★ /mɪs/
mix (n) ★★ /mɪks/
mixture (n) ★★★ /ˈmɪkstʃə(r)/
money (n) ★★★ /ˈmʌni/
musical instrument (n) /ˌmjuːzɪk(ə)l ˈɪnstrʊmənt/
musician (n) ★★ /mjʊˈzɪʃ(ə)n/
negative (adj) ★★★ /ˈneɡətɪv/
never (adv) ★★★ /ˈnevə(r)/
normal (adj) ★★★ /ˈnɔː(r)m(ə)l/
officially (adv) ★★ /əˈfɪʃ(ə)li/
often (adv) ★★★ /ˈɒf(ə)n/
opposite (prep) ★ /ˈɒpəzɪt/
passionate (adj) ★ /ˈpæʃ(ə)nət/
piece of information (n) /ˌpiːs əv ˌɪnfə(r)ˈmeɪʃ(ə)n/
positive (adj) ★★★ /ˈpɒzətɪv/
possible (adj) ★★★ /ˈpɒsəb(ə)l/
productive (adj) ★★ /prəˈdʌktɪv/
racket (n) ★ /ˈrækɪt/
recommend (v) ★★★ /ˌrekəˈmend/
relax (v) ★★★ /rɪˈlæks/
review (n & v) ★★★ /rɪˈvjuː/
right (n) ★★★ /raɪt/
send (v) ★★★ /send/
share (v) ★★★ /ʃeə(r)/
so (conj) ★★★ /səʊ/
sometimes (adv) ★★★ /ˈsʌmtaɪmz/
song (n) ★★★ /sɒŋ/
spend time (phr) /ˌspend ˈtaɪm/
studio (n) ★★★ /ˈstjuːdiəʊ/
style (n) ★★★ /staɪl/
surprising (adj) ★★★ /sə(r)ˈpraɪzɪŋ/
survey (n) ★★★ /ˈsɜː(r)veɪ/
tester (n) /ˈtestə(r)/
theatre (n) ★★★ /ˈθɪətə(r)/
tree (n) ★★★ /triː/
turn left (phr) /ˌtɜː(r)n ˈleft/
turn on (v phr) /ˌtɜː(r)n ˈɒn/
turn off (v phr) /ˌtɜː(r)n ˈɒf/
TV programme (n) /ˌtiː ˈviː ˌprəʊɡræm/
typical (adj) ★★★ /ˈtɪpɪk(ə)l/
usually (adv) ★★★ /ˈjuːʒʊəli/
violent (adj) ★★ /ˈvaɪələnt/
violin (n) ★ /ˌvaɪəˈlɪn/
walk along (v phr) /ˌwɔːk əˈlɒŋ/
wash (v) ★★★ /wɒʃ/
watch (v) ★★★ /wɒtʃ/
website (n) ★★ /ˈwebˌsaɪt/
weekend (n) ★★★ /ˌwiːkˈend/
without (prep) ★★★ /wɪðˈaʊt/

Unit 4

Rooms

bathroom (n) ★★ /ˈbɑːθˌruːm/
bedroom (n) ★★★ /ˈbedˌruːm/
dining room (n) ★ /ˈdaɪnɪŋ ˌruːm/
hall (n) ★★★ /hɔːl/
kitchen (n) ★★★ /ˈkɪtʃən/
living room (n) ★★ /ˈlɪvɪŋ ˌruːm/

Furniture

bath (n) ★★★ /bɑːθ/
bed (n) ★★★ /bed/
chair (n) ★★★ /tʃeə(r)/
cupboard (n) ★★ /ˈkʌbə(r)d/
fridge (n) ★ /frɪdʒ/
radiator (n) ★ /ˈreɪdiˌeɪtə(r)/
shelf (n) ★★ /ʃelf/
shower (n) ★★ /ˈʃaʊə(r)/
sink (n) ★★ /sɪŋk/
sofa (n) ★ /ˈsəʊfə/
table (n) ★★★ /ˈteɪb(ə)l/
toilet (n) ★★ /ˈtɔɪlət/
wardrobe (n) ★ /ˈwɔː(r)drəʊb/

Food and drink

apple (n) ★★ /ˈæp(ə)l/
banana (n) ★ /bəˈnɑːnə/
biscuit (n) ★★ /ˈbɪskɪt/
bread (n) ★★★ /bred/
burger (n) ★ /ˈbɜː(r)ɡə(r)/
butter (n) ★★ /ˈbʌtə(r)/
cake (n) ★★★ /keɪk/
cheese (n) ★★ /tʃiːz/
chicken (n) ★★ /ˈtʃɪkɪn/
chips (n pl) ★★ /tʃɪps/
coffee (n) ★★★ /ˈkɒfi/
egg (n) ★★★ /eɡ/
fish (n) ★★★ /fɪʃ/
honey (n) ★ /ˈhʌni/
ice cream (n) ★ /ˌaɪs ˈkriːm/
jam (n) ★ /dʒæm/
lemonade (n) /ˌleməˈneɪd/
meat (n) ★★★ /miːt/
milk (n) ★★★ /mɪlk/
orange juice (n) /ˈɒrɪndʒ ˌdʒuːs/
pizza (n) ★ /ˈpiːtsə/
salad (n) ★★ /ˈsæləd/
salt (n) ★★ /sɔːlt/
strawberry (n) ★ /ˈstrɔːb(ə)ri/
sugar (n) ★★★ /ˈʃʊɡə(r)/
tea (n) ★★★ /tiː/
tomato (n) ★★ /təˈmɑːtəʊ/
water (n) ★★★ /ˈwɔːtə(r)/
yoghurt (n) /ˈjɒɡə(r)t/

Other words and phrases

a bit (adv) /ə ˈbɪt/
above (prep) ★★★ /əˈbʌv/
abroad (adv) ★★★ /əˈbrɔːd/

accommodation (n) ★★ /əˌkɒmə'deɪʃ(ə)n/
amber (n) /'æmbə(r)/
amount (n) ★★★ /ə'maʊnt/
analyse (v) ★★ /'ænəlaɪz/
behind (prep) ★★★ /bɪ'haɪnd/
boarding school (n) /'bɔː(r)dɪŋ ˌskuːl/
bowl (n) ★★ /bəʊl/
cake tin (n) /'keɪk ˌtɪn/
calories (n pl) ★ /'kæləriz/
can of lemonade (n) /ˌkæn əv ˌlemə'neɪd/
chocolate bar (n) /'tʃɒklət ˌbɑː(r)/
choice (n) ★★★ /tʃɔɪs/
coat (n) ★★★ /kəʊt/
cook (v) ★★★ /kʊk/
cream cheese (n) /ˌkriːm 'tʃiːz/
dairy product (n) /'deəri ˌprɒdʌkt/
dream (n & v) ★★★ /★★ /driːm/
enormous (adj) ★★★ /ɪ'nɔː(r)məs/
expert (n) ★★★ /'ekspɜː(r)t/
fast (adj) ★★★ /fɑːst/
fat (n) ★★ /fæt/
food processor (n) /'fuːd ˌprəʊsesə(r)/
glass (n) ★★★ /glɑːs/
gram (n) ★ /græm/
hard (adj) ★★★ /hɑː(r)d/
healthy (adj) ★★★ /'helθi/
i.e. (abbrev) /ˌaɪ 'iː/
in (prep) ★★★ /ɪn/
in front of (prep) /ˌɪn 'frʌnt ɒv/
inconvenient (adj) /ˌɪnkən'viːniənt/
individual (n & adj) ★★★ /ˌɪndɪ'vɪdʒuəl/
label (n) ★★ /'leɪb(ə)l/
low (adj) ★★★ /ləʊ/
low fat (adj) /ˌləʊ 'fæt/
medium (adj) ★★ /'miːdiəm/
near (prep) ★★★ /nɪə(r)/
next to (prep) /'nekst tuː/
notice board (n) ★ /'nəʊtɪs ˌbɔː(r)d/
nutrient (n) /'njuːtriənt/
of course (adv) ★★★ /əv 'kɔː(r)s/
on (prep) ★★★ /ɒn/
percentage (n) ★★ /pə(r)'sentɪdʒ/
ready (adj) ★★★ /'redi/
realise (v) ★★★ /'rɪəlaɪz/
recipe (n) ★★ /'resəpi/
Reference Intake (n) /'ref(ə)rəns ˌɪnteɪk/
saturated (adj) /'sætʃəˌreɪtɪd/
serving (n) ★ /'sɜː(r)vɪŋ/
side (n) ★★★ /saɪd/
spoon (n) ★ /spuːn/
spoonful (n) /'spuːnfʊl/
stuff (n) ★★★ /stʌf/
team (n) ★★★ /tiːm/
thirsty (adj) ★ /'θɜː(r)sti/
together (adv) ★★★ /tə'geðə(r)/
traffic light (n) /'træfɪk ˌlaɪt/
under (prep) ★★★ /'ʌndə(r)/
unhealthy (adj) /ʌn'helθi/
wall (n) ★★★ /wɔːl/

Gateway to exams: Units 3–4

collect (v) ★★★ /kə'lekt/
collection (n) ★★★ /kə'lekʃ(ə)n/
expensive (adj) ★★★ /ɪk'spensɪv/
popular (adj) ★★★ /'pɒpjʊlə(r)/
signature (n) ★★ /'sɪgnətʃə(r)/
special (adj) ★★★ /'speʃ(ə)l/

Unit 5

Computers

keyboard (n) ★ /'kiːˌbɔː(r)d/
monitor (n) ★ /'mɒnɪtə(r)/
mouse (n) ★★ /maʊs/
printer (n) ★★ /'prɪntə(r)/
scanner (n) ★ /'skænə(r)/
screen (n) ★★★ /skriːn/
screensaver (n) /'skriːnˌseɪvə(r)/
speaker (n) ★★★ /'spiːkə(r)/
touchpad (n) /'tʌtʃˌpæd/
touch screen (n) /'tʌtʃ ˌskriːn/
USB cable (n) /ˌjuː es 'biː ˌkeɪb(ə)l/
USB port (n) /ˌjuː es 'biː ˌpɔː(r)t/
webcam (n) /'webˌkæm/

Using computers

click on (v phr) /'klɪk ɒn/
copy (v) ★★ /'kɒpi/
cut and paste (v) /ˌkʌt ən(d) 'peɪst/
download (v) /ˌdaʊn'ləʊd/
log off (v phr) /ˌlɒg 'ɒf/
log on (v phr) /ˌlɒg 'ɒn/
print (v) ★★★ /prɪnt/
save (v) ★★★ /seɪv/
send an email (phr) /ˌsend ən 'iːmeɪl/

The Internet

blog (n) /blɒg/
password (n) ★ /'pɑːsˌwɜː(r)d/
search engine (n) ★ /'sɜː(r)tʃ ˌendʒɪn/
social network (n) /ˌsəʊʃəl 'netwɜː(r)k/
virus (n) ★★★ /'vaɪrəs/
website (n) ★★ /'webˌsaɪt/

Other words and phrases

access (v) /'ækses/
addictive (adj) /ə'dɪktɪv/
address (n) ★★★ /ə'dres/
already (adv) ★★★ /ɔːl'redi/
animation (n) /ˌænɪ'meɪʃ(ə)n/
app (n) /æp/
audience (n) ★★★ /'ɔːdiəns/
automatically (adv) ★★ /ˌɔːtə'mætɪkli/
background (n) ★★★ /'bækˌgraʊnd/
basically (adv) ★★ /'beɪsɪkli/
boring (adj) ★★ /'bɔːrɪŋ/
bullet point (n) /'bʊlɪt ˌpɔɪnt/
calm (adj) ★★ /kɑːm/
chit-chat (n) /'tʃɪt ˌtʃæt/

comment (n) ★★★ /ˈkɒment/
complicated (adj) ★★ /ˈkɒmplɪˌkeɪtɪd/
computer coding (n) /kəmˈpjuːtə(r) ˌkəʊdɪŋ/
concisely (adv) /kənˈsaɪsli/
conduct (v) ★★★ /kənˈdʌkt/
connect (v) ★★★ /kəˈnekt/
connection (n) ★★★ /kəˈnekʃ(ə)n/
data (n) ★★★ /ˈdeɪtə/
distance (n) ★★★ /ˈdɪstəns/
download (n) /ˈdaʊnˌləʊd/
electricity (n) ★★★ /ɪˌlekˈtrɪsəti/
equipment (n) ★★★ /ɪˈkwɪpmənt/
evaluate (v) ★★ /ɪˈvæljueɪt/
exact (adj) ★★ /ɪɡˈzækt/
experiment (n) ★★★ /ɪkˈsperɪmənt/
fit onto (v phr) /ˌfɪt ˈɒntuː/
font (n) /fɒnt/
font size (n) /ˈfɒnt ˌsaɪz/
gadget (n) /ˈɡædʒɪt/
imagination (n) ★★ /ɪˌmædʒɪˈneɪʃ(ə)n/
impression (n) ★★★ /ɪmˈpreʃ(ə)n/
invention (n) ★★ /ɪnˈvenʃ(ə)n/
length (n) ★★★ /leŋθ/
limit (n) ★★★ /ˈlɪmɪt/
magazine (n) ★★★ /ˌmæɡəˈziːn/
millionaire (n) ★ /ˌmɪljəˈneə(r)/
original (adj) ★★★ /əˈrɪdʒ(ə)nəl/
password (n) ★ /ˈpɑːsˌwɜː(r)d/
permission (n) ★★ /pə(r)ˈmɪʃ(ə)n/
relative (n) ★★ /ˈrelətɪv/
security (n) ★★★ /sɪˈkjʊərəti/
shout (v) ★★★ /ʃaʊt/
size (n) ★★★ /saɪz/
ski (n & v) ★ /skiː/
slide (n) ★★ /slaɪd/
snack bar (n) /ˈsnæk ˌbɑː(r)/
transfer (v) ★★★ /trænsˈfɜː(r)/
tutor (n) ★★ /ˈtjuːtə(r)/
unattractive (adj) /ˌʌnəˈtræktɪv/
via (prep) ★★★ /ˈvaɪə/
visuals (n pl) /ˈvɪʒʊəlz/

Unit 6

Shops

bakery (n) /ˈbeɪkəri/
bank (n) ★★★ /bæŋk/
chemist's (n) ★★ /ˈkemɪstz/
clothes shop (n) /ˈkləʊðz ˌʃɒp/
jeweller's (n) /ˈdʒuːələ(r)z/
newsagent's (n) /ˈnjuːzˌeɪdʒ(ə)nts/
post office (n) ★★ /ˈpəʊst ˌɒfɪs/
shoe shop (n) /ˈʃuː ˌʃɒp/
sports shop (n) /ˈspɔː(r)tz ˌʃɒp/
supermarket (n) ★★ /ˈsuːpə(r)ˌmɑː(r)kɪt/

Shopping

cash (n) ★★★ /kæʃ/
change (n) ★★★ /tʃeɪndʒ/
cheque (n) ★★ /tʃek/
credit card (n) ★★ /ˈkredɪt ˌkɑː(r)d/
customer (n) ★★★ /ˈkʌstəmə(r)/
price (n) ★★★ /praɪs/
purse (n) ★ /pɜː(r)s/
sale (n) ★★★ /seɪl/
shop assistant (n) /ˈʃɒp əˌsɪst(ə)nt/
size (n) ★★★ /saɪz/
wallet (n) /ˈwɒlɪt/

Clothes

boots (n pl) ★★★ /buːtz/
coat (n) ★★★ /kəʊt/
dress (n) ★★★ /dres/
jacket (n) ★★★ /ˈdʒækɪt/
jeans (n pl) ★ /dʒiːnz/
jumper (n) ★ /ˈdʒʌmpə(r)/
shirt (n) ★★★ /ʃɜː(r)t/
skirt (n) ★★ /skɜː(r)t/
sweatshirt (n) /ˈswetˌʃɜː(r)t/
T-shirt (n) ★ /ˈtiː ˌʃɜː(r)t/
top (n) ★★★ /tɒp/
trainers (n pl) ★ /ˈtreɪnə(r)z/
trousers (n pl) ★★ /ˈtraʊzə(r)z/

Other words and phrases

accept (v) ★★★ /əkˈsept/
account (n) ★★★ /əˈkaʊnt/
advertising (n) ★★ /ˈædvə(r)ˌtaɪzɪŋ/
awake (adj) ★ /əˈweɪk/
bait (n) /beɪt/
beauty product (n) /ˈbjuːti ˌprɒdʌkt/
brush (v) ★★ /brʌʃ/
discount (n) ★★ /ˈdɪsˌkaʊnt/
drip (v) /drɪp/
effective (adj) ★★★ /ɪˈfektɪv/
extra (adj) ★★★ /ˈekstrə/
first class (adj) ★ /ˌfɜː(r)st ˈklɑːs/
fix (v) ★★★ /fɪks/
found (v) ★★★ /faʊnd/
go up (v phr) /ˌɡəʊ ˈʌp/
item (n) ★★★ /ˈaɪtəm/
letter (n) ★★★ /ˈletə(r)/
little by little (adv) /ˌlɪt(ə)l baɪ ˈlɪt(ə)l/
lost (adj) ★★ /lɒst/
postcard (n) ★ /ˈpəʊs(t)ˌkɑː(r)d/
product (n) ★★★ /ˈprɒdʌkt/
repair (v) ★★ /rɪˈpeə(r)/
sale (n) ★★★ /seɪl/
sales (n pl) /seɪlz/
scientific (adj) ★★★ /ˌsaɪənˈtɪfɪk/
sell (v) ★★★ /sel/
sign (n) ★★★ /saɪn/
special offer (n) /ˌspeʃ(ə)l ˈɒfə(r)/
technique (n) ★★★ /tekˈniːk/
throw away (v phr) /ˌθrəʊ əˈweɪ/
unnecessary (adj) ★★ /ʌnˈnesəs(ə)ri/

Gateway to exams: Units 5–6

vegetarian (n) /ˌvedʒəˈteəriən/
group (n) ★★★ /gruːp/
delicious (adj) ★ /dɪˈlɪʃəs/
repair (v) ★★ /rɪˈpeə(r)/
safe (adj) ★★★ /seɪf/

Unit 7

Sports

baseball (n) ★ /ˈbeɪsˌbɔːl/
basketball (n) ★ /ˈbɑːskɪtˌbɔːl/
cycling (n) /ˈsaɪklɪŋ/
football (n) ★★★ /ˈfʊtˌbɔːl/
golf (n) ★★★ /gɒlf/
gymnastics (n) /dʒɪmˈnæstɪks/
horse-riding (n) /ˈhɔː(r)s ˌraɪdɪŋ/
ice hockey (n) /ˈaɪs ˌhɒki/
ice-skating (n) /ˈaɪs ˌskeɪtɪŋ/
judo (n) /ˈdʒuːdəʊ/
rugby (n) ★ /ˈrʌgbi/
skiing (n) /ˈskiːɪŋ/
swimming (n) ★ /ˈswɪmɪŋ/
tennis (n) ★★ /ˈtenɪs/
volleyball (n) /ˈvɒliˌbɔːl/

Sports competitions

champion (n) ★★★ /ˈtʃæmpiən/
competition (n) ★★★ /ˌkɒmpəˈtɪʃ(ə)n/
cup (n) ★★★ /kʌp/
final (n) ★★ /ˈfaɪn(ə)l/
match (n) ★★★ /mætʃ/
medal (n) ★★ /ˈmed(ə)l/
player (n) ★★★ /ˈpleɪə(r)/
prize (n) ★★★ /praɪz/
race (n) ★★★ /reɪs/
referee (n) ★★ /ˌrefəˈriː/
team (n) ★★★ /tiːm/
winner (n) ★★★ /ˈwɪnə(r)/

Sports people

climber (n) /ˈklaɪmə(r)/
cyclist (n) ★ /ˈsaɪklɪst/
driver (n) ★★★ /ˈdraɪvə(r)/
gymnast (n) /ˈdʒɪmnæst/
player (n) ★★★ /ˈpleɪə(r)/
rider (n) ★★ /ˈraɪdə(r)/
runner (n) ★★ /ˈrʌnə(r)/
skater (n) /ˈskeɪtə(r)/
skier (n) /ˈskiːə(r)/
swimmer (n) /ˈswɪmə(r)/

Other words and phrases

active (adj) ★★★ /ˈæktɪv/
ago (adv) ★★★ /əˈgəʊ/
army (n) ★★★ /ˈɑː(r)mi/
atmosphere (n) ★★ /ˈætməsˌfɪə(r)/
can't stand (phr) /ˌkɑːnt ˈstænd/
Christmas (n) ★★★ /ˈkrɪsməs/
competitive (adj) ★★ /kəmˈpetətɪv/
constructively (adv) /kənˈstrʌktɪvli/
contribute (v) ★★★ /kənˈtrɪbjuːt/
crafts (n pl) ★★ /krɑːfts/
dead (adj) ★★★ /ded/
depend (v) ★★★ /dɪˈpend/
design (n) ★★★ /dɪˈzaɪn/
dinosaur (n) ★ /ˈdaɪnəˌsɔː(r)/
effect (n) ★★★ /ɪˈfekt/
fact (n) ★★★ /fækt/
feeling (n) ★★★ /ˈfiːlɪŋ/
field (n) ★★★ /fiːld/
fighting (n) ★★ /ˈfaɪtɪŋ/
find out (v phr) /ˌfaɪnd ˈaʊt/
general (n) ★★ /ˈdʒen(ə)rəl/
gentleman (n) ★★★ /ˈdʒent(ə)lmən/
happen (v) ★★★ /ˈhæpən/
interrupt (v) ★★ /ˌɪntəˈrʌpt/
king (n) ★★★ /kɪŋ/
mad about (phr) /ˈmæd əˌbaʊt/
make a contribution (phr) /ˌmeɪk ə ˌkɒntrɪˈbjuːʃ(ə)n/
make somebody mad (phr) /ˌmeɪk ˌsʌmbədi ˈmæd/
marathon (n) ★ /ˈmærəθ(ə)n/
No-man's Land (n) /ˈnəʊ mænz ˌlænd/
order (n) ★★★ /ˈɔː(r)də(r)/
origin (n) ★★★ /ˈɒrɪdʒɪn/
pair (n) ★★★ /peə(r)/
participate (v) ★★ /pɑː(r)ˈtɪsɪpeɪt/
particularly (adv) ★★★ /pə(r)ˈtɪkjʊlə(r)li/
pay attention (phr) /ˌpeɪ əˈtenʃ(ə)n/
pick up (v phr) /ˌpɪk ˈʌp/
respect (n) ★★★ /rɪˈspekt/
role (n) ★★★ /rəʊl/
role model (n) ★ /ˈrəʊl ˌmɒd(ə)l/
salary (n) ★★ /ˈsæləri/
Scottish (adj) /ˈskɒtɪʃ/
second-hand (adj) ★ /ˌsekənd ˈhænd/
serious (adj) ★★★ /ˈsɪəriəs/
soldier (n) ★★★ /ˈsəʊldʒə(r)/
solution (n) ★★★ /səˈluːʃ(ə)n/
strong (adj) ★★★ /strɒŋ/
suddenly (adv) ★★★ /ˈsʌd(ə)nli/
talent (n) ★★ /ˈtælənt/
task (n) ★★★ /tɑːsk/
terrible (adj) ★★★ /ˈterəb(ə)l/
traditionally (adv) /trəˈdɪʃ(ə)nəli/
train (v) ★★★ /treɪn/
training (n) ★★★ /ˈtreɪnɪŋ/
war (n) ★★★ /wɔː(r)/

Unit 8

Jobs

builder (n) ★★ /ˈbɪldə(r)/
bus driver (n) /ˈbʌs ˌdraɪvə(r)/
businessman (n) ★★ /ˈbɪznəsmæn/
businesswoman (n) ★ /ˈbɪznəsˌwʊmən/
chef (n) ★ /ʃef/

engineer (n) ★★★ /ˌendʒɪˈnɪə(r)/
hairdresser (n) ★ /ˈheə(r)ˌdresə(r)/
mechanic (n) ★ /mɪˈkænɪk/
nurse (n) ★★★ /nɜː(r)s/
shop assistant (n) /ˈʃɒp əˌsɪst(ə)nt/
waiter (n) ★ /ˈweɪtə(r)/
waitress (n) ★ /ˈweɪtrəs/

Personal qualities

calm (adj) ★★ /kɑːm/
cheerful (adj) ★ /ˈtʃɪə(r)f(ə)l/
clever (adj) ★★ /ˈklevə(r)/
creative (adj) ★★ /kriˈeɪtɪv/
friendly (adj) ★★★ /ˈfren(d)li/
hard-working (adj) ★ /ˌhɑː(r)d ˈwɜː(r)kɪŋ/
kind (adj) ★ /kaɪnd/
responsible (adj) ★★★ /rɪˈspɒnsəb(ə)l/

Adjectives to describe jobs

badly-paid (adj) /ˌbædli ˈpeɪd/
full-time (adj) ★★ /ˈfʊl ˌtaɪm/
indoor (adj) ★ /ˈɪndɔː(r)/
outdoor (adj) ★ /ˈaʊtdɔː(r)/
part-time (adj) ★★ /ˈpɑː(r)t ˌtaɪm/
skilled (adj) ★★ /skɪld/
unskilled (adj) /ʌnˈskɪld/
well-paid (adj) /ˌwel ˈpeɪd/

Other words and phrases

abilities (n pl) ★★★ /əˈbɪlətiz/
administrative (adj) ★★ /ədˈmɪnɪstrətɪv/
advice (n) ★★★ /ədˈvaɪs/
airline (n) ★★ /ˈeə(r)ˌlaɪn/
anywhere (adv) ★★★ /ˈeniˌweə(r)/
application (n) ★★★ /ˌæplɪˈkeɪʃ(ə)n/
apply for (v phr) /əˈplaɪ fɔː(r)/
astronaut (n) ★ /ˈæstrəˌnɔːt/
attitude (n) ★★★ /ˈætɪˌtjuːd/
brilliant (adj) ★★★ /ˈbrɪljənt/
busy (adj) ★★★ /ˈbɪzi/
by plane (adv) /baɪ ˈpleɪn/
caring (adj) /ˈkeərɪŋ/
change your mind (phr) /ˌtʃeɪndʒ jɔː(r) ˈmaɪnd/
comic (n) ★ /ˈkɒmɪk/
company (n) ★★★ /ˈkʌmp(ə)ni/
congratulations (n) ★ /kənˌgrætʃʊˈleɪʃ(ə)nz/
construction (n) ★★★ /kənˈstrʌkʃ(ə)n/
cost (v) ★★★ /kɒst/
emotionally (adv) /ɪˈməʊʃ(ə)nəli/
experience (n) ★★★ /ɪkˈspɪəriəns/
head (n) ★★★ /hed/
job shadow (v) /ˈdʒɒb ˌʃædəʊ/
league (n) ★★★ /liːg/
menu (n) ★★ /ˈmenjuː/
minimum (adj) ★★ /ˈmɪnɪməm/
news (n) ★★★ /njuːz/
opportunity (n) ★★★ /ˌɒpə(r)ˈtjuːnəti/
organisation (n) ★★★ /ˌɔː(r)gənaɪˈzeɪʃ(ə)n/
panic (v) ★ /ˈpænɪk/
physically (adv) ★★ /ˈfɪzɪkli/
prize (n) ★★★ /praɪz/
professional (n & adj) ★★/★★★ /prəˈfeʃ(ə)nəl/
record shop (n) /ˈrekɔː(r)d ˌʃɒp/
service (n) ★★★ /ˈsɜː(r)vɪs/
skill (n) ★★★ /skɪl/
somebody else (pron) /ˌsʌmbədi ˈels/
space (n) ★★★ /speɪs/
success (n) ★★★ /səkˈses/
technical (adj) ★★★ /ˈteknɪk(ə)l/
ticket (n) ★★★ /ˈtɪkɪt/
time off (n) /ˌtaɪm ˈɒf/
truth (n) ★★★ /truːθ/

Gateway to exams: Units 7–8

chef (n) ★ /ʃef/
coach (n) ★★ /kəʊtʃ/
gymnast (n) /ˈdʒɪmnæst/
hockey (n) ★ /ˈhɒki/
individually (adv) ★ /ˌɪndɪˈvɪdʒuəli/
normal (adj) ★★★ /ˈnɔː(r)m(ə)l/
young (adj) ★★★ /jʌŋ/

Unit 9

Animals and insects

antelope (n) /ˈæntɪˌləʊp/
beetle (n) /ˈbiːt(ə)l/
cheetah (n) /ˈtʃiːtə/
frog (n) ★ /frɒg/
kangaroo (n) /ˌkæŋgəˈruː/
penguin (n) /ˈpeŋgwɪn/
rhino (n) /ˈraɪnəʊ/
rhinoceros (n) /raɪˈnɒs(ə)rəs/
whale (n) ★★ /weɪl/

Parts of the body

arm (n) ★★★ /ɑː(r)m/
finger (n) ★★★ /ˈfɪŋgə(r)/
feet (n pl) /fiːt/
foot (n) ★★★ /fʊt/
hand (n) ★★★ /hænd/
head (n) ★★★ /hed/
horn (n) ★★ /hɔː(r)n/
leg (n) ★★★ /leg/
neck (n) ★★★ /nek/
stomach (n) ★★ /ˈstʌmək/
tail (n) ★★ /teɪl/
toe (n) ★★ /təʊ/
wing (n) ★★★ /wɪŋ/

Geographical features

beach (n) ★★★ /biːtʃ/
desert (n) ★★ /ˈdezə(r)t/
forest (n) ★★★ /ˈfɒrɪst/
island (n) ★★★ /ˈaɪlənd/
lake (n) ★★ /leɪk/
mountain (n) ★★★ /ˈmaʊntɪn/

ocean (n) ★★ /'əʊʃ(ə)n/
river (n) ★★★ /'rɪvə(r)/
sea (n) ★★★ /siː/
waterfall (n) ★ /'wɔːtə(r),fɔːl/

Other words and phrases

across (prep) ★★★ /ə'krɒs/
action plan (n) /'ækʃ(ə)n ˌplæn/
adventure (n) ★★ /əd'ventʃə(r)/
aerial (adj) /'eəriəl/
aggressive (adj) ★★ /ə'gresɪv/
alive (adj) ★★★ /ə'laɪv/
alone (adj) ★★★ /ə'ləʊn/
around (adv) ★★★ /ə'raʊnd/
be able to (phr) /biː 'eɪb(ə)l tuː/
biodegradable (adj) /ˌbaɪəʊdɪ'greɪdəb(ə)l/
cancer (n) ★★★ /'kænsə(r)/
character (n) ★★★ /'kærɪktə(r)/
charity (n) ★★★ /'tʃærəti/
chemical (n) ★★★ /'kemɪk(ə)l/
climb (v) ★★★ /klaɪm/
compete (v) ★★★ /kəm'piːt/
continent (n) ★★ /'kɒntɪnənt/
continental (adj) ★★ /ˌkɒntɪ'nent(ə)l/
die (v) ★★★ /daɪ/
dive (v) ★★ /daɪv/
dome (n) /dəʊm/
dry (adj) ★★★ /draɪ/
environment (n) ★★★ /ɪn'vaɪrənmənt/
escape (v) ★★★ /ɪ'skeɪp/
expedition (n) ★★ /ˌekspə'dɪʃ(ə)n/
explorer (n) /ɪk'splɔːrə(r)/
fit (adj) ★★ /fɪt/
floor (n) ★★★ /flɔː(r)/
fly (adj) /flaɪ/
garbage (n) /'gɑː(r)bɪdʒ/
goldfish (n) /'gəʊld,fɪʃ/
guide (n) ★★★ /gaɪd/
heart (n) ★★★ /hɑː(r)t/
heavy (adj) ★★★ /'hevi/
hole (n) ★★★ /həʊl/
hunt (v) ★★ /hʌnt/
hunter (n) ★ /'hʌntə(r)/
in comparison with (phr) /ɪn kəm'pærɪs(ə)n wɪð/
jump (v) ★★★ /dʒʌmp/
killer whale (n) /'kɪlə(r) ˌweɪl/
land (n) ★★★ /lænd/
length (n) ★★★ /leŋθ/
lift (v) ★★★ /lɪft/
mammal (n) ★ /'mæm(ə)l/
marine (adj) ★ /mə'riːn/
material (n) ★★★ /mə'tɪəriəl/
noise (n) ★★★ /nɔɪz/
North Pole (n) /ˌnɔː(r)θ 'pəʊl/
operation (n) ★★★ /ˌɒpə'reɪʃ(ə)n/
parrot (n) ★ /'pærət/
patch (n) ★★ /pætʃ/
period (n) ★★★ /'pɪəriəd/
piranha (n) /pə'rɑːnə/
plastic (n & adj) ★★★ /'plæstɪk/
platform (n) ★★ /'plæt,fɔː(r)m/
pollution (n) ★★★ /pə'luːʃ(ə)n/
populated (adj) /'pɒpjʊ,leɪtɪd/
powerful (adj) ★★★ /'paʊə(r)f(ə)l/
protect (v) ★★★ /prə'tekt/
recycle (v) ★ /riː'saɪk(ə)l/
reduce (v) ★★★ /rɪ'djuːs/
region (n) ★★★ /'riːdʒ(ə)n/
rubbish (n) ★★ /'rʌbɪʃ/
seabird (n) /'siː,bɜː(r)d/
shark (n) ★ /ʃɑː(r)k/
snake (n) ★ /sneɪk/
species (n) ★★★ /'spiːʃiːz/
speed (n) ★★★ /spiːd/
toxic (adj) ★ /'tɒksɪk/
tropical (adj) ★★ /'trɒpɪk(ə)l/
turtle (n) /'tɜː(r)t(ə)l/
walkway (n) /'wɔːk,weɪ/
water filter (n) /'wɔːtə(r) ˌfɪltə(r)/
weight (n) ★★★ /weɪt/

Unit 10

The weather

cloudy (adj) /'klaʊdi/
cold (adj) ★★★ /kəʊld/
hot (adj) ★★★ /hɒt/
raining (pres part) /'reɪnɪŋ/
snowing (pres part) /'snəʊɪŋ/
stormy (adj) /'stɔː(r)mi/
sunny (adj) ★ /'sʌni/
warm (adj) ★★★ /wɔː(r)m/
windy (adj) ★ /'wɪndi/

Things to take on holiday

gloves (n pl) ★★ /glʌvz/
guidebook (n) ★ /'gaɪd,bʊk/
passport (n) ★ /'pɑːspɔː(r)t/
suitcase (n) ★ /'suːt,keɪs/
sunglasses (n pl) /'sʌn,glɑːsɪz/
sunscreen (n) /'sʌn,skriːn/
swimming trunks (n pl) /'swɪmɪŋ ˌtrʌŋkz/
swimsuit (n) /'swɪm,suːt/
umbrella (n) ★ /ʌm'brelə/

Types of transport

boat (n) ★★★ /bəʊt/
bus (n) ★★★ /bʌs/
car (n) ★★★ /kɑː(r)/
helicopter (n) ★★ /'helɪ,kɒptə(r)/
motorbike (n) ★ /'məʊtə(r),baɪk/
plane (n) ★★★ /pleɪn/
taxi (n) ★★★ /'tæksi/
train (n) ★★★ /treɪn/
tram (n) /træm/
underground (n) /'ʌndə(r),graʊnd/

Other words and phrases

Afghan (adj) /'æfgæn/
Angle (adj) /'æŋg(ə)l/
autumn (n) ★★★ /'ɔːtəm/
Bajan (adj) /'beɪdʒ(ə)n/
Bangladeshi (adj) /ˌbæːŋglə'deʃi/
below (prep) ★★★ /bɪ'ləʊ/
bind (v) ★★★ /baɪnd/
bitter (adj) ★★ /'bɪtə(r)/
blend (v) /blend/
Bosnian (adj) /'bɒzniː(ə)n/
cause (n) ★★★ /kɔːz/
Celt (n) /kelt/
chance (n) ★★★ /tʃɑːns/
Chilean (adj) /'tʃɪli(ə)n /
Chinese (adj) /ˌtʃaɪ'niːz/
conqueror (n) /'kɒŋkərə(r)/
culture (n) ★★★ /'kʌltʃə(r)/
damage (v) ★★★ /'dæmɪdʒ/
Dominican (adj) /də'mɪnɪkən/
dreadlocks (n pl) /'dredˌlɒks/
drive (v) ★★★ /draɪv/
equality (n) ★★ /ɪ'kwɒləti/
Ethiopian (adj) /ˌiːθiː'əʊpiːən/
express (v) ★★★ /ɪk'spres/
fine (n) ★★ /faɪn/
flamingo (n) /flə'mɪŋgəʊ/
flourish (v) ★ /'flʌrɪʃ/
frock (n) /frɒk/
get fit (phr) /ˌget 'fɪt/
Guyanese (adj) /ˌgaɪən'iːz/
heat (n) ★★★ /hiːt/
high-rise (adj) /'haɪ ˌraɪz/
Hindi (adj) /'hɪndi/
hype (n) /haɪp/
in-between (adj) /ˌɪn bɪ'twiːn/
Iraqi (adj) /ɪ'rɑːki/
Jamaican (adj) /ʤə'meɪkən/
Japanese (adj) /ˌdʒæpə'niːz/
justice (n) ★★★ /'dʒʌstɪs/
Jute (adj) /dʒuːt/
keen (adj) ★★★ /kiːn/
Kurdish (adj) /'kɜːdɪʃ/
Maasai (adj) /'mæsaɪ/
Malaysian (adj) /mə'leɪʒən/
melting pot (n) /'meltɪŋ ˌpɒt/
message (n) ★★★ /'mesɪdʒ/
Nigerian (adj) /naɪ'ʤɪəriən/
Norman (adj) /'nɔː(r)mən/
overrun (v) /ˌəʊvə'rʌn/
pain (n) ★★★ /peɪn/
Pakistani (adj) /ˌpɑːki'stɑːni/
Palestinian (adj) /ˌpælə'stɪniən/
peak time (n) /'piːk ˌtaɪm/
Pict (n) /pɪkt/
poem (n) ★★★ /'pəʊɪm/
poet (n) ★★ /'pəʊɪt/
poetry (n) ★★ /'pəʊɪtri/
pray (v) ★★ /preɪ/
remove (v) ★★★ /rɪ'muːv/
rhyme (n) ★ /raɪm/
Roman (adj) /'rəʊmən/
Sadhu (adj) /'sɑːduː/
safari (n) /sə'fɑːri/
Saxon (adj) /'sæks(ə)n/
settle (v) ★★★ /'set(ə)l/
Silures (n pl) /'sɪljəriːz/
simmer (v) /'sɪmə(r)/
sit around (v phr) /ˌsɪt ə'raʊnd/
Somalian (adj) /sə'mɑːliːən/
sort (n) ★★★ /sɔː(r)t/
spare time (n) ★ /ˌspeə(r) 'taɪm/
spice (n) ★ /spaɪs/
spread (v) ★★★ /spred/
spring (n) ★★★ /sprɪŋ/
sprinkle (v) ★ /'sprɪŋk(ə)l/
Sri Lankan (adj) /ˌʃriː 'læŋkən/
stereotype (n) ★ /'steriəˌtaɪp/
stir (v) ★★ /stɜː(r)/
Sudanese (adj) /ˌsuːdə'niːz/
summer (n) ★★★ /'sʌmə(r)/
summer camp (n) /'sʌmə(r) ˌkæmp/
sure (adj) ★★★ /ʃɔː(r)/
taste (n & v) ★★★ /★★ /teɪst/
the Tube (n) /ðə 'tjuːb/
too (adv) ★★★ /tuː/
Trinidadian (adj) /ˌtrɪnɪ'dædiːən/
trip (n) ★★★ /trɪp/
turn up (v phr) /ˌtɜː(r)n 'ʌp/
unequal (adj) /ʌn'iːkwəl/
unity (n) ★★ /'juːnəti/
unpleasant (adj) ★★ /ʌn'plez(ə)nt/
variety (n) ★★★ /və'raɪəti/
verse (n) ★★ /vɜː(r)s/
Vietnamese (adj) /ˌviːetnə'miːz/
vigorously (adv) /'vɪg(ə)rəsli/
Viking (adj) /'vaɪkɪŋ/
want for (v phr) /'wɒnt fɔː(r)/
warning (n) ★★★ /'wɔː(r)nɪŋ/
winter (n) ★★★ /'wɪntə(r)/
wise (adj) ★★ /waɪz/

Gateway to exams: Units 9-10

alive (adj) ★★★ /ə'laɪv/
darker (adj) /'dɑː(r)kə(r)/
deepest (adj) /'diːpɪst/
extremely (adv) ★★★ /ɪk'striːmli/
moon (n) ★★ /muːn/
ocean (n) ★★ /'əʊʃ(ə)n/
rainforest (n) ★ /'reɪnˌfɒrɪst/
submarine (n) ★ /ˌsʌbmər'iːn/
suitcase (n) ★ /'suːtˌkeɪs/
uncomfortable (adj) ★★ /ʌn'kʌmftəb(ə)l/

Unit 1

LISTENING: IDENTIFYING THE CORRECT PICTURE

In this exercise, you listen to dialogues. For each dialogue, there are different pictures. You choose the correct picture for each dialogue.

Step 1: Look at the pictures before you listen. They help you to know the situation and vocabulary in the dialogues.

Step 2: Listen carefully. In the dialogue, there are probably things from both pictures. But only one picture is exactly correct.

Step 3: Usually you listen twice. Do not panic if you do not understand information the first time.

SPEAKING: SPELLING

In speaking exams, the first questions are usually personal questions. One typical question is 'Can you spell your name/surname?' You need to know the alphabet. Practise spelling your name, surname and other words and names.

Unit 2

READING: TRUE/FALSE/NOT MENTIONED ACTIVITIES

In this exercise, decide if the sentences are true or false. In some exercises you decide if the sentences are true, false or if the information is not in the text.

Step 1: Read the whole text quickly.

Step 2: Read the *True/False/Not Mentioned* sentences.

Step 3: Read the parts where you think the answers are. Now read slowly and carefully.

Step 4: Answer all the questions. Put *Not Mentioned* if you can't find the information in the text.

USE OF ENGLISH: CONVERSATION ACTIVITIES

In this activity you have five short dialogues. You choose the right answer to complete each dialogue.

Step 1: Think about where the people are.

Step 2: Think about who the people are.

Step 3: Think about what the first person says, asks or wants.

Step 4: Choose the answer. The grammar in all the answers is correct. Answers are incorrect because they are answers to different questions. They are not right for the situation or the person who replies.

Unit 3

LISTENING: TRUE/FALSE/NOT MENTIONED ACTIVITIES

- In *True/False/Not Mentioned* exercises, read the statements BEFORE you listen. The statements help to give you an idea of what you are listening for.
- Be careful. The words in the statements are not always exactly the same in the listening text. They often express the same idea but in a different way.
- In *True/False/Not Mentioned* exercises, put *Not Mentioned* if the information is not in the listening text.

WRITING: STYLE AND CONTENT

- When you write a letter, message or note to a friend, use contractions (*isn't, don't*) and informal expressions (*Hi!, See you*). When you write a formal or semi-formal letter, message or note, do not use contractions or informal language.
- When a question tells you to put information in your text, you lose marks if you do not include the information. You can use your imagination, but remember to include all the information in the instructions.

Unit 4

READING: MATCHING TITLES AND PARAGRAPHS

In this type of activity you read a text with different paragraphs. Then you match a title to each paragraph.

Step 1: Read the whole text quickly. This gives you a general idea of what it is about. You do not need to understand everything.

Step 2: Read the titles. What does each title talk about?

Step 3: Find the sections of the text with information similar to the information in the titles. Read those sections again slowly.

Step 4: When you finish, read the text with your answers in the correct place. Is the text logical?

USE OF ENGLISH: COMPLETING THE DIALOGUE

In this activity you have a dialogue and sentences. Put the sentences in the correct place in the dialogue. There are usually more sentences than spaces.

Step 1: Read the complete dialogue. This helps you to understand the general situation.

Step 2: Read the sentences. Choose a logical place for each sentence in the dialogue. Cross out each sentence when you use it so that you don't use the same sentence again.

Step 3: Do not leave any spaces blank.

Step 4: When you finish, read the whole, complete dialogue with your answers in the correct place. Is the dialogue logical?

Unit 5

USE OF ENGLISH: MULTIPLE-CHOICE CLOZE ACTIVITIES

In this type of exercise there is a text with gaps. You fill the gaps in the text with one of three words on the page.

Step 1: Read the complete text. Don't stop to think about the gaps. This is to get a general understanding of the text.

Step 2: Look again at the gaps and especially the words which come just before and after the gap.

Step 3: Look at the three options. Decide which is best.

Step 4: Read the sentence again with your answer in the gap to check it. Do not leave any answers blank.

SPEAKING: INFORMATION EXCHANGE

In information role-plays you need to communicate specific information.

- The examiner explains the situation and the information that you need to ask for and give. It is important in the exam that you communicate this information.
- If you don't understand what the examiner or your partner says, ask them in English to repeat or to speak more slowly. Use expressions like: *'Sorry, can you say that again?'* or, *'Sorry, could you speak more slowly?'*
- Remember that it is important to listen to what your partner says. In a conversation, we listen to the other person and then respond to what they say to us.

Unit 6

READING: MATCHING NOTICES AND PROMPT SENTENCES

In this type of activity, you have different notices. You also have sentences which express the message in the notice. You match the notice with the correct sentence.

Step 1: First, read all the notices. Some are possibly quite similar.

Step 2: Think about where the notice could be. Think about who the notice is for.

Step 3: Read the sentences. Do they contain similar information to any of the notices?

Step 4: Read the possible notices for each sentence slowly and carefully. Choose the best answer. Don't use the same notice for more than one sentence.

LISTENING: MULTIPLE-CHOICE ACTIVITIES

In this type of activity you choose the best answer from three or four different options.

Step 1: Read the different answers before you listen. Decide which words you think are important. They can give you ideas about the topic of the text and the vocabulary in it. The questions are usually in the same order as you hear them in the recording.

Step 2: When you listen, do not write the answers immediately. Sometimes the speaker says one thing and then changes what they say or adds new information.

Step 3: You usually hear the text twice. Do not panic if you do not understand information the first time.

Step 4: At the end, check that you have one answer for each question. Never leave answers blank in an exam.

Unit 7

LISTENING: MATCHING

In matching exercises you need to match each speaker to the correct piece of information.

- Read the questions and information before you listen. This helps you to know the words and ideas in the conversation.
- Sometimes extra pieces of information appear in the conversation, but they are not the correct answers.
- Do not panic if you do not understand information the first time. If you don't hear the answer to one question, start listening immediately for the answer to the next question.

WRITING: CHECKING YOUR WORK

It is normal to make mistakes when we write. That is why it is important to read your work carefully when you finish, especially in exams. For example, when you write a story about past events, check that your verbs are in the past tense. Be careful that they don't suddenly change between the past and present.

Apart from tenses, check for mistakes with:

- punctuation
- capital letters
- word order
- spelling
- agreement between the subject and verb (e.g. *he goes*, not ~~*he go*~~)

Unit 8

READING: MATCHING PEOPLE AND INFORMATION

In this type of activity, you have two texts about two different people. Then you decide if information is about the first person, the second or both.

Step 1: First, read both texts quickly to get a general understanding. You need to read both texts because the information can be about both of the people.

Step 2: Read the pieces of information. Look for important words that help you to find the part(s) of the text(s) with the information.

Step 3: When you find the information in one text, check if the information appears in the other text, too. Then mark your answer.

SPEAKING: KNOWING ABOUT EVALUATION

In speaking exams it is important to know how many marks there are for different sections and to know what the examiners want. Usually examiners in speaking exams want to see if you:

- communicate successfully
- speak fluently
- use grammar well
- use vocabulary well
- pronounce words clearly

Unit 9

READING: MULTIPLE-CHOICE ACTIVITIES

In this type of activity, you choose the best answer from three or four different ones.

Step 1: Read the text quickly to get a general idea of the whole text. A time limit can help you to do this. Don't spend a long time looking at each word.

Step 2: Look at the different options. Look again at the section of the text where you think the answer comes. Read it slowly and carefully. Cross out any answers which you know are incorrect. Choose one answer.

Step 3: In exams, always answer all the questions.

LISTENING: COMPLETING SENTENCES

In this type of activity you have sentences with spaces. You listen to a text and complete the spaces with words that you hear in the text.

Step 1: Read the sentences before you listen. Think about the words or type of words that are missing.

Step 2: Read the instructions carefully. How many words can you write? Usually it is between one and three words. Sometimes you can write numbers too.

Step 3: When you write the answers, be careful with spelling.

Step 4: Write an answer for each space. Do not leave answers blank.

Unit 10

USE OF ENGLISH: OPEN CLOZE ACTIVITIES

In this type of activity, you have a text with gaps. You must complete the text with words which are grammatically correct and are logical. Usually the words are:

- prepositions (e.g. *in, on, next to,* etc.)
- articles (e.g. *a/an, the, –*)
- auxiliary verbs (e.g. *be, have, do*)
- question words (e.g. *who, what, why*)
- pronouns (e.g. *he, him, his*)
- linkers (e.g. *and, but, because*)

Step 1: Read the complete text. Don't stop to think about the gaps. This is to get a general understanding of the text.

Step 2: Look again at the gaps and especially the words which come just <u>before</u> and <u>after</u> the gap. Fill in the gap with the best word.

Step 3: Read the sentence again with your answer in the gap to check it.

WRITING: EXAM CONDITIONS

- When you write in exam conditions, you cannot usually use a dictionary or grammar book. If you do not know a word, think of a similar word or a more general word.
- If you are not sure how to use a grammatical structure, think of a different way to say the same thing.
- Answer the question. Sometimes you can get no points if you don't answer the question.
- Pay attention to the maximum and minimum number of words in the instructions.
- Good handwriting and presentation are very important in writing exams.

Unit 2

DEVELOPING SPEAKING

Exercise 4, p30

Student A, describe these people in the photo in this order: 1 a, 2 e, 3 f, 4 c

Gateway to exams: Units 1–2

SPEAKING

Exercise 7a, p35

Student A. Spell these names to your partner.

1 Sturridge
2 Gerrard
3 Allen
4 Johnstone
5 Radcliffe

Unit 3

DEVELOPING SPEAKING

Exercise 6a, p44

Student A: You are at the bus station. You want to go to the shopping centre. Ask your partner for directions. If you don't understand, ask your partner to repeat.

Unit 5

DEVELOPING SPEAKING

Exercise 6a, p70

Student B: Look at the information and answer your partner's questions.

Science Museum

The Science Museum is at 43 Lyall Street
It's open from Monday to Saturday, from 10 am to 7 pm.
You can see 3D films and do different experiments!
It costs £6 for adults and £3 for children under 14
We have a restaurant and a snack bar

Gateway to exams: Units 5–6

SPEAKING

Exercise 6a, p87

Student B: Look at the information and answer your partner's questions.

TECHNOWORLD

We sell computers, laptops, tablets, webcams ...
Our new shop is in the Kirkby Shopping Centre
Open Mon. to Sat., from 9.30 am to 8 pm
Come and see our special offers – 50% off all printers and scanners!

Unit 7

LIFE SKILLS

Exercise 2, p92

Student C. Watch Student B during the exercise and notice these things:

1 Are they listening carefully to Student A?
2 Do they interrupt Student A?
3 Do they look interested?
4 When Student A finishes talking, ask Student B to repeat the main things that Student A said. Can Student A do this?

Unit 9

VOCABULARY

Exercise 3, p117

Geography Quiz!

1 The Mediterranean is a sea.
2 Titicaca is a lake.
3 K2 is a mountain.
4 Sherwood is a forest.
5 Iguazu Falls is a waterfall.
6 The Mississippi is a river.
7 Mallorca is an island.
8 The Kalahari is a desert
9 Copacabana is a beach.

Unit 9

GRAMMAR IN CONTEXT

Exercise 4a, p121

1 The Sahara is the largest and probably the most famous hot desert in the world.
2 China is the most populated country in the world.
3 The Nile is the longest river in the world.
4 Angel Falls is the highest waterfall in the world.
5 Lake Baikal is the deepest freshwater lake in the world.
6 The Galapagos Islands are probably the best islands for unusual species. Charles Darwin went there to study them.
7 The hottest place in the world is Death Valley in the US. It's also one of the driest.

Unit 2

DEVELOPING SPEAKING

Exercise 4, p30

Student B, describe these people in the photo in this order: 1 d, 2 i, 3 b, 4 h, 5 g

Gateway to exams: Units 1–2

SPEAKING

Exercise 7b, p35

Student B: Spell these names to your partner.

1 Rodgers	**3** Driscoll	**5** Brannagan
2 Davies	**4** Rossiter	

Unit 3

DEVELOPING SPEAKING

Exercise 6a, p44

Student B: You are at the bus station. You want to go to the school. Ask your partner for directions. If you don't understand, ask your partner to repeat.

Unit 5

DEVELOPING SPEAKING

Exercise 6b, p70

Student A: Look at the information and answer your partner's questions.

Fantastic new Science Fiction film – 'Skylab'!

Apollo Cinema in Smith Street
7.20 pm or 9.15 pm
Length: 1 hour 45
Tickets just £13 adults, £10.50 children under 12

Gateway to exams: Units 5–6

SPEAKING

Exercise 6b, p87

Student A: Look at the information and answer your partner's questions.

BLUE STAR GRILL

We serve great burgers, hot dogs and American-style food
You can find us in Clarke Street
Open seven days a week, from 11 am to 11 pm
Special offer this month: Free lemonade between 3 pm and 5 pm!

Unit 1

A PERSONAL PROFILE

p19

Style: Informal. Use contractions.

Start: Use *Hello* and then give your name.

Useful grammar: Use capital letters for the pronoun *I*, the start of a sentence, names of people and cities, countries, nationalities, languages, months and days.

Content: Include your name and surname, where you are from, and your age. Then give basic information about your family, pets and hobbies.

Units 2 and 8

AN INFORMAL EMAIL

pp31 (Unit 2) and 109 (Unit 8)

Style: Use contractions.

Start: *Hi, Dear …, Hello*

Useful expressions: To begin, use *How are you?, I hope you're well, Good to hear from you, How are things?*

To change the subject, use *Anyway* or *By the way*.

To say hello to another person, use *Say hi to … from me, Give (him/her) my love/congratulations.*

Useful expressions in 'news' emails: *I've got some great news!, That's great news about …, Did I tell you about …?, How/What about you/your (week)?, How was your (week/weekend)?*

End: *That's all for now, Write back soon, All the best, Best wishes.*

Content in informal emails giving basic personal information:

Suggested paragraph plan

Paragraph 1: Basic personal information and physical description

Paragraph 2: Basic information about school

Paragraph 3: Information about your other interests

Content in informal emails giving news:

First, ask how the other person is. Then give your most important news. Say other things that happened. Finish by asking the other person to tell you about their week/weekend.

Units 3 and 6

A SHORT NOTE

pp45 (Unit 3) and 83 (Unit 6)

Style: Informal. Use contractions. Write short, direct sentences.

Start: Use *Hi, Hello* or simply write the name of the person you are writing to.

Useful linkers: *and* (addition), *because* (reason), *but* (contrast), *so* (consequence)

End: *See you!, All the best*

Content: Include all the practical information that the reader needs to know.

Unit 4

A DESCRIPTION OF A PLACE

p57

Style: Adjectives are important to make our descriptions interesting.

Useful vocabulary: *beautiful, happy, big, comfortable, enormous, special, old, favourite, warm.*

Useful grammar: Adjectives usually come <u>before</u> the noun they describe (e.g. *It's a beautiful room)* or <u>after</u> the verb *to be*, e.g. *The room is beautiful.*

Content: Introduce the place you are going to describe. Say what it is and where it is. Describe what you can see and do there. Give your opinion of the place and explain your opinion.

Unit 5

A QUESTIONNAIRE

p71

Useful vocabulary: *Who, Which, When, Where, Why, How, How much, How many, How often …*

Useful grammar: In questions, auxiliary verbs (*do, does, is, are, can …*) come before the subject.

Content: Give your questionnaire a title. Make all your questions relevant to the questionnaire. If possible, put the questions in order. We usually start with general questions and then we ask more specific things. The last question can ask for a general conclusion.

Unit 7

A STORY

p97

Useful expressions: To say when things happened, use *One day, Then, Next, Suddenly, After (the final), After that, In the end …*

Useful linkers: *and* (addition), *because* (reason), *but* (contrast), *so* (consequence)

Useful grammar: Use the past simple to talk about completed actions in the past.

Content in a story:

Suggested paragraph plan:

Paragraph 1: Explain where and when the story begins. Introduce the characters.

Paragraph 2: Explain the main events in the story.

Paragraph 3: Explain how the story ended.

Unit 9

A BLOG POST

p123

Style: Informal. Use contractions.

Start: Have a title for the blog post.

Useful expressions: To say when things happened, use *Then, Next, After (the final), After that, In the end …*

Useful grammar: Use different present and past tenses to say when things happened. Use the *present simple* to talk about routines, and things that are generally true, the *present continuous* to talk about things that are happening now, the *past simple* to talk about things that happened at a specific time in the past, and the *present perfect* to talk about things that happened at an unspecified moment in the past.

Unit 10

AN ARTICLE

p135

Style: Magazine articles should not be very formal or informal. They can have titles.

Useful expressions: To say when things happened, use *One day, Then, Next, Suddenly, After (the final), After that, In the end …*

Useful linkers: *and* (addition), *because* (reason), *but* (contrast), *so* (consequence)

Useful vocabulary: To describe interesting descriptions of positive experiences, use these adjectives: *amazing, beautiful, brilliant, excellent, exciting, great, ideal, incredible, interesting, perfect, spectacular.*

Content:

Suggested paragraph plan:

Paragraph 1: *Introduction saying what your article is about.*

Paragraph 2: Main point(s).

Paragraph 3: Conclusion – restate the most important points and your opinion(s)

CHECKING YOUR WRITING

Check for mistakes with:

- Punctuation
- Capital letters
- Word order
- Spelling
- Tenses
- Vocabulary
- Missing words
- Agreement between the subject and verb (e.g. *He goes* … not ~~*He go*~~.)
- Style
- Content

Irregular verbs

Infinitive	Past simple	Past participle
be	was/were	been
beat	beat	beaten
become	became	become
begin	began	begun
break	broke	broken
bring	brought	brought
build	built	built
burn	burnt	burnt
buy	bought	bought
catch	caught	caught
choose	chose	chosen
come	came	come
cost	cost	cost
cut	cut	cut
do	did	done
draw	drew	drawn
drink	drank	drunk
drive	drove	driven
eat	ate	eaten
fall	fell	fallen
feel	felt	felt
find	found	found
fly	flew	flown
forget	forgot	forgotten
forgive	forgave	forgiven
get	got	got
give	gave	given
go	went	gone
grow	grew	grown
have	had	had
hear	heard	heard
hide	hid	hidden
hit	hit	hit
hurt	hurt	hurt
keep	kept	kept
know	knew	known
lay	laid	laid
leave	left	left

Infinitive	Past simple	Past participle
learn	learned/learnt	learned/learnt
let	let	let
lie	lay	lain
lose	lost	lost
make	made	made
mean	meant	meant
meet	met	met
pay	paid	paid
put	put	put
read	read	read
ride	rode	ridden
ring	rang	rung
run	ran	run
say	said	said
see	saw	seen
sell	sold	sold
send	sent	sent
shine	shone	shone
shoot	shot	shot
show	showed	shown
sing	sang	sung
sit	sat	sat
sleep	slept	slept
speak	spoke	spoken
spell	spelt	spelt
spend	spent	spent
stand up	stood up	stood up
steal	stole	stolen
swim	swam	swum
take	took	taken
teach	taught	taught
tell	told	told
think	thought	thought
understand	understood	understood
wake up	woke up	woken up
wear	wore	worn
win	won	won
write	wrote	written

Macmillan Education
4 Crinan Street
London N1 9XW
A division of Macmillan Publishers Limited

Companies and representatives throughout the world

ISBN 978-0-230-47085-9

First edition published 2016

Designed by emc design ltd
Illustrated by A Corazón Abierto (Sylvie Poggio Artists Agency) pp8, 10 (l), 17, 24, 29, 35, 36, 44, 62, 64 (r), 77, 122, 129; Tim Bradford (Illustration Ltd) pp68, 90, 121; Dante Ginevra (Advocate Art) pp97, 102; Javier Joaquin (The Organisation) pp16, 25, 55, 81, 82, 95, 113, 128, 133; Mark Ruffle pp6, 7, 9, 39, 48, 50 (l), 51, 57, 59, 64 (l), 74, 85, 99, 102, 111, 125, 126.
Flipped video illustrations by emc design ltd and Mark Ruffle (bedroom).
Cover design by emc design ltd and Macmillan Publishers Ltd
Cover photographs by Getty Images/Image Source (teens);
Getty Images/Travelpix Ltd (tower bridge).
Picture research by Emily Taylor

Author acknowledgments
I would like to give a big thank you to the whole Macmillan team in the UK for their dedication, hard work, and enthusiasm throughout the writing of this course. Thanks also to all the other Macmillan teams around the world for their help, encouragement and always making me feel welcome. Very special thanks to Colegio Europeo Aristos in Getafe, Spain. The daily contact with my students there continues to be a main source of inspiration and I am sincerely grateful to every one of my students, past and present. Massive thanks, as always, to Gemma, Jamie and Becky for their unending love and support.

This book is dedicated to Emily Rosser.

The publishers would like to thank staff and pupils at the following schools in Mexico and Spain for helping us so enthusiastically with our research for the course:
Concha Campos, IES Burgo de Las Rozas, Las Rozas, Madrid; Félix Gaspar, IES Las Encinas; Villanueva de la Cañada, Madrid; Cristina Moisen, IES Joaquín Turina, Madrid; Colegio Montessori Cuautitlán; Colegio Conrad Gessner; Colegio Erasmo de Rotterdam; Colegio Kanic, Centro Educativo Erich Fromm; Universidad Franco Mexicana; Centro Pedagógico María Montessori de Ecatepec; Instituto Cultural; Escuela Maestro Manuel Acosta; Liceo Sakbé De México

The author and publishers would like to thank the following for permission to reproduce their photographs:
Alamy/Allstar Picture Library p11(tm), Alamy/Archimage p28(tl), Alamy/Blend Images pp49(tl), 101(tcr), Alamy/Blickwinkel p114(cr), Alamy/Bill Cheyrou p92(br), Alamy/Frank Chmura p107(tl), Alamy/Corbis/Super RF p115(cheetah), Alamy/Alan Edwards p112(tr), Alamy/EPA p95, Alamy/Stephen Giardina p74(3), Alamy/Scott Hortop p77, Alamy/K-Photos p74(4), Alamy/James Linsell-Clark p11(tl), Alamy/MBI p30(bm), Alamy/Shaun Parnell p139, Alamy/PCN Photography p115(bolt), Alamy/PhotoAlto p74(7), Alamy/Radharc Images p22(d), Alamy/Andrew Twort p54(d), Alamy/Xinhua p34(a);
APEX/Mark Passmore/Courtesy of The Eden Project p123(br); **BananaStock** pp13(harry, amie), 18, 51(14); **Brand X** pp88(tm), 131(english countryside);
Comstock p127(bike); **Corbis** pp51(4), 100(1), 114(7), Corbis/2/Sylvain Cordier/Ocean p116, Corbis/145/Ocean/Rosemary Calvert p74(2), Corbis/145/Ocean/Bjorn Holland p74(1), Corbis/Adoc-photos p89(3), Corbis/Koji Aoki/Aflo p88(5), Corbis/Ausl`ser p69(cr), Corbis/Paul Bonugli/Demotix p106(cl), Corbis/Design Pics/Ben Welsh p91(1.1), Corbis/EPA/Dave Hunt p91(4.4), Corbis/Randy Faris p71, Corbis/Sergi Garcia Fernandez p119(turtle), Corbis/Sigrid Gombert p100(5), Corbis/Chris Hendrickson/Masterfile p22(b), Corbis/Henn Photography p109, Corbis/Mitsuhiko Imamori/Minden Pictures p115(cr), Corbis/Keith Levit/Design Pics p11(b), Corbis/Gabe Palmer p127(3), Corbis/Peathegee Inc/Blend Images p108, Corbis/Geoff Renner/Robert Harding World Imagery p34(b), Corbis/Reuters/Lucas Jackson p91(cl), Corbis/Reuters/Eddie Keogh p89(2), Corbis/Reuters/Suzanne Plunkett p63(tl), Corbis/Akira Sakamoto p106(tcmll), Corbis/John Smith p100(4), Corbis/Splash News p91(4.3), Corbis/Justin Steffman/Splash News p11(tr), Corbis/Unlisted Images p100(9); **Eden Project**/Courtesy of the Eden Project p123(tr); **Getty Images** p51(6, 9, 13), Getty Images/2012 Alvaro Canovas/Paris Match p120, Getty Images/AFP pp96, 106(tcl), Getty Images/Archive Photos p89(1), Getty Images/Blend Images pp28(br), 76(2), 134(1), Getty Images/Tom Bonaventure p121(cm), Getty Images/Mark Bowden p56(tl), Getty Images/Anthony Bradshaw p88(tr), Getty Images/Brand X p22(c), Getty Images/Niels Busch p130(cr), Getty Images/Caiaimage p81(tmr), Getty Images/Collection Mix: Subjects RM p30(tr), Getty Images/Compassionate Eye Foundation/Monashee Frantz p56(tr), Getty Images/Jeffrey Coolidge p74(6), Getty Images/Cultura RF pp100(6, 7), 127(1), Getty Images/Cultura RM p25, Getty Images/Cultura/Tom Lindboe p103(b), Getty Images/John Cumming p7, Getty Images/Peter Dazeley p105(baker), Getty Images/Suzi Eszterhas/Minden Pictures RM p115(bm), Getty Images/Steve Debenport p49(cr), Getty Images/Dorling Kindersley pp54(c), 88(8), Getty Images/F1online RF p105(boy in suit), Getty Images/FilmMagic pp103(tl), 106(br), 138, Getty Images/First Light p88(1), Getty Images/Flickr RF p36(2), Getty Images/David Franklin p126(tm), Getty Images/Glowimages p130(crowd), Getty Images/Jamie Grill p94(tl), Getty Images/Rüstem Gurler p26™, Getty Images/Hemera p62(g), Getty Images/Justin Horrocks p105(doctor), Getty Images/ImageSource p24, Getty Images/iStockphoto pp51(10, 11, 12), 51(19, 20), 76(1), 75(evan), Getty Images/iStockphoto/Alessio Cola p51(8), Getty Images/iStockphoto/Thinkstock p51(1, 2, 3, 5, 7), Getty Images/iStockphoto/Thinkstock/Paul Grecaud p52(background on cereal box), Getty Images/Hemera/Thinkstock/Michael Hoerichs, p79(jeans), Getty Images/iStockphoto/Thinkstock Images/Andrew Mayovskyy p36(tl), Getty Images/iStockphoto/Thinkstock Images/Sally Scott p52(bowl on cereal box), Getty Images/iStockphoto/Thinkstock Images/Dimitri Zimmer p10(teen girl), Getty Images/JoKMedia p26(pencil case), Getty Images/Jasper Juinen p88(br), Getty Images/David Malan p11(a), Getty Images/Moodboard RF p31, Getty Images/Chris Nash p130(cl), Getty Images/Neustockimages p67(tr), Getty Images/OJO Images pp76(3), 101(tr), Getty Images/Allison Michael Orenstein p100(2), Getty Images/Tim Platt p91(1.3), Getty Images/PhotoAlto/Milena Boniek p52(br), Getty Images/Stephen Pond/British Athletics p112(cl), Getty Images/Adrian Pope p130(bcl), Getty Images/John Powell/Liverpool FC p134(3), Getty Images/Purestock p133, Getty Images/Radius Images p23(cr), Getty Images/Redferns pp42, 134(2), Getty Imgages/Oli Scarff p106(tml), Getty Images/Peet Simard p38, Getty Images/Small Frog p100(10), Getty Images/Alina Solovyova-Vincent p88(7), Getty Images/Tetra images RF p13(sophie), Getty Images/Michael Turek p94(br), Getty Images/Ian Walton p90, Getty Images/Yellow Dog Productions p27(tl), Getty Images/Stephan Zabel p22(a); **ImageSource** pp13(jack), 51(18), 54(b), 67(br), 74(5), 92(paper doll chain), 117(5a.5), 122(2); **Macmillan Publishers Ltd** p51(16), Macmillan Publishers Ltd/Australia p51(15), Macmillan Publishers Ltd/Photodisc/Doug Menuez p15(tr); **MakeyMakey**/Courtesy of MakeyMakey p63(br); **PhotoDisc**/Getty Images p51(17), PhotoDisc/Getty Images/Siede Preis p118-119(background); **PlainPicture**/Bildhuset p76(4), PlainPicture/Etsa p60, PlainPicture/Image Source p76(6), PlainPicture/MICK p83(tr), PlainPicture/Bill Miles p127(2), PlainPicture/OJO p92(shona); **Rex Features**/HZ/Pixathlon/Sipa p91(4.1), Rex Features/Shutterstock pp13(cm), 130(bm), Rex Features/Shutterstock/BFAnyc.com p12(bm), Rex Features/Shutterstock/Warming Images p118(inset), Rex Features/Sipa Press p34(c); **Shutterstock/whiteisthecolor p66(background sketch), Stockbyte** p36(3), Stockbyte/PunchStock/Getty Images p81(earth); **The Picture Desk**/20TH Century Fox p107(bm); **Thinkstock** p10(background), 14-15(background), 19(br), 37(background), 40-41(background), 48(background), 66(circles), 67(sticky notes), 70(tl), 78-79(tags at bottom, tags on jeans), 92-93(background), 100(magnifying glass), 104-105(background), 104(tr), 105(avatars), 126(tr), 131(union jack), Thinkstock/BananaStock RF p88(6), Thinkstock/Michael Blann p13(liam), Thinkstock/Brand X Pictures p100(3), Thinkstock/David De Lossy p52(4), Thinkstock/Digital Vision pp117(1.1), 132(cr), Thinkstock/Eyecandy Images RF p70(cr), Thinkstock/Getty Images p91(4.2), Thinkstock/Getty Images/BananaStock RF p61, Thinkstock/Getty Images/Fuse pp19(cr), 22(tr), 23(cl), 36(4), 117(5a.3), 135(tr), Thinkstock/Getty Images/Goodshoot RF p13(henry), Thinkstock/Getty Images/Hemera pp68(tl - inset), 81(tr), 114(background tm), 126(2), Thinkstock/Getty Images/Huntstock pp13(sandra), 19(tl), 23(bl), Thinkstock/Getty Images/iStockphoto pp11(c), 12(cr), 13(anne), 15(map, bm, tmr), 16(cat, phone), 22(e, cr), 26-27(background), 26(notebooks), 26(desk), 36(tm, 1, 5, 6,7), 37(tcr, bl), 40(tm), 43, 44, 48(tr), 52-53(background, veg on forks), 52(2, 3, 6, notepaper, bl, 'O' in food, br), 54(a), 62(foreground, a, b, c, d,f, h, i, j, k), 65(tr), 66(tr), 67(bl), 68(tl), 74(8), 76(5), 78-79(shoppers), 79(tl), 81(tcmr, tcr, br), 86(br, a, f, g), 88(2, 3), 91(1.2), 92(mike, katie), 93(tm), 97, 100(tm, 8), 101(cm), 105(painter, builder), 106(tl), 106(cmll), 107(tr), 114(tm, tr, 1, 2), 115(tr), 117(5a.1, 5a.4, 5a.6, 1.3, 1.4, 1.6), 119(tr), 118(bl), 119(seal), 121(cl), 122(3, 4, 5, 6), 126(1, 3, 4), 127(car), 130-131(background), 130(tm, spices), Thinkstock/Getty Images/iStockphoto/Jani Bryson p41(hugo), Thinkstock/Getty Images/iStockphoto/funstock p23(tl), Thinkstock/Getty Images/iStockphoto/Galinast p41(tania), Thinkstock/Getty Images/iStockphoto/gnagel p114(6), Thinkstock/Getty Images/iStockphoto/Anton Gvozdikov p117(1.5), Thinkstock/Getty Images/iStockphoto/Klagyivik p36(background), Thinkstock/Getty Images/iStockphoto/Pavel Kriuchkov p41(helen), Thinkstock/Getty Images/iStockphoto/Marcus Photography p135(cl), Thinkstock/Getty Images/iStockphoto/Mitchii p114(4), Thinkstock/Getty Images/iStockphoto/MR1805 pp114(3), 117(5a.2), Thinkstock/Getty Images/iStockphoto/Sergey Nivens p23(digital background), Thinkstock/Getty Images/iStockphoto/Paulaphoto p41(jared), Thinkstock/Getty Images/iStockphoto/Tomas Sereda p117(1.2), Thinkstock/Getty Images/iStockphoto/Seregraff p114(8), Thinkstock/Getty Images/iStockphoto/Suttisukmek p41(rose), Thinkstock/Getty Images/iStockphoto/Jacob Wackerhausen p41(rory), Thinkstock/Getty Images/iStockphoto/Lai Leng Yiap p6, Thinkstock/Getty Images/Moodboard RF pp66(desk), 93(br), Thinkstock/Getty Images/Pixland pp12(tr), 103(c), Thinkstock/Getty Images/Purestock p52(1, 5), Thinkstock/Getty Images/Top Photo Group RF p114(5), Thinkstock/Getty Images/Valueline p69(tl), Thinkstock/Getty Images/Todd Warnock p13(ava), Thinkstock/Getty Images/Wavebreak Media pp14(tr), 70(br), 74(tm), Thinkstock/Getty Images/William87 p80, Thinkstock/Getty Images/Kevin Winter p17, Thinkstock/Jetta Productions p22(tm), Thinkstock/Jupiterimages pp13(oliver), 55(cr), 88(4), Thinkstock/Jupiterimages/Brand X Pictures p41(tr), Thinkstock/Monkeybusinessimages p65(cl), Thinkstock/Thomas Northcut p62(e), Thinkstock/Photodisc p103(a), Thinkstock/Ron Chapple Studios RF p91(1.4), Thinkstock/Siri Stafford p79(bm), Thinkstock/Stockbyte pp16(bike), 53(bm), 67(cl), Thinkstock/Maria Teijeiro p55(bl), Thinkstock/Top Photo Group RF p122(1); ™**Transport for London**/Thinkstock/TonyBaggett p132(tl); **Zoonar RF** p127(football).

The author and publishers are grateful for permission to reprint the following copyright material:
Facts about 'Animal Olympic Games' taken from animalsunlimited.co.uk
Extract from 'Rebecca Tunney'. Originally published by Gymnastike on 04 March 2014 © FloSports, 2014. Reprinted with permission.
Extract from 'StageofLife.com Trend Report: High school and college students talk TV viewing habits and their favourite shows' © Stage of Life, 2015. Reprinted with permission.
Extract from 'Super talented British teenage sprinter Asher-Smith eyes success in Eugene' by Emily Moss. Originally published by IAAF Athletics on 26 November 2013 © IAAF Athletics, 2013. Reprinted with permission. www.iaaf.org
'Variety is the Spice' and 'The British' from WICKED WORLD by Benjamin Zephaniah (Puffin, 2000) Text copyright © Benjamin Zephaniah, 2000. Illustrations copyright © Sarah Symonds, 2000.
Extract from Makey Makey website © Makey Makey, 2015. Reprinted with permission.
Extract from 'British teen sells Summly app for millions' by Jessica Winch. Originally published in the Daily Telegraph on 25 March 2013 © Telegraph Group Limited, 2013. Reprinted with permission. www.telegraph.co.uk
Extract from 'Great Garbage Patch: the problem of plastics in the ocean' by Heidi Blake. Originally published in the Daily Telegraph on 06 January 2010 © Telegraph Group Limited, 2010. Reprinted with permission. www.telegraph.co.uk
Extract from 'James Cameron completes record dive but resurfaces six hours early' by Rosa Prince. Originally published in the Daily Telegraph on 26 March 2012 © Telegraph Group Limited, 2012. Reprinted with permission. www.telegraph.co.uk

Printed and bound in Argentina
2022
24